D1645729

ONE WEEK !

3 0 NOV 2006

DEDICATION

To Wendy and Alice, Ben, Dom, Jonathan, Katy, Lucy, Rachel and Sian. Also to Carolyn, Alex, Tim and Jenny. Inadequately we express our gratitude for the love, patience and understanding that sustains us.

THE HISTORY OF PROBATION

Politics, Power and Cultural Change
1876–2005

Philip Whitehead and Roger Statham

Shaw & Sons

Published by
Shaw & Sons Limited
Shaway House
21 Bourne Park
Bourne Road
Crayford
Kent DA1 4BZ

www.shaws.co.uk

© Shaw & Sons Limited 2006

Published February 2006

ISBN 0 7219 1700 3

A CIP catalogue record for this book is available
from the British Library

Printed in Great Britain by
Bell & Bain Limited, Glasgow

CONTENTS

ACKNOWLEDGEMENTS

We have been embarked upon a journey over many years and a number of people, within different probation areas, have been a source of inspiration and help to us. Particular thanks must go to the ever efficient Margaret Coyle, Ian White for his thoughtfulness, Ruth Cranfield, Brian Fellowes, Peter Hadfield, Joyce Harrison, Mike Lauerman, Elaine Lumley, Pam McPhee and Peter Trusler. Paul Leeson deserves special mention for keeping faith over many years. We would also like to thank Liz Rodgers, librarian at Dene House; also Steven Burgess of the West Yorkshire probation library. Ken Harrison made available the Police Court Mission Report Book for 1918 to 1923. Martin Leishman and Shahida Nazir have been attentive trainee probation officers who have contributed more than they realise. We are indebted to the Recorder of Middlesbrough, His Honour Judge Peter Fox QC, for his contribution to Chapter 5. Jamie Thompson is a good friend who is a constant source of help. Finally, we want to thank Crispin Williams of Shaw & Sons for taking us on after discussing our ideas with him.

FOREWORD

by Mike Hough

Director of the Institute for Criminal Policy Research and Professor of Criminal Policy at King's College London

It is a pleasure and a privilege to write a preface to a book of such quality and insight. I only wish that I could be doing so at a time when I had more sympathy with the direction of the government's policy on probation. At the time of writing, with the centenary of the probation service in sight, it looks increasingly unlikely that probation work will continue into its second century in a shape that has any significant continuity with the past.

Probation is in the process of radical 'modernisation'. Those of us who are sceptical about the process are all too readily cast in the role of reactionary backwoodsmen – people who think that things were better 'in their day'. I was most closely involved in the probation service precisely at that period when Douglas Hurd and John Patten were trying to 'move the service centre-stage'. At the time, the service had plenty of weaknesses, but also many strengths. The foremost of these was that probation work was transparently a value-driven occupation. It may sound trite or clichéd, but the workforce wanted not simply to make a living but to make a difference.

These values – or the Probation Ideal – are well described in this book. So too are the processes by which probation values are being eroded. The increasingly populist climate of penal debate has intertwined with the government's New Public Management approach to reforming the public sector to change both the function and the structure of probation work. It is by no means fanciful to think that in few years' time, operatives (for that is what they would probably be called) from commercial security companies might prepare and submit pre-sentence reports to judges and magistrates. These reports would recommend a range of penal options, some based in prisons, some in the community. Some of these might be provided by the report-writer's own organisation, and some by its commercial competitors. In the words of the government, this 'vibrant mixed economy' will drive up probation standards, improve value for money and reduce re-offending. One wonders.

The government vision of correctional services includes a probation system braced by the tensions of market place competition. The tensions are seen as constructive ones that do not necessarily undermine existing institutions or deplete their social capital. We are offered the example of prisons privatisation, whereby competition forced the Prison Service to improve its performance. There is room to question whether it was in fact the threat of privatisation that 'did the trick' in reforming prisons. Leaving this aside, the circumstances of the two services differed widely at the point at which contestability was threatened. Simply put, the prisons workforce controlled their charges a little too much and cared for them much too little. Some private prisons appear now to treat prisoners with more dignity and respect than their public sector counterparts. Arguably, from two successive governments' viewpoints, the problems of probation are the reverse – too much care and too little control. It is questionable, to say the least, whether the same solution will work in the reform of two such different agencies facing diametrically different problems.

One should, of course, keep an open mind about the prospects of success for the government's strategy for reforming probation work. Ultimately, successful organisational reform is more about leadership, trust and commitment and less about structures and processes. If the government and those in charge of NOMS succeed in enthusing and energising the probation workforce, the reforms face a reasonable chance of success. However, the service is still recovering from its last major organisational overhaul in 2001, when the National Probation Service was established. It is questionable whether it has sufficient resilience left to allow it to respond constructively to yet more radical change immediately after the massive upheavals involved in creating a unified service.

Many decisions still have to be made about the way that the National Offender Management Service will organise probation work. In reaching these decisions, it needs answers to four important questions. The first relates to the public as consumers or customers of public services. In a sense, the victims of crime are customers of the criminal justice system; but seen through another lens, the real product of the institutions of justice is *compliance* with the law, not consumption of its services. An effective criminal justice system commands compliance from all of us; it does not simply provide a service to the 'law-abiding majority', protecting them from the 'criminals'. To work, these institutions need to command authority across the population. It remains an unknown whether elements of the system can be successfully parcelled up into contracts for providers in the private and voluntary sectors without damaging its overall legitimacy.

Secondly, there are particularly difficult issues about accountability for those public bodies whose role is to deploy the coercive powers of the state. Clearly, there is a balance to be struck between local and national accountability, but it may be that systems of contestability tip the balance in the wrong direction. Certainly it is hard to reconcile forms of political accountability at local level with systems of contractual accountability located at regional or national level. There are also potential tensions between providers' accountability to the court and their accountability to the national or regional paymaster. These tensions obviously already exist within the current system, but they could be exacerbated within a framework of contestability.

Thirdly, there remains that complex set of issues about organisational values. It is hard to argue convincingly that the competence and commitment of teachers or doctors in the private sector is compromised by the fact that they work for profit-making or voluntary sector bodies. On the other hand, there may be a greater incompatibility between altruism and the profit motive in those 'helping professions' that involve highly personalised relationships – and especially relationships into which the 'customer' is coerced. The trust that a good probation officer can command from an offender may be eroded by the latter's realisation that the former is, ultimately, working for shareholders. Similar considerations might apply to the authority and credibility of pre-sentence reports prepared by employees of commercial organisations with a financial interest in the outcome.

Finally, we do not know whether the provision of correctional services through networks of providers from the statutory, voluntary and private sectors will result in a fragmentation that far outweighs the unifying effects of combining the prison and probation services. Successful probation work may require a sense of joint enterprise, trust between different providers and a commitment to shared goals. To what extent can competition remain friendly and constructive when livelihoods are at stake? We do not yet know the answer to this question.

Historical analysis can provide us with the necessary distance and perspective with which to address fundamental questions of this sort. As the authors say, it is impossible to understand the probation service of the 21st century without spending some time excavating its past. That is why this book is so timely and so valuable. It describes how accident and intent have combined to threaten the values traditionally inherent in probation work. As probation undergoes radical change, it is essential that its core values are preserved and not squandered.

PREFACE

In the spring of 2004 we got together to talk about recent changes within the probation service out of concern for an organisation with which we had been associated for many years. We were mindful that the English probation system would be 100 years old in 2007 but because of the Carter report, published in January 2004, probation would be subsumed within a new organisation: the National Offender Management Service (NOMS). This new organisation would merge prison and probation and we were bothered by the implications of this. At first we simply wanted to produce a piece of work to mark the passing of probation, set against the creation of NOMS and in anticipation of the 2007 centenary. As our deliberations evolved and sparks started to fly, we alighted on the reckless notion of writing a history of the probation service; reckless because of the amount of work that inevitably would be involved.

At the beginning of the project we wanted to address, and hopefully answer, two basic questions. First, what has happened to the probation system since its creation under a reforming Liberal government in 1907, until the creation of NOMS in 2004? At one level we simply wanted to tell a story of an organisation that has worked with offenders over many decades. To put it another way, we wanted to produce a biography of a public sector organisation we knew something about. Secondly, but more importantly, is the 'why' question: if at one level we tell a story of *what* has happened, we also want to know *why* things have happened in the way they have, particularly from 1979 to 2004. We put it like this because we are not historical determinists. In other words, it is possible to envisage a different kind of history to the one we describe and analyse in this book. The probation service of recent years could have been different; it could have existed in a less punitive culture; it could have been oriented more towards welfare rather than punishment; the National Probation Service in 2001 and NOMS in 2004 were not predestined to happen. So what has been going on over recent years, and why, are the two basic questions that interested us.

We must state at this point that we are concerned by the fact that the book has not evolved from within the academic community. Certainly, we make extensive use of the splendid work produced by university academics, as will be made plain. But two people who have worked primarily within the practice community rather than academia have written this book. One of us has worked for the service since 1968 and is a retired Chief Probation Officer; the other commenced training in 1979 and continues to be involved in practice. We have lived through and been directly affected by many of the changes described in Part 2 of the book and hope the reader will perceive this as a strength rather than weakness.

Chapter 1 opens our account with reflections on a number of themes and influences that are relevant for an understanding of probation since the police court missionaries first made their appearance in 1876. Chapter 2 provides a more sequential account of significant events from 1907 to 1979. Consequently, our first two chapters cover a lot of ground to prepare the reader for our more substantive chapters.

Chapters 3 to 6 strike to the heart of the book because we cannot understand the service of the 21st century unless we spend some time excavating the period from 1979. Chapter 3 traces events from the arrival of the radical Conservatives under Mrs Thatcher in 1979 to the Statement of National Objectives and Priorities in 1984 that attempted to provide more central control over the 54 area services. Chapter 4 proceeds to cover the Douglas Hurd, John Patten and David Faulkner period of punishment in the community from 1985 to the Criminal Justice Act 1991. To some this was a land of opportunity for the service as it was reshaped to deliver community punishment with a view to reducing the prison population. By Chapter 5, 1992 to 1997, the penal system experienced a remarkable turn around when John Major and Michael Howard were convinced that prison rather than, or as well as, punishment in the community should be the priority. During this period it was doubtful probation could survive. Chapter 6 makes it clear that it did survive under New Labour from 1997 but within a climate of ongoing punishment that continued where the Conservatives left off; 2001 destroyed its local character when New Labour nationalised, rationalised and centralised the service. We argue that this was the culmination of a process that began in 1984, if not before.

The last two chapters comprising the final part of the book, Chapters 7 and 8, cover 2001 to 2004 and beyond. They explain how the upheaval of nationalisation of 2001 was greeted with further far-reaching changes in 2004 when the Carter report culminated in NOMS. The final chapter summarises the book as well as initiating a discussion about the future of what we refer to as the probation ideal beyond 2005.

This book was motivated by a desire to understand what has happened to an organisation that had, and still has, the potential to make a significant contribution to the criminal justice system by promoting values of decency and humanity. In doing so we touch upon politics, power, central control and a changing culture manifested in new governance arrangements since 2001. We wanted to increase our understanding of what has happened to an organisation and why, from its beginnings in Victorian society to its demise under New Labour. We take full responsibility for all sins of commission, omission and hyperbole in what follows, including failures to analyse and interpret events correctly. In other words, all mistakes are well and truly ours alone. We agree with Richard Tarnas when he says, 'All human understanding is interpretation, and no interpretation is final' (1991 p397).

Philip Whitehead
Roger Statham

NOTE ON AUTHORS

Philip Whitehead

After working as a volunteer attached to the Lancaster probation office during the mid-1970s and a year in a Hostel, he qualified to work as a probation officer at Lancaster University between 1979 and 1981. The Cleveland Probation Service (now Teesside) was the first to offer him employment, where he has remained since. He has published several books and articles in relation to probation, community supervision of offenders, temporary release schemes, and management. In 2001, he was appointed to work with trainee probation officers, culminating in a textbook for trainees and practice development assessors. Philip Whitehead continues to be involved with trainees and probation practice in a rapidly changing service. In future he is interested in forging a new synthesis out of the dissonance that currently exists between the concerns of practitioners when working with people and demands of politicians and managers for accountability. Moreover, as this book affirms, he wants to keep alive the moral dimension of probation work which means talking about the values of decency and humanity, in what is a people-based but increasingly bureaucratic organisation.

Roger Statham

Roger Statham joined the Stoke-on-Trent Probation and After-Care Service in 1968. As the youngest probation officer, he learned about the job from colleagues and through the Home Office Direct Entrant Course and obtained certificates in Social Studies and Criminology from Keele University between 1969 and 1974. He was appointed Staffordshire's first Community Service Organiser in 1974 and moved to be a fieldwork Senior Probation Officer in 1978, before being seconded to Keele University in 1980 to complete the Diploma in Social Work. From 1982 he managed the Rainbow Centre in Hanley, before moving to Cleveland (subsequently Teesside) in 1984 as Assistant Chief Probation Officer. He became Chief in 1989, taking early retirement on 31st March 2001, when the service was nationalised. Roger Statham has served on various committees including: Stoke-on-Trent CAB; Chair of Stoke-on-Trent Adventure Playgrounds Association; Local Review Committee at Stafford HMP; Chair of the Local Review Committee at Durham HMP; Chair of North East Prison After-Care Society; and he was a member of the Parole Board from 1994–2000. Furthermore, between 1984 and 2001, he held a number of positions within the Association of Chief Officers of Probation, including Lead Officer for social policy and later for staffing. Since 2001, he has worked as a consultant and with Her Majesty's Inspectorate of Probation. He is a Trustee of NEPACS and a Fellow of the Royal Society of Arts.

LIST OF ABBREVIATIONS

ACOP	Association of Chief Officers of Probation
ACPS	Advisory Council on the Penal System
ACTO	Advisory Council on the Treatment of Offenders
AO	Accountable Officer
APPO	Assistant Principal Probation Officer
BASW	British Association of Social Workers
CAFCASS	Children and Family Court Advisory and Support Service
CCETSW	Central Council for Education and Training in Social Work
CCPC	Central Council of Probation Committees
CJA 2003	Criminal Justice Act 2003
CJPOA 1994	Criminal Justice and Public Order Act 1994
CQSW	Certificate of Qualification in Social Work
C(S)A 1997	Crime (Sentences) Act 1997
CYPA 1933	Children and Young Persons Act 1933
DTTO	Drug Treatment and Testing Order
ECP	Enhanced Community Punishment
FFP	Foundation Practice Portfolio
FMI	Financial Management Initiative
FMIS	Financial Management Information System
HDC	Home Detention Curfew
HMIP	Her Majesty's Inspectorate of Probation
KPI	Key Performance Indicator
MAPPA	Multi Agency Protection Panel Arrangements
MTSG	Management Training Sub-Group
NAO	National Audit Office
NACRO	National Association for the Care and Resettlement of Offenders
NADPAS	National Association of Discharged Prisoners' Aid Societies
NAPO	National Associaton of Probation Officers
NOMS	National Offender Management Service
NPS	National Probation Service

NSPCC	National Society for the Prevention of Cruelty to Children
NVQ	National Vocational Qualification
OASys	Offender Assessment System
PBA	Probation Boards Association
PDA	Practice Development Assessor
PROBIS	Probation Information System
PSCF	Probation Service Christian Fellowship
PSD	Petty Sessional Divisions
PSR	Pre-Sentence Report
SPO	Senior Probation Officer
SNOP	Statement of National Objectives and Priorities
SMINs	Supporting Management Information Needs
YOP	Youth Opportunities Scheme
YTS	Youth Training Scheme

Part 1

BEGINNINGS AND DEVELOPMENT OF PROBATION 1876–1979

Chapter 1

INTRODUCTION: SOME THEMES AND INFLUENCES

'What a blessing it is then that the Saviour of men lived our life, and knowing all our frailties is able to help us to overcome. I am learning more and more to recommend Him to my fellows as their only hope of overcoming the evil around us and in us, and helping us to walk a clean, straight path.' *(Police Court Mission report book entry for December 1922)*

Introduction

We should acknowledge at the outset of this book that it has been written to mark the centenary of the creation of the probation system in 1907 (1907–2007). One of the main tasks that we have set ourselves is to tell the story (or more precisely *our* story) of probation from the late 1970s to the setting up of the National Offender Management Service (NOMS) in 2004, which effectively brought to an end the existence of an autonomous probation service with a distinctive ethos and primary task to work, in the main, with offenders in the community. This is now, we would argue, compromised by its closer alliance with the prison system due to the creation of NOMS. Consequently, we are allowing ourselves a degree of artistic licence when we talk about the centenary of probation because in reality the system has been in existence for just less than 100 years. Nevertheless, we must make it clear that Part 1 of the book includes a chapter on the period from 1907 to 1979 that will help to establish the background against which our main and more contemporary concerns will be explored. A book on probation history cannot eschew these important early years that we need to consider for the sake of completeness and also to facilitate an understanding of our main themes.

It should also be acknowledged that there are a number of informative books on the history of probation, many of which we have hunted down during the preparation of our own contribution: Leeson (1914); Le Mesurier (1935); Glover (1956); King (1964); Monger (1964); Jarvis (1972); Bochel (1976); Haxby (1978); the McWilliams' quartet of essays (1983, 1985, 1986, 1987); Radzinowicz and Hood (1990) Part 7; May (1991); Worrall (1997); Brownlee (1998), specifically Chapters 3 and 4; Crow (2001), Chapter 5; Raynor and Vanstone

(2002); the informative monograph by Oldfield (2002); Chui and Nellis (2003); and Whitehead and Thompson (2004) for more contemporary issues from a training perspective. For those who want a guide as to which to read first then we suggest Bochel's excellent historical introduction; the McWilliams' quartet is essential reading on the history of ideas in probation; Raynor and Vanstone is also a good introduction; Chui and Nellis provide the reader with a contemporary overview of practice issues that is very helpful. At this point we simply want, in a discursive manner, to draw attention to a number of recurring themes and influences that have shaped probation between the 1870s and 1970s, the first hundred years of the system. We do so to prepare the ground for what is to come in later chapters as we proceed to delve deeper into our central concerns. Let us begin with religion.

Evangelical Theology and Saving Souls   *Religion*

The popular, traditional, orthodox, somewhat idealistic and yet inspiringly comforting view of the genesis of the probation system in 1876, is of a handful of well-meaning police court missionaries who worked with inebriated offenders within the late Victorian penal system for purely religious and humanitarian reasons. It has to be said there is an element of truth in this orthodox account, but the reality is more complex as we will attempt to elucidate. When isolating the theme of religion as we begin to excavate some of the influences that shaped probation during the early years, it is important to acknowledge that religious sensibilities determined the first prominent ideology that exercised a powerful rationale from the 1870s to the 1930s (McWilliams 1983). The importance of a religious outlook on the consciousness of probation during the early period should not come as a surprise because the first missionary employees were provided by the Church of England Temperance Society and other religious bodies. Furthermore, David Garland says that Victorian society (1837–1901) was underpinned by a tripartite ideology explicated as laissez-faire economics, utilitarian philosophy and evangelical religion; and it is the latter that has a specific resonance for us here (Garland 1985 p41).

In his 1983 essay, the first in a significant quartet of papers that trace the history of dominant ideas in probation from 1876 to the 1970s, Bill McWilliams (1983, 1985, 1986 and 1987) argues cogently that the police court missionaries had a religious philosophy articulated as saving offenders' souls by divine grace which, of course, is tantamount to the third limb of Garland's tripartite Victorian ideology. Even though

McWilliams argues that this underpinning religious philosophy was influential for the first sixty years of the probation system, he also says that its major influence can be discerned during the first decade of the 20th century, prior to the emergence of the phase of scientific diagnosis and professionalism. Since the early phase of religion, the service has metamorphosed through a number of other distinctive ideological periods that can be reconstructed by alluding to the following typology:

1876–1930s: saving offenders' souls by divine grace;

1930s–1970s: casework, diagnosis, rehabilitation and positivism;

1970s: collapse of the rehabilitative ideal;

1980s: alternatives to custody;

1991–1997: punishment in the community; penal pessimism;

1997f: punishment; renaissance of rehabilitation; evidence-based practice.

At this stage let us try to reconstruct the mind-set and belief system of evangelical theology. Christian theology (specifically its evangelical variant) states that the offender, like all other human beings, is made in the image of God to live in a specific way, which is to be faithful to the God who has created him and to offer worship. Unfortunately the offender, also like other human beings, does not always live up to these high expectations. In fact he misses the mark (the Greek word for sin – *hamartia* – means missing the mark), falls by the wayside, behaves in a sinful manner and therefore does not conform to the will of God. As a sinner the person must be brought back to God by God's saving grace, through faith in Jesus Christ. The life, death and resurrection of Jesus Christ, through whom it is believed God acted uniquely and decisively in human history, has effected atonement and by accepting this saving act in faith fallen human beings, no matter who they are or what they have done, can be redeemed, saved, changed, restored and made into a new person; a better and good person who will play by the rules.

These are the essential components constituting evangelical theology and what may be referred to as Christian essentialism, rooted in biblical theology. This means that the existence of God is assumed as a basic given of reality (a revealed truth and in fact *the* ultimate reality) and that human life has intrinsic meaning indisputably grounded in being made in God's image. In other words, it is unquestionably assumed that meaning is given to human beings by the reality of God. Therefore life must be lived, in fact it can be posited that one is created and destined to live, in a particular manner that encompasses a specific belief system and mode of behaviour so that offending behaviour is considered incompatible. In fact this essentialist Christian view of the world can be succinctly summarised by turning to St Augustine when he said in the Confessions that 'you [God] made us for yourself and our hearts find no peace until they rest in you' (Saint Augustine 1961 p21). Therefore to live in a Christ-like way is incompatible with being an offender, but God can change things through faith.

We should, of course, contrast this Christian essentialist position by referring to the existentialist perspective (the atheistic variety) that proceeds upon the basis that existence precedes essence. In other words, meaning and purpose are not *given* with existence because God does not exist. Rather human beings are burdened by the freedom to determine who they are, why they exist, thus shaping their own lives by their own decisions. Human beings have not been created, nor are they destined to live, in a particular way, to be a certain kind of person, to endorse a particular belief system. Instead they are free to make of themselves what they will and this presents itself as both a responsibility and a burden (Sartre 1973; Stevenson 1974; Kung 1976 for an intelligent guide to Christian belief in the modern world; Tarnas 1991 and the location of the Christian world view within the context of western civilisation from the Greeks to the modern era).[1]

At this point we need to illustrate the cogency of the organising idea of evangelical religion during the early years of the probation system and wider criminal justice system. When reflecting on the influence of Christian religion it needs to be contextualised within a much broader historical framework that embraces the sociology of punishment. Garland (1990) and Hudson (2003), for example, explore punishment from different perspectives by referring to the Durkheimian tradition of moral outrage, emotion, passion and vengeance, in addition to punishment's solidarity promoting effects and expression of collective feeling. Next Weber draws attention to the rule-based, impersonal, rational efficiency and bureaucratic nature of punishment. The Marxist approach draws attention to the class-based nature of punishment and the way it functions, it is reasoned, to control the working class and thus sustain a specific socio-economic order that benefits the few, not the many. There is also a Foucauldian perspective that emphasises discipline, power, knowledge and normalisation. Furthermore, and this is our salient point, the understanding of the sociology of punishment in general, and the history of probation in particular, would be incomplete unless we also take cognisance of religious, ethical and accompanying humanitarian sensibilities. Consequently, Rod Morgan says that when excavating the history of imprisonment it is important to attend to the religious motivation of penal reformers in the 18th century and the links between religion and humanitarian impulses (2002). This point can be illustrated by turning to John Howard (1726–1790), Elizabeth Fry (1780–1845) and the association between spirituality, religious vocation, philanthropy and penal/prison reform (Ignatieff 1978). Fraser draws attention to the religious motivation of those involved in working with individuals at the bottom of the social pile in Victorian society such as orphans, climbing boys, tramps, drunks, prostitutes and lunatics, and comments that this religious motivation was a 'stimulus to Victorian philanthropy' (1973 p118). Garland enriches our theme when he expounds that 'Evangelicals were in the vanguard of reforming movements both in Britain and in the USA, helping to ameliorate conditions of captivity or to aid prisoners upon their release, and later developing alternatives to imprisonment such as probation, which began as a form of missionary work funded by church-based temperance societies' (1990 p204).

In the 1930s Le Mesurier expressed an essentialist perspective when she acknowledged that 'the foundation of successful probation work must be the religious spirit in the best sense' (1935 pp61–62). Even though the religious phase of saving souls was left behind for a more scientific and therefore secular approach by the 1950s, it is intriguing to observe that Glover's book, *Probation and Re-education* (1956), contains a specific chapter on Faith in which a form of Christian essentialism can be discerned: 'Religion is not like a ripe plum which can be had for the picking. People who give up the search live, as it were, only half a life, losing what those who have it deem to be the most worthwhile thing in life ... Everyone who seeks spiritual enlightenment should be advised to pray, and prayer is the most effective way in which any probation officer who has himself a faith in the Living God can help his probationers' (1956 p254). Moreover, McWilliams recounts the story of a former principal probation officer who told him that 'when he was interviewed as an applicant for Home Office training for probation work in 1950 he was questioned in detail about his religious beliefs' (1985 p272). Finally, Radzinowicz and Hood bring us back to the first phase of the probation system by underlining that 'The motivation of the missionaries was deeply religious, to save sinners and bring them to salvation' (1990 p642). Therefore, the influence of religion in general and Christian metaphysics in particular is an important theme during the period under discussion in this opening chapter. It may well be the case that a number of contemporary employees are motivated by religious conviction, not just the Christian variety (and we know some colleagues who are). Nevertheless religion, understood as the organising principle or hegemonic ideology underpinning probation practice, is now passé.

Before developing the theme of religion a little further, even though evangelical theology provided some of the glue that held Victorian society together, it is of interest to consider a wider perspective. For example, and first, the 17th century enlightenment or age of reason in Europe, promoted a secular and scientific view of the world that challenged religious explanations. Secondly, the German philosopher Friedrich Nietzsche (1844–1900) rejected Christianity by announcing that God is dead. Next, Charles Darwin (1809–1882) caused not a little disquiet for the Victorians by his evolutionary views that were in conflict with the God-centred creationism of evangelical theology, supported by a literal interpretation of the Bible (this conflict prevails to this day between evolutionists and creationists). Fourthly, Bertrand Russell (1872–1970), British philosopher, considered that religion was harmful. Moreover, and finally, there was the view that religion was simply a phase en route to true scientific enlightenment. Therefore, even though religion was important to the police court missionaries during the early years of the probation system, it did not have all its own way because it was being challenged on different fronts. As Roy Hattersley says in his admirable account of *The Edwardians*, during the early years of the 20th century there was 'a growing scepticism about the power of prayer and the redemptive quality of faith' (2004 p63).

Before turning to our next theme we must remain with religion for a little while to illustrate further the cogency of this idea during the early decades of probation work. Due to one of life's inexplicable, unexpected, yet pleasant contingencies, during the course of writing this book we were provided with an opportunity to read a Police Court Mission report book that covers the period April 1918 to April 1923. It is a comprehensive account, in diary form, of police court mission probation work compiled by two unnamed officers who worked in the Borough of Sunderland. We assume two people because after the entries for April 1918 to September 1922 the handwriting noticeably changes to cover October 1922 to April 1923 when the accounts come to an end. The document provides us with fascinating insights into probation work in the North-East of England that overlaps with the work of the 1922 Departmental Committee (Home Office 1922, but there is no reference to this Home Office document in the text). In an orderly, readable, and sometimes moving, manner, it provides a monthly account of the job; a statistical digest on a daily basis in relation to eight variables: new arrivals, remands, men, women, boys, girls, protestant and catholic (but sometimes Jews). There is also a statistical monthly summary of work undertaken in addition to references to a number of cases the two officers were working with. Let us illustrate our findings by taking the reader back to December 1918 to hear what the first officer has to say: 'Alice Elliot, age 16, charged at the Court with stealing a quantity of clothing, on account of her youth was remanded to see if something could be done to help to save her. The Clerk suggested I get her into a Home. She consented to go to the Gosforth Home and was taken on the 30 December.' Furthermore, perhaps it can be suggested that religious and humanitarian impulses are in evidence as we recount the entry for the month of February 1920: 'Abdulla Mahomed, an Arab, came to the police station, being destitute and homeless. Mr Barker asked me to get him lodgings and food for the weekend. I tried two or three places to get him lodgings, but on account of him being a Black man they refused to take him. I then took him to the Seamen's Mission High Street and saw the Chaplain, and he was taken in and lodged for three days until Tuesday morning, and as he could not get a ship I sent him on to South Shields and helped with food and lodgings to get a ship. A young girl Laura Ivy Waters charged with (two others) soliciting prostitution. She promised the Justices that she would go to a Home. I arranged with the Salvation Army Matron for admission. She was taken the following day and received into the Home.'

When turning to the entries of the second officer, what we encounter is particularly illustrative of our religious theme. Let us commence with the first of four consecutive entries that begin in October 1922: 'I commenced my duties as Police Court and Probation Officer on the first of this month, and so far have found the work congenial to my nature. I have visited the homes of all the young men under my care, and in every case have found myself a welcome visitor by the young men, their parents and friends. By seeing them in their homes I have been able to get into close touch with them, and find out their troubles and difficulties, as well as the causes; and in some small measure, at any rate, I believe I have been able to help them, materially, morally and spiritually. Nearly all of them are in great distress through being out of work, and most of them I found badly in want of boots and clothing. This want I have been able to relieve to some extent by the prompt and liberal response to an appeal I made in the Daily Echo for cast-off clothing. I have distributed 45 parcels during the month, and they have been gratefully received.'

Then at the end of November 1922 the officer says: 'At the end of my second month I find the work becomes more and more interesting, and furnishes one with opportunities of doing good to the bodies and souls of my fellows. I am sorry to have to say the great depression still continues, and nearly all the cases under my care are out of work, and consequently more or less in need – and badly in need of boots and clothing. I am pleased to say that through the generosity of those ... I have been able to distribute 41 parcels of clothing, also 15 pairs of boots. There is no question that this depression is a cause of a great deal of theft, especially coal stealing, and we rejoice that orders for ships are being secured by most of the shipbuilders, and in a month or two we hope that many of the hands will soon be able to find employment.'

The entry for the month of December 1922 is particularly poignant when we read that 'I feel more than ever that to keep heart in this work, one needs to keep in constant touch with the Saviour of men. Human nature is such a weak and frail thing and of itself is so insufficient for the fight that unless we are strengthened by Him we are sure to go under. What a blessing it is then that the Saviour of men lived our life, and knowing all our frailties is able to help us to overcome. I am learning more and more to recommend Him to my fellows as their only hope of overcoming the evil around us and in us, and helping us to walk a clean, straight path. On the 8th of this month Stanley Wilson went to sea on the S.S. *Skarv*. He was convicted of stealing jewellery and remanded for this purpose.'

Our final entry is from the end of January 1923 and reads: 'The New Year is beginning with rifts in the clouds of depression that have hung over us for so long a time, and we are hoping that as the year advances the trade outlook will become brighter and brighter. I believe that most men have learned some good lessons from the hard times, and that a return to better times will do a great deal now to help them to live better and straighter lives. As we give to each other the seasons wishes for a bright, happy and prosperous year, God grant us grace to help each other to a better life. I have seen the Captain of the S.S.

Skarv and he says that Stanley Wilson is doing well, and gives every promise of making a good seaman and a good man.'

These entries illuminate the way in which faith in the Saviour of men underpinned probation work being undertaken by one officer specifically in the economically depressed North-East of England. Even though there is some acknowledgement of an association between economic conditions and crime (stealing coal presumably to keep warm in winter) the view being expressed, if our exegesis is correct, is that offenders known to the probation officer need Christian salvation to live a morally good and straight life. There is no argument for radical political change in the diary; rather spiritual and therefore moral reform is necessary for men who are victims of the vagaries of trade to withstand those temptations related to difficult social circumstances. Therefore salvation facilitates playing by the rules and social control. One last point: we made reference above to the 1922 Departmental Committee and will return to this document in the next chapter. Nevertheless, it is thematically significant to record at this juncture, because it overlaps with the period covered by the diary, that the 1922 Committee endorsed the position that the probation officer should be a person of missionary spirit and religious conviction.

The Politics of Probation

Religion was an important theme in probation for many years, but it was not the only influence at work shaping the developing system. Probation has never existed in a vacuum; it has never been a free floating structure within a hermetically sealed unit. In other words, we cannot understand probation unless we touch upon the wider political, social, economic context, even at its inception during 1876. To illuminate this point, a summary of Garland's 1985 text, *Punishment and Welfare*, is instructive. In this significant book he discerns a 'strategic fit' between Victorian penality and the wider political context. The central theme of the book is to explain the transition from the late Victorian penal system that was dominated by a repressive prison, to what he describes as the penal-welfare system that emerged towards the end of the 19th century and therefore coterminous with the emergence of probation. To be precise, this transition occurred between 1895 and 1914, a significant period in British political, social and penal history (Hattersley 2004).

Victorian penality, says Garland, operated with a particular view of the offender that was dominated by the themes of individualism, moral weakness, freedom and equality under the law, individual responsibility, absence of state aid (but there was selective charitable giving) and the classical view that offending is a form of behaviour freely and rationally chosen. The argument advanced is that there was a fit between these penal ideas and practices and the wider structures of social life, namely a laissez-faire economic system, minimalist state, freedom of the individual in a political system dominated by a free market, deterrent and less eligible social policies. The book proceeds to describe the complex processes that brought about the transition from the Victorian to the penal-welfare complex after 1895 as a consequence of change occurring at different levels, for example:

- An economic downturn after 1880 – recession.

- Growing realisation of poverty (Charles Booth's survey in London; Benjamin Rowntree in York; and Lady Florence Bell in Teesside revealed that poverty was widespread).

- Deprivation.

- Inequality and the need for social reform.

- The threat of working-class agitation and social revolution.

- The questionable legitimacy of the repressive Victorian prison.[2]

In other words, argues Garland, the cumulative weight of these events precipitated a crisis within British society that focused on the role of the state in relation to social and economic issues, accompanied by the important issue of the management, containment, regulation and control of problem populations, including working class offenders (1985 p65). Garland argues that there were four main responses to the crisis that emerged towards the end of the Victorian period: the new criminological science of positivism as opposed to classicism; social work; social security; and something that is no longer on the political agenda – eugenics. In his chapter that deals with Resistances, Manoeuvres and Representation (1985 Chapter 6) he explains the complex processes that created the new political, social, economic and penal arrangements during the early 20th century. Consequently, out of this crisis that was occurring at different levels, a more interventionist and ameliorative state emerged that was manifested in a number of social policy developments: school meals (1906); old age pensions (1908); National Insurance Act – health and unemployment (1911); all the result of a reforming Liberal government in power between January 1906 and 1915 (Fraser 1973; Hattersley 2004). Additionally, it was in this context of change that the probation system was placed upon a statutory footing by the Probation of Offenders Act 1907, thus establishing an important alternative to prison for predominantly working class offenders.

Therefore, the point being established within the context of this opening chapter as it traces a number of influences that were shaping probation during the first one hundred years, is that we need to complement the positive glow emanating from religious and humanitarian impulses with a dose of reality that comes from the political process. It may be theorised that the social and penal changes that occurred during the early years of the 20th century ameliorated the conditions of the working class and gave them a greater stake in society, whilst concurrently legitimising new forms of political power and control over those sections of society that supplied the probation and criminal justice system with its clientele (Raynor and Vanstone 2002; Vanstone 2004). Or, as Roy Hattersley puts it, 'Improvements in welfare have always resulted from a combination of altruism and political expedience' (2004 p129). Probation can not be solely analysed and has never simply existed as a humanitarian movement to counter the repressive nature of the Victorian penal system because there has always been a political dimension that draws us along the path of acknowledging its role in managing, containing and controlling 'problem' populations on behalf of the state. However, the period that we are exploring was more politically benign than the political culture that emerged during the 1970s. The point we make here is that the political dimension, the realities of power and control, can not be divorced from the development of probation from 1876; in fact, the story of probation is one of incremental political control from the centre, the story of which will be traced in the substantive chapters of this book.

Criminology, Reform and Rehabilitation

The third constellation of influences we want to allude to takes us beyond religion and politics into the area of changing criminological discourses and the accompanying concepts of reform and rehabilitation. We have already encountered how Garland analyses the 'fit' between Victorian penality and the wider structures of social life. Furthermore, there are other complementary features that can be identified as we begin to explore the late Victorian emphasis on individual responsibility, rational choice, the work of the missionaries and evangelical religion within the framework of classical criminology and the notion of reform

(Whitehead and Thompson 2004, specifically Chapter 1). Therefore, let us begin this section with an exploration into classical criminology.

The 19th century classical criminology paradigm did not, in its purest form, differentiate between the criminal and non-criminal in the sense that all criminal acts (there were exceptions) occurred because the offender, both rich and poor, made a free and deliberate choice to behave in a certain way. The individual, within this paradigm, was perceived as a rational actor freely choosing to offend with the result that the punishment should be proportionate to the seriousness of the act. This is the post-enlightenment tradition of Bentham and Beccaria (for a detailed exposition of these ideas see: Taylor, Walton and Young 1973; Garland 1985 p14; Morrison 1995; Walklate 2003).[3] At this stage the point that must be established is the fit between the approach of classical criminology and the framework of evangelical religion that initially shaped the work of the police court missionaries after 1876, embracing notions of reform rather than rehabilitation. Often the language of reform and rehabilitation is used interchangeably but for our purposes a conceptual distinction can be drawn. According to Hudson there is an echo of classicism in the notion of reform in the sense that it depends upon an understanding of the free will of the individual. Therefore 'the criminal *can* repent, *can* become a good citizen, only if he *will*' (1987 p3). He is even free and will therefore not be coerced to accept God's grace, to put his faith in God and be saved; it is a matter of individual choice. Human freedom and volition are intact. So even though the influence of positivism was being felt towards the end of the 19th century, the tenets of which will be explored shortly, we should not overlook the influence of classical or neo-classical thinking on the inchoate probation system, accompanied by the language of reform. Where the latter concept is concerned, Garland clarifies that 'reformation was seen as a process of moral atonement rather than behaviour modification, to be brought about through moral exhortation and the grace of God, and not through positive techniques of transformation' (1985 p127).

Let us return to the work of McWilliams (1983), albeit briefly. We have already seen that the police court missionaries' ideology was based upon saving offenders' souls by divine grace. Yet during the 20th century a new set of ideas began to establish themselves that took the probation system away from its original mission rooted in evangelical theology. McWilliams explains that, as the 20th century progressed, the idea took hold that those factors associated with offending (for example, alcohol) determined offending. In other words, drink was perceived as a stumbling-block (the Greek *skandalon*) that may have to be removed by coercion and human intervention, rather than as a consequence of the offenders' free will, faith and God's transforming grace. So this becomes what McWilliams refers to as the 'ontological flaw' in the missionary ideology of saving souls by divine grace, because here we encounter a determinist conception that paved the way for the period of scientific diagnosis and the growing influence of positivism as opposed to classical principles. The transition is captured by Garland when he says that 'the process of reform no longer attended upon the visitation of God's grace or the return of true reasoning, but instead mobilised its own positive techniques of intervention and human transformation' (1985 p79).

So what do we mean by positivism? Positivism as it started to emerge towards the end of the 19th century rivalled those ideas associated with the classical paradigm. As we were in the process of discovering those scientific laws that explain physical objects in the natural world, so it was believed that positivism within the context of social science could discover scientific laws that explain human behaviour. It is the approach that specifies certain positive factors are associated with crime; the focus was on the search for 'facts' as though crime is some material object or hard rock-like structure out there in the world, a naturally occurring entity that is waiting to be discovered, as opposed to thinking about crime as a culturally conditioned and socially constructed phenomenon (Young 1999). In other words, as Jock Young would argue, no aspect of human behaviour is inherently criminal; rather a crime is only a crime when someone in a position of power defines the item of behaviour as a crime (changing attitudes towards fox hunting seems to be a good example of this position, illustrating that crime is more analogous to a sponge that changes shape, a consequence of complex political and social processes, than hard rock). By contrast positivism directs attention to the offenders' characteristics rather than the offence, the person rather than the deed; offenders are different to law-abiding people; it challenged the classical view of individual responsibility in favour of biological, psychological and sociological determinism (Gelsthorpe 2003). Therefore, the response of the criminal justice system should be treatment rather than punishment for individuals of questionable responsibility for their actions. Of fundamental importance was the notion of aetiology, the search for the causes of crime, and that the criminal justice system should be left to the 'experts' in human transformation, including probation officers. This was the criminological context that influenced what may now be considered as the halcyon days of the probation service between the 1930s and 1970s. It is the period of 'science', positivism (even though neo-classical thinking remained as part of the system), casework and rehabilitation (as opposed to reform). Tony Bottoms helps us with this distinction when he says that 'In the post-war period, "reform" became rehabilitation – that is, religious and moral impulses in reformation became secularised, psychologised, scientised' (1980 pp1–2). This was the period of the highly influential rehabilitative ideal with its connotation of individualised treatment.[4]

The period in question being considered in this first chapter, specifically the years leading up to the crisis decade of the 1970s, Garland and Sparks (2000) refer to as 'modern' criminology. The central themes of modernism are described as: social progress; an aversion to punishment and retribution; a focus upon the individual and treatment. The problem of crime was understood and articulated in terms of poorly socialised and maladjusted individuals who created problems for society that required correction. In fact, the general principles of modernist criminology are neatly captured in the following summary of the position: 'It focused upon deep-rooted causes, distant childhood experiences and psychological conflicts ... If there was a central explanatory theme, it was the welfarist one of "social deprivation" and subsequently "relative deprivation". Individuals became delinquent because they were deprived of proper education, or family socialisation, or job opportunities, or proper treatment for their social and psychological problems. The solution for crime was a welfare state solution – individual treatment, support and supervision for families, and the enhancement of the plight of the poor through welfare reform' (Garland and Sparks 2000 p9).

Therefore, within this context there was a broad consensus between the political parties on the approach that the criminal justice system should take; a commitment to the welfare state after 1945; the need for state intervention and social services; a commitment to the welfare and treatment of individual offenders expressed in the rehabilitative ideal both in the community through probation and in prison. The probation system was at the heart of this enterprise, and it is helpful for the reader to study David Garland's summary of the penal-welfare system to appreciate the importance of the rehabilitative ideal in this process.[5]

So far we have alluded to the themes of evangelical religion, the politics of probation, and latterly to criminology, reform and rehabilitation.

The next step is to enquire into the tension between the psychology of the individual and the dimension of the social, a tension that has always prevailed in probation work.

Psychology

It may be argued that three of the most important academic disciplines that have impacted upon probation during its long history are criminology, sociology and psychology.[6] New recruits to the service need to be grounded in these disciplines primarily because they make an intellectual contribution to assessing, understanding, interpreting and explaining human (offending) behaviour. Of course, probation practitioners require an eclectic knowledge base that also includes the criminal justice system, penal policy, rationales of sentencing, sociology of punishment and legislation, in addition to more ineffable features (for a discussion of different types of knowledge in the probation service, see Whitehead and Thompson 2004). We turn now to the pervasive influence of psychology throughout the history of probation as we continue with the theme of our first chapter, which is to identify a number of significant influences.

Hollin takes our journey almost back to the beginning of the probation system as he states that it was during the early 1900s that psychology was established as an academic discipline in British universities (2002 p145). The history of probation has been closely associated with an emphasis on the psychology of the individual, which means that explanations for offending have, on the whole, been conceptualised within a framework of faulty and maladjusted individuals rather than the wider social structure. To some degree this tradition continues into contemporary approaches with offenders because since 1997 evidence-based practice has focused on teaching the individual thinking, social, and problem-solving skills. The reason for this is that offending, like other forms of behaviour, is considered to be learned; therefore the acquisition of certain skills will help the individual to unlearn a repertoire of dysfunctional offending behaviours. This is the cognitive-behavioural approach that is rooted in psychology and primarily focused on the individual. In fact one may ponder the difference, if any, between a religious approach that seeks the moral and spiritual transformation of the individual, and the secular cognitive-behavioural approach that seeks to straighten out the individual offender's thinking. It can be argued that the same objective is being pursued, which is *individual change* with a view to more acceptable forms of behaviour; conformity to an established norm.

If we return to an earlier period then it is interesting to recall that Dorothy Bochel (1976) tries to keep our feet on the ground by reminding us that in the 1920s and 1930s probation officers were aware of the problems being created by social factors, namely unemployment. In fact this observation can be illustrated by returning to the Police Court Mission report book. First, an entry from February 1921 reads: 'I have a number of youths and lads who are unemployed, asking my help to get them work but under the depressed state of the works in the town I am unable to give them help to find work.' Then in April 1922: 'Two youths I took to the Labour Exchange and to the Shipping Federation, also to the Customs Office to try to get them to sea. But there were no vacancies due to the slackness of trade.' Finally, June 1922: 'One of my difficulties in seeking to help boys or youths to get employment is no work. I have visited both the Labour Exchange and also the Shipping Federation and the Customs Office of the Board of Trade. I have taken youths who wished to go to sea, but the reply is that there are so many on their books waiting. I am glad to say that an ex-convict who was given employment by a J.P. that the man and his wife are very thankful for such help being given to get him employment – he is doing well.'

However, by the late 1920s there was an emerging preoccupation with psychology and casework (Bochel 1976 p121). In fact, Joan King concludes that as the probation system emerged from the economic depression of the 1930s with its well-documented material and social problems, so much greater emphasis was placed upon the personal, mental and psychological factors in criminality (1964 p19f). It was during this period that the system was moving beyond the mission of saving souls to the age of diagnosis and the medical-treatment model with its connotations of rehabilitation through casework (Whitehead and Thompson 2004, Chapter 1; Oldfield 2002 p31f). Le Mesurier in the mid-1930s comments that 'A study that is becoming increasingly necessary to all engaged in the work of education is that of psychology, and to few can it be more important than to probation officers … They must realise that there are unconscious motives as well as conscious ones, and that these affect their own conduct as well as that of those whom they are trying to help' (1935 p62). With Le Mesurier's reference to unconscious and conscious motives we stray into the orbit of Freud and psychoanalysis, thus reminding us of the importance of those early years in the formation of human character that can be significant, particularly if there has been a traumatic incident. Marx believed that the behaviour of human beings is determined by one's location within the economic system; Skinner that we are conditioned by the environment. It was Freud who pointed towards those factors in the mind he considered determine behaviour that can be hidden from ourselves – the determining influence of the unconscious (Stevenson 1974). We know that the Police Court Mission Training Scheme (as opposed to the Home Office Training Scheme that was established in 1930) taught prospective probation officers a number of subjects including the Psychology of Criminal Tendencies with a view to investigating, understanding and correcting the individual in the direction of conformity to acceptable standards. By the 1930s the discipline of psychology embraced the practices of mental testing, IQ scores, intelligence and mental deficiency, some of the tools that could be used to facilitate an understanding of the criminal (Le Mesurier 1935). In other words, these psychological tools facilitated a journey of inwardness into the soul to establish why the individual did not conform to the norm. Consequently, the individual could be corrected and changed by behaviour modification techniques, for example, to establish conformity (Kendall 2004).

Glover's (1956) window onto probation work in the late 1940s and early 1950s refers to the links between behaviour and social or material conditions. However, there is a focus on changing, ameliorating, treating and reforming the individual (but it is interesting to note that there are no references to rehabilitation or casework in Glover's book). Glover acknowledges the impact of socio-economic conditions on health. Furthermore 'in this country at the present time the greatest toll of ill-health comes from emotional causes' (p87). She also proceeds to make the point that 'The greatest contribution which psychology has made from the point of view of probation is that it has led us away from the purely legal or moral approach to delinquency to the scientific or curative one' (p19). A further reference can be made to Stott (1952), who said that the main task of the probation officer is diagnostic. According to Stott, diagnosis 'means that the probation officer must be able to measure the emotional and moral state of the offender' (p208). The picture that emerges in Stott is one where the probation officer, in order to diagnose problems, needs an understanding of psychology, as opposed to 'Freudian occultism' (p209). According to Stott, delinquency is rooted in emotional problems within the individual or family and it is the discipline of psychology that facilitates the process of explanation; it makes a contribution to aetiology. Therefore, during the period under discussion, there is a surfeit of evidence that crime is understood mainly as an individual, emotional and moral, rather than social, problem (McWilliams 1985) that requires the insights that can be drawn from psychology.[7]

The Social Dimension: a brief comment

On the whole, the search for the aetiology of criminal behaviour has predominantly concentrated on the maladjusted individual and 'problem family', and the assertion that the discipline of psychology has been conducive to such an approach. By contrast, it should be remembered that Guerry and Quetelet, in the second half of the 19th century, concluded that crime was a result of social causes. Moreover, during the early years of probation, the preoccupation with psychology did not preclude the possibility of social reform (Garland 1985 Chapter 3). Garland refers to the influence of Bonger and Ferri during the early 20th century to add weight to the concentration on the social dimension. Of course, a more contemporary exposition of this approach can be found in Walker and Beaumont (1981), who provide us with a Marxist analysis of probation work. Nevertheless, the main focus within probation work over many decades has been the preoccupation to change the individual rather than change the wider political, social and economic factors that are associated with criminal behaviour. Moreover, Garland (1985 pp175–181) explains the process that, in the early years of probation, closed off social reform in favour of individual reform.[8]

Summary and Conclusion

We begin this book by covering ground that other authors have excavated empirically in some detail over recent years, yet we feel it is important to draw attention to some of the major influences that have been at work shaping the probation enterprise during the first one hundred years. We have drawn attention to the influence of Victorian religion in conjunction with Christian evangelical metaphysics, essentialism, humanitarianism and anti-custodialism with the birth of the probation order in 1907. The influence of religion continues into the present in the form of chaplains in prisons and religious organisations within probation, but religion is no longer the dominant ideology it was at the beginning.[9] Even when it was the dominant ideology, the original mission of saving souls did not exist in a vacuum, which is why we have alluded to politics, state power and control. In other words, probation work can not be disassociated from prevailing political, social and economic priorities and the methods available to the state to manage, contain, regulate and control recalcitrant populations who drift into offending. Probation has always been involved in the exercise of political and social control by one group over another; by one section of society over another (Garland 1985; Young 1976; Walker and Beaumont 1981) on behalf of the state.[10]

Next are a set of related influences within the orbit of classical and positivist criminology, changing criminological perspectives, reform and rehabilitation. Furthermore, we have touched on the tradition of psychology in probation whilst not overlooking the wider social dimension within which to understand crime. The argument can be advanced that it has always been more manageable, and of course politically acceptable, to transform the individual to conform to social mores, to blame the individual and locus of the family for criminal behaviour, rather than to ameliorate those social conditions and structures that insightful probation officers realise affect behaviour. Furthermore, psychology could be harnessed to the purpose of social control in the way it focused upon dysfunctional, maladjusted and degenerative human beings, rather than the political system that produces winners and losers (Vanstone 2004).

There is little doubt that probation existed in a relatively benign political world for many decades and that the centre, in the form of the Home Office, provided a light touch in local probation areas that on the whole slowly emerged in the decades after 1907. However, as we move towards the end of the 1970s this situation was about to change in a significant way that perhaps few of us could appreciate at the time, particularly the years after 1984. With the benefit of hindsight, probation work, specifically after 1979, was embarking on a journey into a world where the landscape was beginning to change. Within a short period of time a new atmosphere began to pervade the organisation, a new language and different priorities emerged, but we knew little of this as the 1970s came to an end. Therefore, against the background of our exploration of numerous themes and influences, the next chapter will look in a more sequential way at the period 1907–1979 before turning to our substantive chapters in Part 2.

NOTES – Chapter 1

[1] What is both interesting and arguably paradoxical about the reliance upon evangelical theology and Christian metaphysics during the early years of the probation system within Victorian society, is the wider context of European culture and thought that was in the process of becoming more secular, scientific and anti-God. Tarnas (1991) traces this process from the 15th century renaissance through the 17th century enlightenment and then the 19th century pronouncements of Nietzsche that God is dead and Darwin's assault upon the Christian essentialist edifice. He also draws attention to the scientific revolution. Therefore at a wider level we can observe a philosophical and scientific movement away from the Church and Christian theology. Yet it is within this wider context that the probation system began in 1876 with a distinctively religious ideology of saving offenders' souls by divine grace. Secularisation has progressed even further into the 20th century and the probation service no longer justifies its existence by resorting to religious ideas, even though a vestige of religious sensibility remains, of course, within society (Christianity and Islam, for example) and also in probation work.

[2] Garland's 1985 thesis can be expanded upon by saying that without locating the book in a Marxist framework, yet influenced by Marxist concepts of the relationship between political, social, economic structures and social-penal policy, in addition to the presence of Foucauldian themes, he explores the relationship between political, social, economic, ideological, penal and social policy change between 1895 and 1914. What appears to be happening is a completely different basis for the role of the state than previously: more interventionist, reformist, inclusive, with a focus on managing, containing, regulating, normalising and controlling, as opposed to the exclusionary and repressive punishment of the Victorian prison system. What emerges is a different basis for the state's control of the poor, a new form of legitimacy with the religious outlook of the police court missionaries forming part of this process, as was the creation of the probation service and probation order in 1907.

[3] It needs to be acknowledged that, since the 1980s, we have witnessed the renaissance of classical criminological ideas in the form of Right Realism that will be alluded to in subsequent chapters.

[4] When distinguishing between reform and rehabilitation throughout the history of the probation service it is instructive to refer to the four important Departmental Committee Reports (Home Office 1909, 1922, 1936 and 1962) that are considered in more detail in Chapter 2. In the 1909 report probation is perceived as a powerful instrument for the reformation of individual offenders. The 1922 report supported its predecessor in its commitment to the principle of reformation. By the time of the 1936 report it was stated that 'The object of probation is the ultimate re-establishment of the probationer in the community and the probation officer must accordingly take a long view' (p58). In 1962 the Morison committee confirmed the principles articulated in the three

previous reports, which are of a service concerned with treatment, reformation *and* the rehabilitation of offenders – see paragraphs 8–24, 53–59.

5 The 'modernist' agenda was characterised by rehabilitation and correctionalist criminology. David Garland (2001 pp34–44) provides the reader with an excellent overview of its central tenets, in addition to which he draws attention to the historical conditions that structured the framework for this approach within the criminal justice system for many decades. The 'conditions of existence' for the penal-welfare system were: social democracy, inclusivity and welfare; humanitarian motivations; informal controls exercised within the family, school and workplace; favourable economic conditions in the 1950s and 1960s; respect for professional groups and so-called 'experts'; political support and a discernible consensus between the main parties. Additionally, the perceived effectiveness of rehabilitation and correctionalism was a factor. By contrast, it has been argued that the period after the 1970s has witnessed the transition from the category of the 'modern' to 'late modern'. Jock Young (1999) describes this transition in terms of a shift from a more inclusive and assimilative society to exclusion. He also says that 'There is a predominant train of thought shared both by those on the left and the right of the political spectrum that the last third of the twentieth century has been a period of decline' (1999 p48). The indices of this decline include unemployment, the breakdown of the family and community, disrespect, declining standards, disorder and insecurity, and of course the phenomenon of rising crime.

6 A note on etymology is perhaps helpful here. Criminology literally means 'word about crime'; sociology 'word about social realities existing apart from the individual'. Additionally, psychology comes from two Greek words that literally mean 'word about the heart, soul or mind'. Therefore psychology takes us on a journey of inwardness within the individual.

7 A further note on psychology may be considered helpful here. Lorraine Gelsthorpe reminds us that, according to Freud, crime reflects 'the notion of the offender as having a weak conscience' (2003 p23). She also helps to define the parameters of psychological theories by referring to 'personality, reasoning, thought intelligence, learning, perception, imagination, memory and creativity' (2003 p23). Additionally, McWilliams confirmed the view in the second of his quartet of papers that crime, during the probation system of the 1920s to 1960s, was located in the individual not the social. He stated that crime was a 'manifestation of psychological or psycho-social disease' (1985 p260). There is also a very helpful paper by Maurice Vanstone (2004) in the *Probation Journal* that draws attention to the important relationship between the emergence of the probation system and the discipline of psychology.

8 Bill McWilliams (1983 p133) makes a reference to Brian Harrison (1971) and his book *Drink and The Victorians*: 'hordes of prostitutes and drunkards ... were not psychological aberrations but the product of a particular socio-economic structure' p355). See Stewart and Stewart (1993), in addition to

Mair and May (1997), for more contemporary evidence that adds weight to the social determinants of certain types of crime.

9   It should be acknowledged that the influence of Christianity continues in the probation service. This can be illustrated by referring to the Probation Service Christian Fellowship that celebrated its 50th anniversary in 2004. Personal correspondence with the chair of the PSCF in November 2004 revealed that it was during the early 1950s that a probation officer in London had a vision of the need for a fellowship of Christians within the service. 'People began to pray and in February 1954 the PSCF was founded that was a gathering together of a small group of people united by their faith. The focus was on prayer for the work of offenders and families ... I firmly believe that the need remains for Christian witness within the Service and for informed prayer for its work and workers. So God is still calling his people into this work and we have seen many Christian Trainee Probation Officers join the Fellowship: Praise the Lord!' In November 2004 we were informed that there were 136 members. For further details see: www.pcsf.org.uk; e-mail address: enquiries@pscf.org.uk.

10   When exploring probation history, particularly the early years, it is important to draw a distinction between *orthodox* and *revisionist* accounts. For example, Jarvis grounds the work of police court missionaries within a religious and humanitarian framework and states that 'a care and concern for the socially disadvantaged is still at the core of its being' (1972 p69). However, other factors must be taken into account that are elucidated by, for example, Vanstone (2004) and to which we have alluded in this chapter.

Chapter 2

REFORMING LIBERALS TO RADICAL CONSERVATIVES: 1907 TO 1979

'All the cases who are on probation are behaving remarkably well and are trying to obey the order of their recognisances.'
(Police Court Mission Report Book entry for July 1922)

Introduction

In December 1905, four years into the reign of Edward VII, the Conservatives resigned from office. At the general election on 13th January 1906 the Liberal party won a landslide victory when Henry Campbell-Bannerman became Prime Minister until replaced by Asquith in 1908. The result of the election was: Unionists 157 seats; Labour 53; Irish Nationalists 83; Liberals 377 – which gave the Liberals a 132-seat majority. During the Edwardian period 77% of the population of England and Wales lived in urban areas (Hattersley 2004 p69) and textiles, coal, iron and steel, in addition to shipbuilding, were important for the economy. These were the years when the suffragettes were agitating for votes for women; education was becoming important; the trade unions and labour movement campaigned for the protection of their rights. It was also the time for the fledgling motor car (for example, Rolls and Royce) and the aeroplane (the Wright brothers). The Liberals ushered in a number of social reforms including the probation system; and yet, to our surprise, Hattersley (2004) does not mention the latter at all. So it is down to us to say that probation was born at a time of rapid political and social change.

The Probation of Offenders Act 1907

We can trace the first police court missionary to 1876, but the first time the word 'Probation' was added to the lexicon of legislative terms was on 8th August 1887 when the Probation of First Offenders Act received Royal Assent. Unfortunately this legislation did not enable offenders to be supervised by probation officers but it was a step in the right direction. We had to wait until the reforming Liberal Government that had come to power in January 1906 for the Bill that was to culminate in the creation of the probation system. In fact it was Herbert Gladstone, as the newly elected Home Secretary, who sponsored the Bill that was to become the Probation of Offenders

Act, receiving Royal Assent on 21st August 1907. However, the Act was not implemented until 1st January 1908 when, for the first time in British penal history, it was possible for the courts to impose a Probation Order that contained a supervisory element. At this introductory stage of this chapter it is worth pausing to clarify some of our language because, on 1st January 1908, we did not have an organised probation service that was being administered or managed throughout the United Kingdom in a consistent manner. Rather, what we did have was the possibility of a Probation Order, Probationer, and a fledgling Probation Officer. We also had an established court system (courts of summary jurisdiction, quarter sessions and assizes) that had the power to make such an order and appoint an officer; but we must stress that we did not have a probation service in the way we have come to understand the term. Subsequently, of course, a number of local area services emerged that, as late as 2001, were melded into a National Probation Service, tightly controlled by a central authority. But in 1907 and for many decades to come there was little sense of a complete organisation, an organic whole. It was a case of small but important beginnings.

When we look back at the language and philosophy of the initial primary legislation it is instructive, particularly from the vantage point of the 21st century. The Probation of Offenders Act 1907 (7 Edw. 7, c. 17) gave courts the power to appoint probation officers and initially a number were appointed on a part-time basis. But the new concept of placing offenders under the supervision of a probation officer was accepted only slowly. The essence of the new order was that it was not a punishment and not a sentence, even though the charge was proved. Nevertheless, there had to be consent, rather than compulsion, because the latter is tantamount to punishment. The name of the probation officer appeared on the probation order itself and the probationer had to give a signed undertaking to be of good behaviour. It was also possible for the order to include various conditions as to residence, avoiding alcohol, or other matters the court deemed necessary to prevent re-offending. Section 4 of the 1907 Act explained the duties of the probation officer, which are worth repeating as follows:

(a) to visit or receive reports from the person under supervision at such reasonable intervals as may be specified in the probation order;

(b) to see that he observes the conditions of his recognisance;

(c) to report to the court as to his behaviour;

(d) to advise, assist and befriend him, and, when necessary, to endeavour to find him suitable employment.

By 1907 the developing penal-welfare system under the Liberals was in the process of creating new court disposals that expanded the late Victorian penal system (Garland 1985) by adding, in addition to probation, borstal training; preventive detention; detention in an inebriate reformatory and for mentally defectives; licensed supervision and supervised fines; to the death penalty; penal servitude; prison; reformatory schools; whipping for adults and birching for juveniles; recognisance and fine. Consequently there was a recognisance with and without the element of supervision and it was the latter form, prior to the 1907 Act and towards the end of the Victorian period, under which the police court missionaries were being used to provide informal supervision of offenders.[1] The recognisance with supervision was the probation order that required the probationer to promise to be of good behaviour. It was a time of trial and the testing out of the promise made prior to being readmitted to full citizenship (Oldfield 2002). The work of these early probation pioneers involved working with inebriates in trouble with the courts, matrimonial disputes, prison aftercare, helping to find work, and the making of enquiries for courts, within a religious framework of saving offenders' souls by divine grace (as we elucidated in our first chapter). It is also important to state that from its inception probation was being used as an alternative to custody (Downes 1988 p6). Even though the Bill that culminated in the 1907 Act was sponsored by the Home Secretary, the only vestige of Home Office central control at this stage of the system was the power to make Rules for putting the new Act into effect (Bochel 1976 p30). In fact, section 7 stated that 'The Secretary of State may make rules for carrying this Act into effect, and in particular for prescribing such matters incidental to the appointment, resignation, and removal of probation officers, and the performance of their duties, and the reports made by them, as may appear necessary'. After only 14 months the new probation system became the subject of a review, the first of four Departmental Committees that we will consider in the course of our journey towards 1979.

Report of the Departmental Committee on the Probation of Offenders Act 1907 *(Home Office 1909)*

On 8th March 1909 the Home Secretary, who remained Herbert Gladstone, appointed a Departmental Committee comprising five members to enquire into the operation of the 1907 Act. It reported on 23rd December 1909 to the Secretary of State. It was discovered that some courts were using the probation order more than others, which culminated in the report recommending that the Home Secretary write to all magistrates with a view to encouraging them to make greater use of the new disposal. It also considered the appointment and remuneration of probation officers and anticipated the creation of a national association. Some witnesses advocated the appointment of a chief probation officer to improve the organisation of the system, but this was rejected. It was the Committee's view that probation was already proving to be of value at this inchoate stage and suggested that justices should arrange for the oversight of probation work that anticipated the emergence of the probation committee system (Central Council of Probation Committees 1987). It was also stated that the Home Office should be responsible for the general supervision of probation developments and the probation order was ideologically perceived as a powerful instrument in the reformation of offenders. Probation officers were also encouraged to keep a record of cases and work undertaken.

The probation officer appointed after 1st January 1908 could also be the agent of a voluntary society: Church Army, Church of England Temperance Society, Police Court Mission, Discharged Prisoners' Aid Societies, Catholic Societies, Salvation Army and NSPCC. Therefore the probation officer could have two masters: the appointing court supported by the local authority that paid him, in addition to a voluntary society. This was known as dual control and was a feature of the early years of probation, particularly until 1936 (as we shall see presently). We have just seen how the 1909 Committee suggested the formation of an association of probation officers. This suggestion was shortly to be taken up and requires a brief word of explanation.

National Association of Probation Officers

A recommendation made by the 1909 Committee culminated in the creation of a society to promote probation. First, in 1910 an undated NAPO publication of recent years states there was a meeting of ten probation officers at a house in Croydon that discussed the creation of a staff association. Subsequently, in an article located in the journal *Probation*, Bochel (1962) reminds us that on 22nd May 1912 about forty probation officers gathered at Croydon Town Hall, where they heard Sydney Edridge, Clerk to the Borough Justices, press the cause for a national association of probation officers. Later, in December 1912, the first meeting of prospective members was held at Caxton

Hall, Westminster, where 70 out of 180 officers who had expressed an interest attended to adopt a constitution:

(a) for the advancement of probation work;

(b) for the promotion of a bond of union amongst probation officers, the provision of opportunities for social intercourse, and the giving of friendly advice;

(c) to enable probation officers from practical experience by collective action to bring forward suggestions on probation work, and on the reformation of offenders.

By 1913 the first newsletter was produced and in 1929 the first probation journal appeared with the help of the Earl of Faversham. Therefore, a journal produced by the National Association of Probation Officers has been in existence ever since and is currently known as the *Probation Journal*, which is published four times a year. It has acquired a national and international reputation for disseminating good practice in probation and wider criminal justice matters.

The Criminal Justice Administration Act 1914 (4 & 5 Geo. 5, c. 58) made amendments to the 1907 Act by recognising a condition of residence in a probation order, in addition to making provision for a fines supervision order. Of course, during the next four years, 1914–18, the country was at war in Europe, so compared to these events the development of the probation system was hardly a national priority. In 1918 the Conservatives were returned to power with a large majority. Then, after being less popular in the 1922 and 1923 elections, the general election of 1924 witnessed a large Conservative majority that was to last until 1929 when Labour was the largest party in the Commons for the first time, yet without an overall majority.

Before moving on to consider the second of the Departmental Committees (referred to earlier), we shall return to the aforementioned Police Court Mission diary to illustrate probation work towards the end of the First World War and into the early 1920s. In fact we begin with the first entry in the diary, dated April 1918, which says: 'John Dunn a boy aged 15 whose father is in France. The mother dead. At the desire of the Justices the boy was found good lodgings and also work at Mr Bartram's ship yard. He is now doing well and he was charged with gambling. He had been sleeping in common lodging's houses previous to being charged at the court.' We include this entry because of our assumption that the boy's father was caught up in the

European war that impacted upon the work of the probation officer. Further illustrations from the report book will follow shortly. It is also important to acknowledge that during the early years, that is by 1920, probation was mainly used for young people under 21 years of age (Matthews 1999 p156).

Report of the Departmental Committee on the Training, Appointment and Payment of Probation Officers *(Home Office 1922)*

On 22nd November 1920 a Departmental Committee was appointed by the Home Secretary, Edward Short, and it reported on 30th January 1922. Again, it was discovered that the use being made of the probation order by magistrates was uneven and it was recommended that probation officers should continue to be appointed by the courts and paid by local authorities. It reinforced the 1909 Committee in its view that probation was a reformative measure but went on to state that every court should have a probation officer at its disposal because many courts did not have access to such a service; remuneration should be improved; and central government should provide a grant towards the cost of the service. Furthermore, and importantly, it was recommended that each Bench of magistrates should appoint a number of justices to form a committee to organise and oversee probation work in their area. In the month that the Committee was appointed, we read the following entry in the Police Court Mission diary, which provides an insight into the scope of probation work in the North-East of England at this time:

'Summary November 1920

Visits to cells, remand homes, adults and juveniles 34

Prisoners in cells seen and conversed with 114

Remand cases which have been seen in the cells from day to day 35

Persons conversed with at the Borough and County Courts 156

Juveniles conversed with at the Borough and County Juvenile Court 32

Discharged prisoners met with who have been to prison 7

Visits made to homes of cases etc. 58

Visits from cases and other persons seeking advice or help 35

Visits from cases who are on probation or bound over 64

Visits to lodging houses or boarding houses 2

Attendance at Courts, adults and juvenile 38

Letters written to cases or on behalf of cases 15

Persons who have signed the pledge or promised to give up drink 3

Youths and men assisted with food, clothing or lodgings 8

Girls or women assisted with food, clothing or lodgings 1

Youths, lads and men assisted, advised, to try to find work 5

Young people visited at the request of friends etc. 6

Young women taken to a Home 1

Married couples conversed with to settle their differences 12

Boys sent to the Industrial School 3

Boys sent to Reformatory Schools 0'

What is of interest is the paucity of clear references to probation reports or enquiries in the diary. In fact, one of the few references is located in the entry for January 1921 that reads: 'I was written to by the police court missionary of the Bow Street Police Court, London, about a youth who lived at 23 Lawrence Street, who was locked up. He was remanded by the magistrates for enquiries as to his character as he said he knew me. He was charged with wearing H.M. uniform unlawfully. I saw the parents and wrote to the missionary and I learn he was discharged and has arrived at his home. He is a sailor and the chaplain of the Seamen's Mission will no doubt succeed in getting him a ship.' A brief comment on probation enquiries is required at this point. Joan King says that the work of police court missionaries prior to 1907 involved being used by magistrates to report on the homes and other circumstances of offenders (1964 p5). Moreover, Bill McWilliams (1983) states that, around 1889, missionaries were being used to undertake pre-sentence investigations. Rule 37 of Probation Rules 1926 adds: 'A Probation Officer shall make such preliminary enquiries, including enquiries into the home surroundings, as the Court may direct in respect of any offender in whose case the question of the making of a probation order may arise.' There is a section on court reports in Le Mesurier (1935) and, as we will see later in this chapter, the Streatfield Committee (Home Office 1961) extended the provision of reports beyond the determination of suitability for a probation order to include other sentences. Consequently, we may rightly claim that the provision of information to courts has always been a significant probation task (also see Oldfield 2002 p21).

The Criminal Justice Acts of 1925 and 1926 started to establish a more standardised administrative probation system by the way it was made compulsory for the first time that every court had access to the services of a probation officer, including a woman officer if possible. The legislation also confirmed that the local probation committee was responsible for paying and appointing probation officers, and that the committee would comprise justices from either one or more than one court area. In fact the Home Secretary was given the power to combine two or more Petty Sessional Divisions to create probation areas in the interests of administrative efficiency. But, as the Central Council of Probation Committees was to remind us, 'In a service which was small and organised in local units, there was no managerial hierarchy and it was for this reason that special committees, to be known as cases committees, were established in each PSD to exercise direct supervision over the work of individual officers. Probation committees and case committees developed side by side with the latter eventually evolving into the probation liaison committee' (1987 p3; see also Le Mesurier 1935 p35 for more information on the importance of the probation committee during the 1920s and 1930s).

The costs of the developing area services were to be covered by the local authorities, which would raise money from local ratepayers but with a grant of 50% made by central government. The financial mechanisms instituted made the local authority the banker of probation so that the probation committee set the budget and local authority treasurers managed the financial processes, setting protocols for financial control. Consequently these arrangements made treasurers powerful players in the budget-setting process and they were able to influence the size and shape of probation spending plans. This did not seem to matter greatly during the early decades but as the system began to expand there was a need for more finance. Furthermore, some principal probation officers in years to come were committed to innovation, with the result that local services grew at differential rates, and there were few checks on growth if local authority treasurers and elected members were content to see a little extra added to the local rate bill that met with little opposition from the Home Office. Financial management also operated differentially because probation areas adopted the accounting practices of their sponsoring local authorities. This not only influenced the size of budgets but also practice in relation to budget management and accounting practices. For example, virement, the procedure by which money could be moved from one budget head to another after the budget had been set, was more flexible in some regimes than others. Consequently, some developing probation areas operated under financial and therefore operational constraints that could hamper new developments and organisational needs.

Following the above legislation, the Probation Rules of 4th June 1926 were published by the Secretary of State under the 1907 Act and Part I of the Criminal Justice Act 1925. These are comprehensive Rules that deal with a range of issues including probation committees, the appointment and qualifications of probation officers, leave arrangements, duties, court reports and records. It is worth quoting Rule 60 in full because of the reference to salaries, inequality between the sexes and the development of a hierarchy within the service, as follows: 'Full-time probation officers shall be placed on a scale salary rising from the minimum to the maximum of the scale by annual increments of £10 a year. The minimum of the scale shall not be less than £180 nor more than £220 for men, and not less than £150 nor more than £200 for women. The maximum of the scale shall not be less than £330 nor more than £370 for men and not less than £230 nor more than £270 for women. Provided that with the approval of the Secretary of State a special salary scale may be fixed for a Principal Probation Officer who may be appointed to supervise the work of other probation officers or to a probation officer with approved University qualifications.' By 1928 a Home Office Circular drew attention to the fact that the probation order was not simply intended for first offenders or juveniles. In 1930 the first Home Office Training Course for probation officers was established; it was thus being acknowledged that the probation officer required something more than religious conviction and enthusiasm (see Whitehead and Thompson 2004, specifically Chapter 1, for a succinct history of training arrangements in probation from 1930 to the creation of the Diploma in Probation Studies towards the end of the 1990s). The Children and Young Persons Act 1933 emphasised a central role for the growing probation system in the supervision of juvenile offenders subject to probation orders. Before turning our attention to the third

Departmental Committee report, it is worth drawing the readers' attention to a significant publication by Mrs Le Mesurier in 1935 that is a rich source of information for probation work from the missionary period into the mid-1930s.

Report of the Departmental Committee on the Social Services in Courts of Summary Jurisdiction *(Home Office 1936)*

On 9th October 1934 yet another Departmental Committee was appointed by the Home Secretary, Sir John Gilmour, which reported to the new Secretary of State, Sir John Simon, on 13th March 1936. This document constituted a major review of the service and established two main principles: first, the developing service needed trained staff; and, secondly, that it must be a wholly public service that would bring to an end the system of dual control and therefore split loyalties between courts and voluntary societies. Some of the main proposals were that it was important to retain local probation committees; more senior and principal probation officers were required; Home Office supervision should be maintained but should be strengthened by the introduction of powers of inspection, thus initiating the Home Office Inspectorate. Moreover, in 1936 the theme of efficiency was emphasised, which would come to assume much greater significance after 1979 (as we shall see in the next chapter). Where the probation committee was concerned, Bochel says that it was its failure to keep in contact with its probation officers through lack of supervision that resulted in the proposal for the development of a supervisory grade to complement the work of the committees (Bochel 1976 p214). Again it should be noted that it was perceived there was value in probation in keeping offenders out of custodial institutions.

Prior to taking the next step on our probation journey, it is necessary to reflect on an important shift that was beginning to occur in relation to the organisational structure of the service from the 1930s. From 1907 until the 1930s we can discern a horizontal model of organisation that can be diagrammatically presented:

Probation Officer———Probationer———Justices' oversight

Within this model, the individual supervising officer was effectively the representative and manifestation of the probation system before the courts. By contrast, from the mid-1930s a different model of organisation was slowly emerging, which was vertical and hierarchical rather than horizontal because it started to comprise the following dramatis personae:

Principal Probation Officer

Assistant Principal Probation Officer

Senior Probation Officer

Main Grade Probation Officer.

However, and this point will assume greater significance as the book unfolds, at this stage the emerging vertical and hierarchical structure facilitated and enabled the professional task of the individual probation officer to do the job. In other words, we are not describing the beginnings of a management structure; rather it was a framework for professional consultation in what was a court-based social work service, influenced by religion, rehabilitation and emerging casework. It was a form of enabling supervision and oversight, not management by objectives and targets (McWilliams 1992). The individual officer maintained a considerable degree of autonomy and the links with local courts remained intact. In fact, the probation committee exercised a great deal of influence over its officers for many years to come.

The Conservatives were still in power, having won the elections of 1931 and 1935, the last before the start of the Second World War. The Summary Procedure (Domestic Proceedings) Act 1937 extended the statutory duties of probation officers to matrimonial conciliation. In 1938 the Home Office published *The Probation Service – Its Objects and its Organisation* (Home Office 1938). This slim document was addressed to all Justices of the Peace in England and Wales and was sent to Clerks to the Justices on 25th April 1938 by the Under Secretary of State at the Home Office. The document was a significant milestone in the development of probation. Reading it in the 21st century, it is certainly a child of its time, yet it was an attempt to reinforce the philosophy of probation as well as being another exhortation to sentencers to use a sentencing option that had now been in existence for 30 years. The Objects document ran to 55 pages and, in addition to reflecting on the achievements of the first three decades, it was also an attempt to progress the organisation against the background of the recommendations of the 1936 Departmental Committee. The fact that it could draw upon newly commissioned statistics served to add to its authority.

The Objects document dealt with a wide range of issues including the value of probation and its results; preliminary enquiries; additional requirements; the quality of supervision and enforcement. It proceeded to describe the probation officer as a conciliator in Domestic Courts and other duties included: preliminary enquiries; investigation into means and collection of monies; applications in bastardy; adoption enquiries; the supervision of juveniles; aftercare and the value of residence conditions. There was also a section on the organisation of probation. But what could be said about the results of the relatively new system? In 1933 the Home Office, in conjunction with 15 Courts of Summary Jurisdiction, wanted to know how many probationers commit further indictable offences during a period of three years following the termination of an order of 12 months' duration. Statistics were collated on 2,311 probationers and it was discovered that over 70% were judged successful. Interestingly, yet perhaps not surprisingly, the success rate rises with age:

Children under 14	65.3%
Young persons	68.2%
Age 17 and under 21	73.3%
Age 21 and over	81.8% *(Home Office 1938 pp12–13)*

There was an interesting subtext in that, of the 2,311 probationers, only 438 had been charged with a previous indictable offence and the success rate was about 54%. This evidence of success was used to suggest that an even greater number of offenders should be placed on probation. Interestingly, in 1935, of the 44,306 offenders found guilty of an indictable offence, 7,712 or 17% were placed on probation (p11). Some 51% of those aged under 17 similarly convicted in 1935 were placed on probation. Therefore, looking at these figures it is possible to say that the new probation system had been a success during its first 30 years, certainly if judged by the modern concept of market share. But these data suggest that the service was dealing with offenders who were relatively lightly convicted and there was already an indication that probation was likely to be less successful with those who were more heavily convicted.

Even though the Objects document was an exhortation to use probation, it also provided a reminder to magistrates that they should both decide who was to be placed on probation and how they should be supervised: 'It rests with the Justices not only to decide the cases in which the probation method can properly be used, but also largely to control and supervise the manner in which the method is carried out. The success or failure, therefore, of the probation system lies to a large extent in their hands' (1938 p11). Equally, there was a warning to magistrates about the 'extravagant' use of conditions attached to probation orders, as the following examples clarify. 'A young man of eighteen charged with attempting to steal one shilling's worth of cigarettes was bound over on condition that he should not smoke cigarettes for twelve months, that he should be in the house winter and summer at nine o'clock and that he should go to church at least once every Sunday'. Moreover, 'Two boys placed on probation for theft were ordered not to attend a cinema for two years' (p18). A word on recruitment is also instructive when it says that 'The Court cannot expect successful probation work from unsuitable or ineffective probation officers. The Justices acting through their Probation Committee must take care to appoint men and women of fine personality, well equipped for the difficult work required of them. And equally must be prepared to encourage, stimulate and when necessary, to criticise the work which is being done' (p21). A section on enforcement of orders reinforced the need for probationers to be brought back to the sentencing court promptly and to be sentenced for the original offence if there was a breach of the court order (p21). Consequently, this document provides us with an intriguing glimpse into probation work some thirty years after its introduction.

Whilst the first part of the document devotes itself to the value of probation and reinforcing good practice, the second part turns to organisational matters in light of the recommendations of the 1936 Departmental Committee. There is a clear exhortation to single areas where the Justices have continued the practice of appointing their own staff to combine to make larger units. There were also a number of criticisms. For example, some probation committees failed to meet regularly and there were concerns about the personnel of probation. The latter related to poorly qualified, poorly paid and overworked staff and one outcome of the staffing problem was to reinforce the importance of the training programme for probation officers that had been established in 1930. A Probation Training Board was set up consisting of members of the reconstituted Probation Advisory Committee, in an attempt to stimulate university training opportunities. It also reinforced the recommendation of the review in 1936 by referring to the role of Principal Probation Officer in areas where there were significant numbers of staff, and the role was to supervise the work of other probation officers.

The optimism and high aspirations of the Objects document were soon to be overshadowed by the commencement of the Second World

War and national preoccupations turned away from the subject of probation and penal reform. But by 1938 it may be argued that probation had come a long way from its missionary and religious beginnings in 1907, and that some important aspects of a governance structure had emerged. Consequently, a number of building blocks had been put in place as a result of the Departmental Committees of 1909, 1922 and now 1936, in addition to relevant legislation that we have alluded to so far. Before proceeding with our story of probation, it is interesting to remind ourselves that during the Second World War it was classified as a reserved occupation, therefore the system was not disbanded. In fact, the first conference of Principal Probation Officers was initiated by the Home Office in December 1942 (Jarvis 1972 p61), which suggests that the service continued to develop during the war years. Lord Windlesham comments that between the two World Wars the probation system was thriving (1993 p66) and that there had been a positive atmosphere in relation to penal policy and reform. However, from 1945 crime was rising and more people were being sent to prison, in that the daily average prison population in 1944 was 12,915; by 1947 it was 17,000; pre-war it was between 10,000 and 11,000. This is the context within which the Criminal Justice Bill was introduced in 1947 when J. Chuter Ede was Home Secretary, culminating in the Criminal Justice Act 1948.

Criminal Justice Act 1948

The Criminal Justice Bill 1938 that would have given effect to the proposals contained in the Departmental Committee of 1936 was aborted because of the war. However, this was rectified to some extent by the Criminal Justice Act 1948 (11 & 12 Geo. 6, c. 85) that was an attempt by the post-war Atlee government to bring new socialist thinking to tackling crime. Some of the changes to the penal system included abolishing birching, penal servitude, prison with hard labour and whipping, thus dismantling the Victorian penal system. By contrast, it introduced the detention centre and attendance centre order and encouraged the courts to use the borstal training system rather than prison for young offenders. Furthermore, the 1948 Act introduced corrective training and the maximum period of preventive detention was raised from 10 to 14 years. Therefore, despite elements of a tougher attitude in the post-war period, the Labour government also created the welfare state that complemented the rehabilitative ideal that influenced both probation and prison. Where the probation order was concerned, the name of the officer no longer appeared on the order itself, replaced by the Petty Sessional Division, yet the consent of the prospective probationer was still required before the order could be imposed. Consequently, the 1948 Act amended the legislative basis of probation first instituted in 1907.

It should be acknowledged that the section in Joan King's second edition on probation (1964) that covers 1948–58 describes this period as one of consolidation and extension. She reminds us that the 1948 Act superseded the 1907 Act and that the First and Fifth Schedules clarified procedural and organisational matters. Therefore, it signals an attempt at legislative consolidation after the war years. The fifth Schedule to the 1948 Act focused on 'Administrative Provisions As To Probation' and clarified the definition of probation area, which allowed the Secretary of State to use statutory instruments to confer formally 'Area' status on petty sessional divisions that wished to combine. It also clarified the roles and responsibilities of probation and case committees. Membership of these bodies was largely made up of local Justices but the Schedule allowed for co-options of not more than a third of total membership, thus extending influence beyond the sentencers. There were important measures governing the appointment of staff, their remuneration and expenses. Again, the importance of local authorities was reinforced through a range of defined administrative functions related to payments and expenses. Paragraph 4 of the Schedule outlined the role of case committees in the selection of probation officers for specific cases. It is intriguing to observe that there was a clear statement that the case committee selected the probation officer for each case and would subsequently determine whether or not the case should be moved to another officer in any circumstances in which it was thought that this might be appropriate. This is undoubtedly intriguing in light of the emerging hierarchy of the service alluded to above because it adds credence to our point that it was most certainly not facilitating modern notions of managing staff. Probation Rules followed in 1949 and it may be suggested that the 1950s began with clear governance structures in place. It is also worth emphasising that the notion of 'advise, assist and befriend' remained an important probation officer task; and the themes of welfare, rehabilitation, in addition to the centrality of the officer-probationer relationship, were endorsed. The minimum period of probation was fixed at 12 months and maximum remained at 3 years (but on 15th May 1978 the minimum period was further reduced to 6 months).

The 1950s

As we move into the 1950s the probation service began to get involved in assisting the Divorce Courts to make decisions about the welfare of children in marital disputes. Eventually, a Divorce Court Welfare Service within the probation system emerged in addition to the probation officer being appointed as guardian *ad litem* of a child to safeguard the child's interests. It was the Matrimonial Proceedings (Children) Act 1958 that provided the legislation for the preparation of reports in custody, access and satisfaction cases, thus extending the probation officer role beyond criminal work. Nevertheless, we need to remind ourselves that by this stage probation officers had been involved in matrimonial work for some time (disputes between the parties; domestic violence). Furthermore, in 1954 the Probation Christian Fellowship met for the first time, thus confirming and preserving an important thematic link with the religious beginnings of the system in 1876. This brings us to the brink of the 1960s and 1970s, which signalled even greater change in a system that had begun with a handful of officers in 1907. However, before bringing our story into the more modern period, we think it is important to pause at the end of the 1950s by referring to a 1959 document – *Penal Practice in a Changing Society* – against the background of reported crime that had risen from half a million to three-quarters of a million during the last ten years despite the welfare state, commitment to education and rising material prosperity (Home Office 1959). According to Windlesham this document 'stands as the high watermark of what later became known as the treatment model', with its emphasis upon aetiology and the need to determine the most appropriate method for working with individual offenders (1993 p72).

This 1959 Home Office command paper (Cmnd 645) begins by lamenting the growth in crime, although the increase during the 1939–45 war years was greater than 1945–59. Furthermore, there were concerns about rising convictions amongst the 16–21-year-old age group, in addition to a rising custodial population, leading to prison overcrowding and resources being overstretched in borstal, approved schools and probation. For example, the prison population and borstal combined in 1956 was 21,000; in 1959 it was 26,000 (Home Office 1959). The document moves on to talk about the weapons being used in the fight against crime, such as the police; the criminal law; and the penal system itself. There is even a reference to Mr Justice Streatfield's committee that had been appointed to look at the courts and reports. Additionally, it referred to current research interests and the recently established Home Office Research Unit. There is an interesting reference to concerns about the victims of crime (paragraph 24) and the prospective Ingleby Report is mentioned (Home Office 1960). But a large proportion of the document is devoted to the prison system rather than probation. Despite the concerns towards the end of the 1950s in relation to rising crime, a number of developments as we leave the 1950s created an atmosphere of a more welfare oriented period, particularly when responding to young people who found themselves in trouble with the law. Importantly, it should be acknowledged that this welfare orientation began under the Conservatives towards the end of the 1950s, and continued into the mid-1960s when the Labour Party of 1964–1970 endorsed the theme of welfare rather than punishment. These developments were to affect probation and were to elicit an interesting response from the service, perhaps with the benefit of hindsight an unexpected and unpredictable response. We need to pick up our story at the beginning of the 1960s.

Into the 1960s

The Ingleby Committee was established in 1956 to enquire into the juvenile courts and deprived children, but it did not report until 1960. It boldly recommended that the age of criminal responsibility should be raised from 8 to 12 years and then to 14. Below this age it was envisaged that civil proceedings would replace criminal (Pitts 2003). We can argue that Ingleby presaged radical proposals during the 1960s that were of a decriminalising and de-stigmatising nature (radical anti-labelling impulses), particularly where young offenders are concerned, that found its apotheosis at the end of the decade in the Children and Young Persons Act 1969 (that will be discussed in more detail in the next chapter in contrast to the Criminal Justice Act 1982). In fact the age of criminal responsibility was raised from 8 to 10 in the Children and Young Persons Act 1963. However, it is of interest to acknowledge that the Criminal Justice Act 1961 actually increased the maximum level of fines for juveniles and the minimum age for the attendance centre order was reduced from 12 to 10 years, while the number of hours increased. Furthermore, the minimum age of imprisonment was raised from 15 to 17 and greater use of borstal was encouraged instead of prison for offenders under 21. However, the minimum age of borstal admission was reduced from 16 to 15 – not what we could construe as either decriminalising or de-stigmatising measures. Therefore there is some conflict here between Ingleby's thinking for the future of young offenders and what was in fact being introduced in the Criminal Justice Act 1961.[2]

The Streatfield Report (Home Office 1961) was mainly concerned with the higher courts yet the findings were applicable to the magistrates' courts as well. This Inter-Departmental Committee said that the role of the probation officer is to provide relevant information through court reports; assess the culpability of the offender; consider how offending behaviour can effectively be checked; and express an opinion, if knowledge and experience will allow, on the likely effects of various sentences and treatment. It is interesting how McWilliams, writing in 1992 and looking back on the work of Streatfield within the context of the rise of policy and managerialism in probation, argued that the document developed a national policy for Social Enquiry Reports that replaced local and traditional customs, a point that we will return to towards the end of this chapter. Nevertheless, after Streatfield probation work in the courts expanded and court duty became an important dimension of the probation officers' role as the services' influence in the process of sentencing grew.

Report of the Departmental Committee on the Probation Service *(Home Office 1962)*

The year 1962 brings us to the fourth and last major Departmental Committee Report that we must peruse. On 27th May 1959 the Home Secretary, R.A. Butler, and the Principal Secretary of State for Scotland, J.S. Maclay, appointed a Committee under the chairmanship of R.P. Morrison QC to enquire into all aspects of probation work, which included its functions, organisation, administration, recruitment, training, salaries and conditions of service. The first point to emphasise was that the rationale of probation was understood and confirmed in terms of treatment, reformation and rehabilitation (paragraphs 8–24, 53–59), and the role of the probation officer was defined as a professional caseworker, utilising skills that he had in common with other social workers. The notion of casework is articulated 'as the creation and utilisation for the benefit of an individual who needs help with personal problems, of a relationship between himself and a trained social worker' (paragraph 56). Not only was the probation officer–client relationship important but the teaching establishments promoted thinking on psychodynamic and therapeutic relationships (the psychodynamic courses at the Tavistock Institute, for example; Stevenson 1981 p33). Furthermore, the duties of a probation officer during the early 1960s were described as follows:

Social Enquiry Reports for criminal courts

Probation supervision

Supervision Order under the CYPA 1933

Money Payment Supervision Order

Supervision of children in matrimonial proceedings

Aftercare: prison, approved school and borstal

Enquiries in adoption cases for the Divorce Court

Matrimonial conciliation

Attendance at court

Escort duty to approved schools

Finding lodgings.

The 1962 Morison Committee interestingly considered the possibility of a national service (paragraph 169) because it was thought that this would be conducive to a more economic form of administration. However, the Committee deliberated that, whatever the merits of this suggestion, they were outweighed by 'the desirability of preserving the employer–employee relationship between magistrates and probation officers'. The 1936 Committee, as we saw earlier, acknowledged the role of the Home Office in the development of the probation service, and one of its central tasks was to ensure efficiency, a point that had already been emphasised in 1936. But Morison interestingly, in paragraph 180, referred to a strained relationship between the Home Office and probation committees, including the Home Office and wider service, due to four main factors: the volume of work within the service; pay and conditions as a consequence of the interests of national economic policy demanding pay restraint; the financial controls over committees; and a perceived lack of support and interest in the service. By 1962 there were 14 Home Office Inspectors.

The early 1960s was proving to be a busy time for the service because, in addition to the report of the Departmental Committee in 1962, the Advisory Council on the Treatment of Offenders (Home Office 1963) published its report on aftercare that would come to have a major impact on the future development of probation services. Given the importance of this report, we feel that we need to devote some attention to this subject, but first we note the comment expressed by Windlesham that 'The report was not without influence, as it contributed to the transition of the probation service from a group of self-employed social case workers into a nationally organised and publicly funded service' (1993 p104).

The Voluntary Aftercare Tradition

Prisoners' Aid Societies were founded towards the end of the 18th century and beginning of the 19th, but the work of local aid societies had to wait until the Discharge Prisoners' Aid Act of 1862 before receiving statutory recognition. The Gladstone Committee of 1895 (the same Herbert Gladstone who was Home Secretary in 1907) considered the work of aid societies and, whilst it acknowledged the benefits to prisoners, lamented the lack of organisation. The Central Discharged Prisoners' Aid Society was established in 1918 which, in 1936, became the National Association of Discharged Prisoners' Aid Societies (NADPAS). Between 1862 and 1935 the aid societies were financed by monies received from charitable sources and grants from public funds, but by 1950 most societies were experiencing financial difficulties. The Maxwell Committee, in 1953, recommended that NADPAS appoint social workers at local prisons, with training and qualifications similar to probation officers, and known as welfare officers. Therefore, by 1962, prison welfare officers, employed by NADPAS, were in post in all local prisons (Whitehead et al 1991).

Compulsory Aftercare for Young and Adult Offenders

In 1901 borstal emerged, as we have already observed, and an Association of Visitors was created by Sir Evelyn Ruggles-Brise to befriend young offenders on release and help them to find employment. By 1903 the Association of Visitors became the Borstal Association. The Prevention of Crime Act 1908 placed borstal training on a statutory footing and borstal licence was introduced that in fact persisted until 24th May 1983, by which time the Criminal Justice Act 1982 was implemented and borstal replaced by the sentence of Youth Custody (a further change of name occurred in 1988 when Youth Custody became a Young Offender Institution). The central objective of the Borstal Association was rehabilitation. Interestingly, the aftercare of convicts released on licence from convict prisons was the responsibility of the police. With the Criminal Justice Act 1948 compulsory aftercare, until this time applied to lads released from borstal in addition to the sentence of preventive detention, was extended to men and women released on licence from sentences of corrective training and the new form of preventive detention created by the 1948 Act, and persons under 21. It was decided that the three aftercare organisations – Borstal Association, Central Association for the Aid of Discharged Convicts and the Aylesbury Association (for women) – should be rationalised into one body called the Central Aftercare Association. Consequently, this was the position in 1963 when the ACTO report on aftercare was published. By 1967, as a result of an ACTO recommendation, an expanded probation service was renamed the Probation and After-Care Service (reverting to the Probation Service in 1982 as a result of changes made by the Criminal Justice Act of the same year) because it became responsible for all forms of compulsory supervision and aftercare. By 1969, probation began to fill social work posts in remand centres, detention centres and borstal allocation centres. We should comment at this point that these developments during the 1960s are significant, particularly when we begin to trace the emergence of managerialism as a dominant force in probation (explored in more detail towards the end of this chapter, and in Part 2 of the book).

Further Developments in the 1960s

We have already touched upon the Ingleby report in 1960. Subsequently, in 1964, Longford's report proposed the abolition of juvenile courts, to be replaced by family services to respond on an informal basis to young people in trouble. Additionally, the 1965 White Paper on *The Child, The Family and the Young Offender* supported the decriminalising initiative of Longford. In fact, the Labour government's White Paper extolled the virtues of a welfare approach for young people in trouble that would have avoided the stigmatising effects of the penal system. Nevertheless, it was a combination of lawyers, the Magistrates' Association, in addition to NAPO, that objected to the proposal to abolish juvenile courts. The probation service was independent of social services and had a long tradition, by this stage, of service to the courts 'and it was from this standpoint that their critique was made' (Bottoms 1974). The result was that the radical 1965 White Paper was not pursued.

Next we see the appearance of the Criminal Justice Act 1967 and some of the key measures were attempts to compel the courts to resort to non-custodial disposals. Preventive detention and corrective training were abolished but, by contrast, the suspended sentence and discretionary parole were introduced to reduce the prison population. Moreover, the notion of rehabilitation in prison, and therefore subsequent release where there were signs that the treatment was working, was an important theme; as was the ongoing ideology of rehabilitation and treatment in probation that had been an important feature of the work for many decades. Therefore it can be claimed that by the mid-1960s the service was at the heart of the Labour government's penal policy, exemplified by the creation of the Probation and After-Care Service in 1967.

We have just commented that the 1965 White Paper was not pursued. Subsequently, however, another attempt to address juvenile crime was attempted in the 1968 White Paper, *Children in Trouble*, but this time the juvenile court was retained. However, it persisted with the related themes of decriminalisation and de-stigmatisation; and prepared the way for the introduction of intermediate treatment and the supervision order, the latter replacing the probation order for juveniles in 1969. One of the implications of this period is that probation remained very much involved in the supervision of young offenders, as it had been, of course, since 1908. What happened in practice is that social workers, in some areas, supervised the 10–13-year-old age group; probation the older 14–17-year-old group.

Moreover, by 1969 the probation service in Scotland lost its independence by becoming assimilated into a new social work service. There was also the possibility that a similar development would occur in England as a consequence of the Seebohm Report (Home Office 1968; Murch 1969). In fact it can be argued that Seebohm presented probation with an acute dilemma in that, if it rejected proposals for a combined social services department, it risked not being involved in mainstream social work by becoming more and more identified with the penal system. Alternatively, if it said yes to Seebohm it risked losing its autonomy and identity, which is what occurred in Scotland. The end result of tense debates was that probation retained its independence. When the British Association of Social Workers (BASW) was formed in 1970, seven of the eight associations in the Standing Conference of Social Work Organisations of Social Workers relinquished their separate identity. Only the National Association of Probation Officers remained outside, although members were permitted to join BASW (Stevenson 1981 pp31–32). Whilst the generic base for both social work and probation training continued, it may be said that probation had severed its umbilical cord from the rest of social work. By pressing this point further the House of Commons Expenditure Committee in 1971, on probation and aftercare, saw no reason to change the independent status of the service but suggested that this could be re-examined in light of changing circumstances (Home Office 1976 p19). Furthermore, by 1972 it was announced that probation would continue to operate as a separate service organised in local areas under committees of magistrates (Home Office 1976), by which stage the government grant towards the costs of the service was increased from 50% to 80%. It is clear looking back that the 1960s was a challenging decade, replete with many changes. Nevertheless, despite the ongoing rise in crime, it may be said that the 1960s remained optimistic in tone where the criminal justice system and penal policy were concerned. On the whole, offenders could be dealt with in a positive manner through classification that would culminate in more effective treatment, to which the social enquiry report would make a contribution. Unfortunately this positive approach was undermined as we moved into the 1970s.

The 1970s

During the mid-1960s the Home Secretary made a request to the Advisory Council on the Treatment of Offenders to consider ways of expanding the range of non-custodial sentences.[3] Consequently, a sub-committee was formed under Baroness Wootton, reporting in 1970, in which the central position of the probation and aftercare service was confirmed in relation to the provision of non-custodial disposals, in addition to which plans for further expansion of the service were announced (Home Office 1976). The Wootton Report was reflected in the Criminal Justice Act 1972 that introduced the community service order,[4] the suspended sentence supervision order, bail hostels, day training centres, in addition to the deferred sentence, within the context of reducing pressure on the prison system. We need to emphasise that community service was a major innovation for probation and was initially introduced in six experimental areas before being made more widely available in 1973. There had been a debate about which organisation should take it on and the choice of probation was to have far-reaching implications (Frayne 1993 p19). Philosophically, whilst the new sentence contained an element of punishment (a radical departure from the rationale of probation), reparation and rehabilitation were also part of the penological mix. Building upon the experience of the six experimental areas, each local service developed its own community service scheme in 1974, thus adding additional costs. These costs were effectively foisted onto local authorities through the statutory responsibility placed on probation areas to make this sentencing provision available to the courts. Not all local authorities responded generously, it should be said, to the new expectations, with the result that some areas were forced to ration courts in the making of community service orders because demand outstripped operational capacity.

By the end of the 1970s probation was building on its experience of running community service schemes, which had demonstrated the value of helping offenders develop skills. But community service was more than skills development and the first of two national seminars was held at Keele University, 20th–22nd April 1979 and then 21st–23rd March 1980. These seminars provided an opportunity for debate and exploration of issues, some of which were dividing the service (Statham 1980b; McWilliams 1979). At the first seminar Pease and Statham (1979) reflected on whether community service was an alternative to custody; whether the offender should be matched to a project to benefit therapeutically; and whether it was morally right for offenders to do work that otherwise would have been paid for by the recipient organisation. Therefore, there were numerous dilemmas that needed airing. Community service also exercised the Conference of Chief Officers of Probation that produced a paper in 1979 to inform debate at the second conference, which contained 21 recommendations, one of which drew attention to the question of whether community service should only be used as an alternative to custody. In 1980 drama (Statham 1980a) was used to illustrate operational tensions: the Chief Officer wanted efficiency; more throughput; less emphasis on nebulous social work concepts; more ancillary workers. By contrast the CS organiser wanted meaningful work for offenders; was bothered about ancillaries doing referrals; and recognised the need for more and better public relations with the courts. The drama concluded with a dialogue between the offender and CS supervisor that illustrated the value of both the work and working relationship in helping the offender to change. These seminars were significant developments in relation to a relatively new sentence of the court that highlighted certain tensions in the service which had surfaced elsewhere. One of them was the fear that probation officers were in danger of becoming 'screws on wheels'.

We need to retrace our steps at this point by saying that, in 1972, J.B. Butterworth (Department of Employment 1972) was looking at the salaries of probation officers compared to that of other social workers, but it was the Younger Report (Home Office 1974) that could have had radical implications for the role of probation officer. The first point that needs to be made is that the Younger Report was yet another piece of work produced by the Advisory Council on the Treatment of Offenders (ACTO) but this time considering Young Adult Offenders, reviewing the treatment of 17–21-year-old offenders. Probation staff of a certain generation will recall that the two main proposals were for a Custody and Control Order in cases where it was considered that a custodial sentence was unavoidable. However, the proposal that caused not a little consternation amongst probation officers was the Supervision and Control Order, which had more control than probation supervision. Moreover, it did not include an obligation to obtain the consent of the offender and, additionally, the probation officer would be given the power to obtain a warrant to secure the detention of an offender for up to 72 hours in circumstances where he was in danger of breaching the order; where a breach had occurred; or if the probation officer thought that a new offence was likely to be committed. It is interesting to recall that there was a special edition of the *Probation Journal* dedicated to Younger's proposals in December 1974, and it is not a surprise that NAPO objected to the idea. The Report acutely brought into the open the now distant debates on the tensions between care and control for many probation staff, in addition to the notion of social work values and the nature of community supervision. Many were relieved when the Report was not implemented. Furthermore, 1974 was also the year in which local government was reorganised, which had implications for probation because the number of area services was reduced from 79 to 56. These changes cemented the well-established financial arrangements for channelling money to area services. Local authorities provided budgeting systems and, within their own accountancy arrangements, managed cash flows. However, despite the fact that local authority treasurers were charging central government for the supply of these services, the burgeoning costs of expanding services were beginning to create tensions with local authority partners. By 1975, notwithstanding the announcement of an expansion of probation as recently as 1970, a deteriorating economic situation was restricting the growth of the service at a time when probation committees were provided with opportunities to introduce community service schemes in their local areas.

Prior to drawing this chapter to a close, we draw the reader's attention to two other documents that are worth perusing when reflecting on the history of the service during the 1960s and 1970s. First, in 1976, a Home Office Working Paper reviewed Criminal Justice policy during the previous decade (Home Office 1976). It contains interesting material on probation during this ten-year period (some of which has been referred to earlier in this chapter). Secondly, in September 1976 yet another special edition of the *Probation Journal* appeared, but this time to draw attention to the centenary of the police court missionaries in 1876: 'Probation – 100 Years On'. Much had happened during this period and this edition of the journal appropriately reflected on some of these events.

Before turning our attention to the post-1979 period in Part 2, we need to consider a number of related issues that form a bridge for what is to come in subsequent chapters. There are five main areas of concern that we think should be addressed: an attempt to trace the evolution of managerialism, which has assumed hegemonic status in probation during the last few years; the implications of empirical research for the rationale of probation work; emerging models of probation in light of research into the questionable efficacy of probation supervision as understood in terms of rehabilitation; history of ideas; and the evolution of Home Office control that becomes an important feature of the 1984–2004 period (which we need to anticipate here).

The Road to Managerialism

It may be argued that, from the 1960s, the professional-supervisory model of organisation that had been evolving since the 1930s was transmuted into a more managerial and bureaucratic model that, over recent years, has had major implications for the probation service (McWilliams 1992). We concur with McWilliams that a professional-administrative model of organisation is illustrated in the Morison report of 1962 (McWilliams 1992 p10); but, as we have seen earlier in this chapter, since the 1930s a hierarchical structure was advocated, a response to the needs of an expanding service (Bochel 1976 p214). However, this hierarchical and vertical model was not tantamount to public sector management as we understand the term today and as it began to emerge in the 1960s. McWilliams suggests that the Streatfield Report (Home Office 1961) facilitated the development of a national policy on social enquiry reports that replaced local and traditional customs so that 'Under the new policy it was no longer the individual offender who was considered for a social enquiry report, but rather classes of offenders defined by reference to the policy categories' (1992 p5). Then, in 1963, the ACTO report on aftercare (Home Office 1963) drew attention to categories of prisoners (borstal, prison, detention centre and approved school) rather than individuals. It is therefore suggested that a developing, changing and expanding service required policies, objectives and, by implication, managerial control.

According to Haxby, developments since 1963 have taken the service beyond court allocated work (specifically the probation order) into much closer cooperation with the penal system and thus 'introduced new lines of accountability and put the senior officer in a middle management position' (1978 p42).

McWilliams expands the discussion by saying that it was as a result of the fallout from the prison escape of the spy George Blake on 22nd October 1966 that Lord Mountbatten's report (Home Office 1966) questioned prison administration because it did not use modern management techniques. Subsequently it is suggested that the fiasco of 1966 resulted in the prison service developing management techniques and that prior to this probation 'had largely been excluded from the managerial revolution which took root in the public and voluntary sectors from the late 1950s onwards' (McWilliams 1992 p3). When perusing the Journal of the National Association of Probation Officers, Malcolm Brown (1969) was reflecting on Management and the Probation Officer. After looking at the transition from probation officer to senior probation officer, at a time when the latter continued to supervise a small caseload, he observed that the service had become more bureaucratic and resorted to the language of the SPO as middle manager, the administrative role, servicing policies and goals. This led Miss Thornborough (1970) to consider 'The Satisfaction of Being a Senior Probation Officer', in response to Brown's article. She puts up a strong defence to allow the SPO to retain a handful of cases even though the first duty of the SPO is to staff. The role, as she understands it, should consist of casework supervision; communication and the sharing of ideas; the development of new thinking; but also to find time to read. Next NAPO published *The Future Development of the Probation and After-Care Service* (National Association of Probation Officers 1970). After extolling the virtues of an independent service (post-Seebohm), it acknowledges that the service has become more bureaucratic whilst accepting that the probation officer retains a measure of autonomy in excess of other social workers. It reflects that the morale of the service has suffered due to uncertainty, but is committed to the principle of a court social work service. The casework relationship is endorsed as the basis of the job, consistent with Morison (Home Office 1962); and there is a call for an expanded service to deal with the growth in crime.

Colley et al picked up some of the concerns of the NAPO publication in an article called 'Administration and Individual Responsibility' (1970). Concerns were expressed that the structures of the probation service had become rigid at the expense of individual initiative and additional concerns over standardisation and conformity. Whilst maintaining a defence of the importance of the main grade officer, a warning note was sounded against the background of appointing more senior probation officers simply to attract more graduates: 'Implicit in this is the danger that they will see their function as managerial and directive, rather than consultative and administrative' (Colley 1970). There was even an article on the role of 'The Assistant Principal Probation Officer and Middle Management' (Clarke 1971) articulated in terms of communicator, supervisor of staff, consultant, initiator, and someone with specialist responsibilities. However, and importantly, Clarke says that 'Unquestionably a deal of value can be gained from study of other organisations, their administration and management, but the probation service is concerned with people'.

By 1973 Malcolm Brown talked about a management structure having been imposed on the service over recent years 'but this has been very gentle with little bite, and one might say, almost ineffective' (Brown 1973 p5). After reflecting somewhat negatively on the level of Home Office control, Brown argues that the managerial function must reside within the service itself and not the Home Office, and the managerial task is to create policy, determine local needs, set priorities, allocate resources and evaluate performance. This is because 'operating with tight Home Office control, the service, over the years, has formulated no objectives' (p6). If the rationale of the service is understood as the prevention and treatment of crime, he seems to be saying that a bureaucratic form of organisation with power at the top to determine objectives is required. Finally, in the same year as Brown was addressing the structure and management of the service, Weston produced a paper on style of management which is interesting for its belief that there should be three main grades of staff: the main grade professional probation officer; the senior probation officer who administers and supervises a team; the principal probation officer who administers and supervises at area level. Importantly he says that 'In a service such as the Probation and After-Care Service, the objectives of the main grade officer and those of the chief officer are essentially the same' (Weston 1973 p70). There is therefore some evidence to indicate that from the 1960s a professional-administrative structure was slowly being transformed into a more managerial and bureaucratic model of organisation because of change, expansion and developing complexity. Managerialism was put firmly on the probation agenda and it was being discussed within the service.

Rehabilitation, Treatment and Research

It is not necessary to provide a copious account of the empirical research studies that started to question the efficacy of probation interventions, but a summary is relevant, mainly because of their implication in forcing the service to re-conceptualise itself (for more information see, for example, Whitehead 1990 p12f). First, Wilkins (1958) found no significant differences in the reconviction rates of two matched samples of probationers and other offenders, most of whom were sent to borstal and prison. Secondly, the Home Office study of probation began in 1961 and doubts were subsequently raised about the effectiveness of probation to prevent recidivism. Thirdly, the IMPACT study – Intensive Matched Probation and Aftercare Treatment (Folkard et al 1974 and 1976) – demonstrated that more intensive treatment was not tantamount to higher success rates, so once again the service was having to cope with negative research findings that led Clarke and Cornish to comment that 'Given the results of their own earlier researches and the increasing scepticism amongst criminologists about the value of probation treatment, the directors of IMPACT would hardly have been surprised by its largely negative results ... The project's main significance for them may have been that it marked the end of the probation research programme which had begun in some optimism fifteen years before, and which, in the search for effective treatment, had proceeded up so many inviting avenues only to discover they were dead ends' (1983 pp28–29). Fourthly, most of the readers of this book will have heard of Martinson's work (1974) that was construed negatively, in conjunction with the theme of 'What Works?'. Finally, Brody (1976), after evaluating nearly 70 studies from various countries, cast doubt upon the rehabilitative efficacy of different treatment programmes, specifically if probation is used for first offenders and confirmed recidivists.

It may be concluded that the combined weight of these research findings were not irredeemably negative in that some forms of treatment do work sometimes, but there is not one form of treatment that works for every offender all the time (refer to the review of criminal justice policy, Home Office 1976). Therefore, it would have been surprising if the service did not feel anxious and confused during the 1970s about its *raison d'être* that had, for many decades, been understood as treatment via casework leading to reformation and rehabilitation. Within this confusing context a number of what may be described as models of probation emerged to fill the ideological vacuum rapidly being created by the findings of empirical research (see, for example, Senior 1984; Raynor 1985; Whitehead 1990). We now turn to consider some of these models at the end of the 1970s and early 1980s, before referring to the SNOP model of probation towards the end of the next chapter.

Models of Probation

Robert Harris (1977, 1980) said in two important papers that, because of the expansion of the probation service and its closer association with the penal system since the mid-1960s, it was in the grip of occupational and moral dissonance. By this he meant a growing gap had emerged between the justice ideology of society and the welfare ideology of social work; between care and control. The service had been through many changes that had created tensions and conflicts that enabled Harris to argue for the separation of care and control, which would be manifested in the creation of two separate agencies: one agency would offer a caring social work service to all offenders in need; a second agency would supervise the statutory orders imposed by the courts. Despite the attraction to many probation officers in providing a caring service to clients as an end in itself, it may be suggested that this was never a politically tenable solution to dissonance; nor, to be fair, was it intended as such by Harris.

Next Bryant et al (1978) advocated a two-contract model of probation in which the primary contract would be with the courts to adhere to the court order; but there would also be a subsidiary contract between the probation officer and probationer for social work help and welfare. Thirdly, one year after the Bryant model, perhaps the most significant re-conceptualisation of probation work was articulated by Bottoms and McWilliams (1979) in their non-treatment paradigm for probation practice. Against the background of the questionable efficacy of the rehabilitative and treatment approach of the 1960s and 1970s, Bottoms and McWilliams eschew the imposition of social work treatment onto offenders by so-called 'experts' and without consultation. Therefore, in this model, treatment becomes help; 'expert' diagnosis becomes shared assessment; the client's dependent need as the basis for social work action becomes a collaboratively defined task. Importantly, the work of the probation service in providing alternatives to custody is endorsed within a person-centred philosophy. In other words, the previously articulated view of Weston that offenders are people was endorsed as an important ethical principle.

Fourthly, the themes of surveillance and control were also advocated from within the service in marked contrast to more social work and welfare-oriented perspectives. It is important to recall that probation work from the very beginning was associated with the management, containment and control of working class probationers (Garland 1985). The debates during the 1970s and 1980s focused on the nature and extent of control within a probation system that was influenced by a social work ethos and service to clients. Therefore some of us can remember lively debates and heated exchanges that tried to reconcile a set of ideas associated with the following: the notions of 'advise, assist and befriend'; social work help and understanding; the religious and humanitarian impulses within probation work, on the one hand, and the demands of law, justice, punishment, discipline, authority and state control, on the other, in the post-rehabilitative era. Where control and punishment are concerned, we have already alluded to the radical proposals of Younger (Home Office 1974) that were rejected; we can also refer to Davies (1982) and Griffiths (1982a, 1982b), who advocated control and surveillance of offenders as the primary rationale of probation.

Previously, in 1978, David Haxby was advocating a community correctional service and, finally, by 1981, Walker and Beaumont were arguing for a form of socialist practice that analyses probation work as an arm of the state for controlling working class offenders. Therefore, one main task of probation work should be: to mitigate the worst excesses of what can be a harsh criminal justice system; to engage in social action; to use the breach process as a last resort; and to understand the structural aspects of crime. In fact, the authors want probation officers who are 'prepared to state publicly that prison is destructive, that there are unjust laws, that law enforcement is discriminatory and even that the probation service cannot cope with the poverty and hardship our work uncovers' (1981 p169). In fact Bill McWilliams, in the last of his excellent quartet of essays on the history of ideas in probation (published in 1987), draws attention to three contrasting models that became significant: the Personalist perspective echoing the social work oriented approach of Harris, Bottoms and McWilliams; the Radical, alluding to the socialist probation practice of Walker and Beaumont; and the Managerial, which has in fact become the dominant model – but not exclusively so because the personalist and socialist perspectives remain in evidence to some degree, alongside surveillance and control.

At this point we need to say a little more about the history of underpinning ideas in probation.

History of Ideas

We should remind ourselves that from 1876 the police court missionaries operated within a religious context (McWilliams 1983; Oldfield 2002) manifested by the way in which they brought moral and spiritual influences to bear upon inebriated offenders with a view to changing lives. By the 1920s and 1930s the influence of religion had not suddenly disappeared. Rather, other elements began to make their presence felt, such as the development of a more scientific outlook associated with positivism, and psychology and Freudian influences; hence the need for something more than a well-meaning religious amateur. In other words, we see the beginnings of a more professional service that required a trained workforce (Whitehead and Thompson 2004). During the post-war era the language of rehabilitation and casework was in vogue, within the wider political context of welfare. Influenced by Freudian psychoanalysis, the probation officer (although not a psychoanalyst) worked with clients on a one-to-one basis to penetrate the presenting problem to get to the underlying problem with a view to providing insight. This involved working back to childhood experiences to yield an understanding of problems so that the client could seize control over their behaviour with a view to changing it.

Casework in probation persisted for many years (Whitehead 1990) and was associated with the medical-treatment model. It was overly individualistic and psychological, complemented by a professional mindset that perceived crime as a disease. There was a profound sense of value in the therapeutic casework relationship held by some during the 1960s and 1970s and perhaps beyond. It was also considered that a relationship between worker and client could transcend the existential dross of those under supervision. In fact, some charismatic probation officers could inspire change in individuals who were socially isolated; and one of us, as a senior probation officer of a probation team, witnessed the change in people's lives as they began to believe in their own sense of worth.

Millard (1977) provided a challenging insight into the dynamics of supervision, reminding us that the process is capable of operating at various levels. The idea being explored here is that therapeutic imagination and, by contrast, the technician, operate as the bookends of the supervisory spectrum. Those with therapeutic imagination have the capacity to absorb the dissonance created by their own role and social position, yet remain able to maintain a statutory supervisory relationship that enables clients to achieve self worth and make some sense of their own situation. Alternatively, those lacking this imagination, either by inclination or training, are more disposed to act as technicians with the consequent diminution of the capacity to inspire change. This distinction provokes an interesting debate around whether the therapeutic imagination can be taught; learned; or is it an innate quality? Moreover, is it something that can be measured? If it can, should it? These are interesting lines of enquiry (that we pursue in later chapters) but then, as now, the therapeutic imagination provided a sense of hope and the inspiration to do the job. Such qualities, associated with casework, included the acceptance of the individual offender regardless of age, class, gender, colour, race or beliefs (Biestek 1961). The therapeutic imagination did not discriminate but attempted to meet human need.

Subsequently, under the weight of empirical research during the 1970s that questioned whether probation was effectively rehabilitating offenders, the 1980s emphasised the idea of alternatives to custody (but this must wait until the next chapter). Therefore since 1876 different sets of ideas have underpinned probation practice.

Home Office Control

We have already reflected on the way in which the Home Secretary sponsored the Probation of Offenders Bill in 1907 and that the only vestige of Home Office control at this stage was an amendment giving the Home Secretary the power to make Rules for putting the 1907 Act into effect (Bochel 1976 p30). The 1909 Departmental Committee proposed that there should be one official at the Home Office who would keep in touch with probation, and the 1922 Committee accepted the need for a central authority in the form of the Home Office in addition to a government grant of 50%. However, a Home Office Circular issued at the time stressed that Home Office control would be kept to a minimum to encourage local initiatives (King 1964 p18) and the mechanism of the Home Office Circular was used to guide the development of the probation system. Then the 1936 Committee stated the following: 'In its present stage, the probation service, which is now developing rapidly, needs the direction and guidance of an active central authority to ensure efficiency, to act as a clearing house for new ideas and to coordinate the work of the various authorities. There is much to be done in the next few years and no step is more likely to contribute to the development of an efficient service than that the Home Office should accept greater responsibility for its general administration, supervision and direction' (Home Office 1936 paragraph 152). Subsequently the Home Office inspectorate came into being. However, it is of interest to note that, before the creation of the inspectorate after 1936, Home Office officials travelled the country to meet magistrates and probation officers (Jarvis 1972 p43).

At a time when the relationship between the Home Office and the service was strained, the 1962 Committee stated that the purpose of Home Office control was twofold: to ensure efficiency and safeguard the interests of the exchequer (paragraph 180 at p71f and paragraph 194 at p76). Nevertheless, because the probation committee was working satisfactorily, a number of Home Office controls could be abolished (Bochel 1976 p212f). In 1972 the central government grant increased from 50% to 80% and it can be argued that, by the time of the Statement of National Objectives and Priorities in 1984 (considered in more detail in the next chapter), this was the first attempt to impose from the centre a qualitatively different level of control than hitherto. In other words, SNOP was the outcome of a more interventionist Home Office approach to probation at a time when Leon Brittan and not William Whitelaw was Home Secretary (the former leaning towards more scrutiny from the centre than the latter). Therefore, we can summarise by saying that in the pre-SNOP period – 1907 to 1984 – the mechanisms of Home Office control can be enumerated as Rules,[5] grant aid by the exchequer, Home Office Circulars; and the work of the Inspectorate. In the post-SNOP period, the subject matter of Part 2, additional mechanisms emerged: the Financial Management Initiative; focus on efficiency; Grimsey report on the Inspectorate in 1987; the work of the Audit Commission; the notion of achieving value for money; key performance indicators; national standards; cash-linked targets; and performance league tables. We should also anticipate a future discussion by mentioning at this point the creation of the National Probation Service in 2001 that attenuated the power, control and initiatives of chief officers in the 56 area services, followed by the imposition of the National Offender Management Service in 2004.[6] But more of this later.

Summary and Conclusion

Beginning with the Probation of Offenders Act 1907 under a reforming Liberal government in Edwardian society and culminating at the threshold of the election of a radical Conservative government in May 1979, we have selectively told the story of the emergence and development of the probation system. From small beginnings in a 'gentler age' (Windlesham 1993) our journey has visited a number of signposts including four Departmental Committees; the creation of a national association; the influence of the Home Office and relevant legislation. Furthermore, we have traced an emerging governance structure and differential rates of growth in area services; the role of the local probation committee; all within a framework of changing ideologies from saving souls through rehabilitation, treatment and beyond.

The first two chapters that comprise Part 1 should have made it clear that the probation system has never existed within some hermetically sealed unit, untouched by disparate pressures and influences. On the contrary, the story of probation is also the story of political power and legitimacy, the wider criminal justice system, rising crime rates, the changing nature of penal and social policy, in addition to government's need for efficiency. It is a story that must take account of the noticeable expansion of the probation service during the mid-1960s when, under a Labour government, it was considered to be at the heart of its penal policy; the introduction of community service in the early 1970s; and the declining influence of the rehabilitative ideal.[7] It was this latter event (in religious terms it had the Nietzschean impact of being told that God is dead), coupled with the seemingly inexorable rise in recorded crime in the post-war period, that elicited various responses by the end of the 1970s. It also precipitated questions such as: Why does the service exist? What is it for and what role does it have to play in the criminal justice system and the government's fight against the enemy of crime? Consequently, along a care-control continuum with Harris and NAPO located at one end, and the controlling agendas of Younger, Davies and Griffiths applying pressure at the other, responses were being made to the dynamics of change, expansion and dissonance.

Yet we want to argue that it was the changing organisational structure, within the context of expansion, change and increased complexity, that was significant by the time we arrive at the end of the 1970s. We have seen how during the first 30 years the service had a horizontal model of organisation. In this model the probation officer was at the centre of the probation system, in fact *was* the probation system in court, and the justices eventually, in the form of the probation committee, provided support, guidance and supervision to their officers. After 1936 a horizontal model evolved into a vertical model that started to comprise principal, assistant principal and senior, in addition to main grade probation officers. This model initially supported a professional-administrative-consultative model of organisation, not a hierarchical managerial bureaucracy (McWilliams

1992). The probation officer continued to experience a fair measure of autonomy and discretion when working with clients. However, from the 1960s this hierarchical model was transformed to serve other ends beyond that of facilitating the professional practice of the individual probation officer. In other words, the probation service began to engage with policies and language of priorities that, in turn, required new forms of leadership and management. Of course there were fears that such developments would facilitate the emergence of a culture of bureaucracy, characterised by standardisation and conformity with a corresponding diminution of autonomy in what was ostensibly a people-based organisation built upon constructive one-to-one relationships, social work principles and values. Nevertheless management had most certainly arrived on the scene.

By the end of the 1970s the context within which the probation service existed was one of rising crime, a concern with juvenile delinquency, and an expanding prison population. There was uncertainty about the rationale of probation because of theoretical critiques and empirical research; less money for welfare due to economic problems that impacted on the ethos of rehabilitation and treatment; the ever pressing demand for efficiency. Additionally, the justice model (Pitts 2003) was eroding the treatment model. Some of these factors will be expanded upon in the next chapter following the election of a new-right, neo-liberal government. If it can be suggested that the service experienced discernible change between the ACTO report on aftercare (Home Office 1963) and the new politics of 1979, Part 2 of our book will make it clear that this was just the beginning.

NOTES – Chapter 2

1 Under section 1 of the Probation of Offenders Act 1907 that deals with the 'Power of Courts to permit conditional release of offenders', the courts had the power to: (i) dismiss the information or charge; (ii) conditionally discharge upon the basis of the offender entering into a recognisance up to three years. Section 2 deals with 'Probation Orders and Conditions of Recognisance' and this is the recognisance or probation order with supervision. Therefore the 1907 Act distinguishes between a probation order with supervision in section 2 from the recognisance or bind over to be of good behaviour which of course is another form of probation or promise to be of good behaviour.

2 We have already seen that Lord Windlesham in Volume 2 of *Responses To Crime* (1993) considers that the 1959 Home Office publication on *Penal Practice in a Changing Society* was the high watermark of the treatment model. Moreover, he says that the Criminal Justice Act 1961 was a progressive measure because 'Its main thrust was directed towards revising the powers of the courts to deal with young offenders; their detention and treatment in a range of institutions other than prison, notably detention centres, borstals or approved schools; and their supervision in the community by the Probation Service. All young offenders released from a detention centre were to get one year's compulsory after-care' (pp74–75).

3 The Advisory Council on the Treatment of Offenders (ACTO) was in existence from 1944 to 1966. It was replaced by the Advisory Council on the Penal System (ACPS) that produced nine reports between 1966 and 1978: Detention of Girls in a Detention Centre (1968); Regime for Long-Term Prisoners in Conditions of Maximum Security (1968); Detention Centres (1970); Non-Custodial and Semi-Custodial Penalties (1970); Reparation by the Offender (1970); Young Adult Offenders (1974) (the Younger Report); Powers of the Courts Dependent on Imprisonment (1977); The Length of Prison Sentences: Interim Report (1977); Sentences of Imprisonment: A Review of Maximum Penalties (1978). The function of the ACPS was to advise the Home Secretary on penal matters.

4 'To the politicians of the early 1970s, the notion of community service by offenders was an attractive one. Combining relative novelty with practicality, it seemed evidently constructive as a way of repaying society for a wrong done, while at the same time bringing the offender within reach of the voluntary organisations which are a peculiarly English way of providing services of value to a wider community' (Windlesham 1993 pp122–123).

5 Probation Rules were published, for example, in 1908 following the Probation of Offenders Act 1907; May 1923 following the 1922 Committee; June 1926; June 1937; the 1949 Rules clarified the duties of the Principal Probation Officer and Senior Probation Officer etc.

6 Despite our analysis of the various mechanisms of Home Office control since 1907, Burnham (1981a, 1981b) argues that by the early 1980s the movement

was *away* from central control rather than towards because during the 1970s: (a) there was local government reorganisation in 1974, followed by (b) restrictions on the growth of the service in 1976 due to national economic problems. Consequently, by 1981 Burnham states that 'the image of the Probation Service as a unified national service "led" by the Home Office is rapidly fading'. Moreover, during the early 1970s Jarvis could talk about the service retaining 'its independence of central government' (1972 p69). Therefore, these analyses serve as a corrective to other perspectives discussed in the text above. However, the position of Burnham and Jarvis could not be sustained after 1983/84, as we will see in Chapter 3.

[7] It should be acknowledged that there were approximately 1,000 probation officers in the 1950s, which had expanded to 5,000 by 1976 and then over 7,000 by the mid-1990s.

Part 2

POLITICS, MANAGEMENT AND CENTRAL CONTROL 1979–2001

Chapter 3

LAW, ORDER AND EFFICIENCY: MAY 1979 TO THE STATEMENT OF NATIONAL OBJECTIVES AND PRIORITIES 1984

'The probation and after-care service has never been free from change, but at present it is at a crucial stage in its development. Many changes have been imposed on it recently by legislation and administrative decision, and other changes are impending.' *(Haxby 1978 p15)*

Introduction: The Changing Political and Social Context

The general election of May 1979 signalled a decisive break with the political climate of the previous 30 years. The tectonic plates were sliding and the political, social, economic and cultural furniture was rearranged. This is because, at a macro level, the policies of the newly elected Conservative government took a clear yet qualified stance against post-war central planning, state regulation and control, in addition to managerial, bureaucratic and state interventionism (Seldon and Collings 2000 explore the contradiction at the heart of this statement).[1] It extolled the virtues of monetarism at the expense of Keynesianism (it was the latter that postulated that governments could ensure that people had jobs by controlling public expenditure) and had something to say about welfare dependency, the trade unions, and an anti-enterprise culture that had emerged since the war. In fact, by the summer of 1979 Mrs Thatcher's analysis of the country was that 'Taken together, these three challenges – long-term economic decline, the debilitating effects of socialism, and the growing Soviet threat – were an intimidating inheritance for a new Prime Minister' (Thatcher 1993 p9).

As the 1980s unfolded public spending was reduced from 44% of GDP in 1979 to 40% by 1990. Privatisation reversed the growth of nationalisation that developed under socialism after 1945, with the result that there was more competition and the contracting out of services to the private sector. What is significant for our book is the application of market disciplines after 1979 in pursuit of greater efficiency, and the related doctrine of value for money touched the spheres of welfare, education and the National Health Service.

Therefore, efficiency audits and the political pressure for greater accountability in the public sector entered the consciousness of the workplace, a development that was to impinge upon the people-based probation service in the years ahead. This rapidly changing macro political context after 1979 (a change not simply of degree but of kind, we suggest) is very different to the milieu that gave us evangelical religion, positivism, reformation and rehabilitation, welfare and Freudian psychology that we touched upon in the discursive introductory chapter.

Against the background of political seismic shifts from 1979 were widespread debates about crime. There were 2.5 million crimes recorded in 1980 compared with 1.6 million in 1970 and 0.5 million in 1950. Rises in the prison population were also a concern in that the sentenced prison population had more than doubled from 18,400 in 1950 to 41,796 in 1978. Therefore the cost of criminal justice was growing and the new government was determined to reduce public spending. It is also important to recall that in 1970 the unemployment rate was 2.7% (640,000) but by 1981 had reached 11.4% (2,734,000) and did not dip below 10% until 1988 (Grieve Smith 1997 p80). The post-war years of full employment were at an end. But it was the rapidity of change that was so alarming in that in 1979 the unemployment rate was 5.7% (1,300,000) yet by 1982 it was 13% (3,119,000). It was inevitable that such changes would have the greatest impact on the most vulnerable in the labour market and offenders on probation caseloads were some of the most vulnerable of all. Consequently, the number of unemployed offenders known to probation rapidly increased and probation officers were being presented with problems that militated against the rehabilitative process, which culminated in a growing sense of despair. This was reflected in wider political debates between government and trade unions that spilled over into class war. During the 1960s and 1970s the trade unions had political clout but by 1979 there was a political leader who was prepared to take them on, culminating in the pitched battles of the miners' strike in 1984/85, which saw the demise of the miners' union.

These issues were highly pertinent for the probation service. By this stage one of us was working as a probation officer in Stoke and had assiduously built up contacts with personnel departments in the Potteries, which were prepared to give offenders the chance of settling into jobs. The other had worked as a probation volunteer attached to the Lancaster probation office towards the end of the 1970s whose job it was to tap into local firms with a view to providing opportunities for lads released on borstal licence, mainly from Deerbolt at Barnard Castle. Work was not simply a means of earning money (that was important, of course) but a means by which personal growth and responsibility could be enhanced. Disaffected youth may not be willing to listen to parents, teachers, policemen, or even probation officers; but the environment provided by the workplace might help the offender to mature through contact with other workmates that, in turn, would provide a stake in society and something to lose. These conditions helped the probation officer. The value of work as a socially defining activity and providing personal power is explored by Allatt and Yeandle (1992). They also remind us that the deep-seated ideology of work that helped to define people's lives also created a social elite from those who were in employment (p121). However, the swelling ranks of the unemployed began to feel marginalised and despised by a government whose proposed solution was to get on their bikes to find work. The picture of the growing social divide was never more graphically illustrated than in the 'Boys from the Blackstuff' and Yossers' famous line, 'gizza job'. By the end of the 1970s we were unwittingly embarked upon a journey of acceptance of a permanent underclass of out-of-work people, illustrated in TV character Rab C. Nesbit: 'I know I am scum'.

At the end of the 1970s the probation service was engaging in attempts to deal imaginatively with the problems presented by unemployed clients. After 1979 the shape of probation work began to change because there were not the same lengthy queues on reporting evenings as unemployed offenders were now available during the day for routine home and office visits. In the North-East of England, for example, the rate of unemployment on probation caseloads stood at 71.5% during the 1980s when for the population generally it stood at 14.4% in the Northern region (Association of Chief Officers of Probation, North-East Region, Occasional Paper 1987). The challenge of tramping the streets of council housing estates in inner city areas when visiting unemployed probation clients was an acute problem during the 1980s, and the newly formed Association of Chief Officers of Probation (created in 1982 to replace the Chief Probation Officers' Conference) chose to press release the Conservative Party Conference in 1982, deprecating the still-rising levels of unemployment and its harmful social effects (Association of Chief Officers of Probation 2001 p3).

Those of us in being on 4th May 1979 when the Conservatives were returned to power (the previous time being the Heath government of 1970–74), in addition to being involved in probation work (one of us was preparing to begin the two-year CQSW course at Lancaster University to qualify as a probation officer after working with old lags for 12 months in a Hostel and as a volunteer at the Lancaster probation office; the other had already been in the job since 1968 and was now an SPO in Stoke), could not have imagined the kind of change that was about to evolve politically, and which would in turn affect probation services. Even if we were exceptionally prescient, we could be forgiven for our failure to anticipate the period covered by the next four chapters because of the conciliatory language used by the newly elected Prime Minister on the steps of Downing Street: 'where there is discord may we bring harmony; where there is error may we bring truth; where there is doubt may we bring faith; where there is despair may we bring hope'.[2] For many people there would indeed be despair during the next few years, particularly amongst the growing numbers of unemployed people. If you were an offender and unemployed then you were doubly disadvantaged in certain areas of the country after 1979.

From Modern to Late Modern

As we try to impose a layer of meaning onto the macro level political changes that were about to evolve and within which to understand the place of probation since the end of the 1970s, it is helpful to resort to the construction of the *late-modern* world from 1979. Garland and Sparks (2000), Garland (2001) and Young (1999) draw our attention to a number of features that illustrate the shift from the *modern* to the *late-modern* that occurred during the crisis decade of the 1970s: for example, more unstable economic circumstances illustrated by recession, unemployment and sometimes riots in the streets; changes in family life and increasing divorce rates; the rise of the teenager phenomenon and increased consumerism; developments in transport and therefore mobility and leisure; new technology and the growing influence of the media; the declining influence of religion and particularly Christian metaphysics that was accompanied by the inexorable spread of secularism and moral relativism. Consequently, it has been cogently argued that we have entered a period over recent years characterised by 'pluralism, debate, controversy and ambiguity' (Young 1999 p2). These changes, largely a consequence of cultural change in the 1960s and then profound economic change in the 1970s, combined to create a markedly different political, social and economic context as we journeyed into the 1980s.[3]

It is within this changing situation that certain commentators have resorted to the language of ontological insecurity, marginalisation and the rise of the underclass in addition to exclusionary tendencies within society (Young 1999), accompanied by rising crime and declining welfare benefits. This uncertain state of affairs led Garland and Sparks to comment that: 'the political reaction of the 1980s and 1990s has shaped the public perception of these troubling issues persuading us to think of them as problems of control rather than welfare; as the outcome of misguided social programmes; as a result of an amoral permissiveness and lax family discipline encouraged by liberal elites who were sheltered from their worst consequences; as the irresponsible behaviour of a dangerous and undeserving underclass ...' (Garland and Sparks 2000 p16).

Conservative Manifesto Priorities

Before running ahead too quickly we need to recall that a Conservative policy paper produced in 1978 – 'Law and Order: A New Perspective' – was prepared in anticipation of the manifesto the following year. Lord Windlesham explains that William Whitelaw suggested 'The Protection of the Citizen' rather than the language of 'Law and Order'. Windlesham proceeds to say that there is apparently no record of the ensuing discussion around these different terms 'but the phrase "law and order" was too deeply engrained to be displaced from general currency' (1993 p136). Therefore, during 1978 the prospective Conservative government expressed five areas of concern that can be enumerated as: 1. support for the police; 2. the guilty must be convicted; 3. punishment and prison for the right people, in other words serious offenders; 4. treatment is important as well as punishment. Where point 4. is concerned, do we see the more liberal hand of Whitelaw in wanting to preserve an attitude of compassion within the context of an emerging tougher approach? Notwithstanding this speculation the document said that deprivation is not an excuse for criminal behaviour, with the result that there should be a firm attitude towards law and order. Finally, point 5. turned to discipline in schools and the fact that young people commit a disproportionate amount of offences (see the discussion in Windlesham 1993 from page 135 which is illuminating).

Subsequently, it was the Conservative manifesto in 1979 that offered a change of direction to the previous Labour government and the post-war consensus (Thatcher 1995 p440), illustrated by the way in which it drew attention to five key areas:

1. The need for a sound economy and a balance between trade union rights and duties.

2. Restore incentives.

3. Uphold the rule of law.

4. Welfare for the most needy.

5. Strong defence (1995 p447).

Dwelling on the first of these manifesto commitments, i.e. a sound economy, it should be acknowledged that after the election an Economic Strategy Committee ('E' Committee) was chaired by the Prime Minister and the theme of efficient management was significant (Thatcher 1993 p47). Resources, in other words taxpayers' money, had to be used efficiently and government departments had to find savings (Thatcher 1993 p51). In fact, financial savings were agreed for 1979/80 and the government at this early stage was even looking as far ahead as the 1983/84 period. By the time of the budget in 1981 a change to the planning of public expenditure had been agreed 'in cash rather than what were called "volume" terms. Each minister would be given a cash budget within which to keep his expenditure' (Thatcher 1993 p137). This is the concept of cash limits, which would determine the volume of services that could be provided in any given area. Cash limits are inextricably linked to efficiency because if you are given a set amount of money to spend on services – a budget with clearly determined parameters – then you must get as much as you can for your money (particularly if it is the taxpayers' rather than the government's money; in fact the government does not have any money of its own anyway). This is the principle of good housekeeping, which means that cash limits determine what a department can do, and it encourages the development of policies and priorities to achieve this objective. In time this thinking was to permeate the probation service (as we will see as this chapter progresses) as well as other public sector organisations. In fact, we should acknowledge that cash limits were a product of International Monetary Fund intervention during 1976 to 1979 when the Labour government was troubled with inflation and public expenditure cuts. Consequently, a new system of financial control was introduced and Howard Glennerster explains that 'The Conservative government later developed this into a tougher system of cash planning targets set for several years ahead but the first steps happened in 1976' (2000 p161).

Therefore, as we begin to focus on the substantive chapters of our book, which cover the 1979–2004 period (from the election of a new Conservative government to the creation of the National Offender Management Service), we think it is important to draw the reader's attention to change at a macro political level. It is within this broad context that we can begin to locate and understand a change of attitude towards the criminal justice system in general and probation in particular, as we trace the growing emphasis on efficiency alongside the emotive theme of law and order.

Before taking this chapter to its next explanatory level, it is important to draw attention to the criminal justice and penal policy-making process that, it can be said, is a convoluted business. This is because it involves different players with different interests, including the House of Commons and House of Lords in a legislative capacity; numerous individuals and pressure groups (for example, NACRO and NAPO) in addition to public opinion, the media, reformers and campaigners (Ryan 2003). Additionally, the attitude adopted towards criminal justice is affected by: political ideology and changing social-economic circumstances (already alluded to) (Garland 1985, 1990 and 2001); the personality of the Home Secretary in power; Home Office civil servants; numerous politicians and ministers including the Prime Minister; and, importantly, the priorities of the Treasury should not be overlooked. In fact, after the election of 1979, pressure was brought to bear upon the Home Office and criminal justice system in the name of efficiency (as we will see in more detail below) but at this point Windlesham reminds us that the 'hand of the Treasury is never far away' in the form of the Chancellor and Chief Secretary to the Treasury (1993 p29). For example, it was the focus on efficiency (but also certain centralising tendencies) that culminated in a number of quangos (quasi-autonomous non-governmental organisations) being disbanded on the grounds of efficiency after May 1979; but perhaps it was also due to a growing distrust of the independent expert who could get in the way of political priorities. It was against this background that the Advisory Council on the Penal System became a casualty of the efficiency drive by central government but particularly the pressure being exerted by the treasury. Furthermore, Jeremy Paxman (2002 p198) records Gerald Kaufman saying that out of all the Whitehall departments 'the Treasury is the mightiest' because it has control over all government income and expenditure.

Nevertheless, it is instructive to observe what can only be described as a contradiction within the Conservative government in the post-

1979 period, illustrated in an interview that the *Probation Journal* was granted with Leon Brittan after replacing William Whitelaw as Home Secretary in 1983. Notwithstanding the emphasis upon efficiency and the need to reduce public expenditure in the period following May 1979, the money was found to spend on expanding the prison estate during the 1980s. This apparent contradiction did not pose too much disquiet for Mr Brittan when talking to Nigel Stone, primarily because 'the government attached very considerable importance to law and order issues' (Stone 1984 p3). This is an opportune moment to turn to other issues that will focus more specifically on the theme of law and order.

Political Consensus and Differences on Law and Order

The empirical investigations of Downes and Morgan (1997, 2002) reveal that between 1945 and the 1970s there was a discernible consensus in British politics between the major parties that coalesced around a commitment to full employment, the welfare state (Family Allowances Act 1945, National Insurance Act 1946, National Health Service Act 1946, National Assistance Act 1948), educational provision, a mixed economy, public sector intervention and state control (Fraser 1973; Sked and Cook 1979). Additionally, and importantly, during the elections of 1945, 1950, 1951, 1955 and 1959 'Crime and criminal justice were minor, taken-for-granted aspects of this consensus' (Downes and Morgan 1997 p89). We need to recall, by dragging the point from the introductory chapter, that the consensus being referred to here is the rehabilitative ideal within the criminal justice system that provided probation and prison services with a clear working ideology and legitimacy. Therefore for many years after 1945 the party manifestos analysed by Downes and Morgan said little about law and order. To some degree it was an apolitical subject that did not excessively exercise the minds of public or politicians. Whilst the post-war governments established the legislative parameters of criminal justice and the work of the probation service, beginning with the Criminal Justice Act 1948 (see Whitehead and Thompson 2004, particularly Chapter 4, for a genealogy of legislation during the 20th century affecting the probation service), the day-to-day operation of the system was left in the hands of the 'experts' (Bottoms 1980). Law and order, the rationale of probation and prison, the operation of the criminal justice system, sentencing and penal policy did not constitute a site of political conflict. They were not subject areas used by the main political parties to beat their opponents, score political points, cause embarrassment or inflict damage to win elections. Law and order matters were relatively quiescent areas of concern in a relatively quiescent political world.

But if (as we have just considered above) there were the beginnings of political, social, economic and cultural change during the 1960s and 1970s that came to a head towards the end of the 1970s with the election of a new-right Conservative government, similarly the criminal justice system experiences discernible change. The two set of changes are, of course, connected (Garland 2001). Downes and Morgan in their extremely helpful accounts explain that incrementally during the 1960s the theme of law and order creeps into the party manifestos. Then as we move into the 1970s the fault lines begin to appear between Labour and Conservative perspectives. Under the Labour government of 1974 to May 1979 debilitating problems emerged, set against the background of the oil crisis in 1973, problems with the unions and strikes, the International Monetary Fund loan, in addition to rising crime, that culminated in the winter of discontent (Sked and Cook 1979; Brake and Hale 1992). Downes and Morgan state that whilst Labour – to be precise *Old Labour* – continued to fuse together the themes of social deprivation and crime in the sense that the former provided the explanatory context for the latter; by contrast the Conservatives from 1979 articulated a more right-wing agenda that was manifested in the language of law and order, the fight against crime, individual responsibility, the need for discipline and authority, tougher sentences for young people, that initially appeared in the Criminal Justice Act 1982 (considered in more detail below). Consequently 'The 1979 Conservative manifesto brought "law and order" to the fore as a major election issue and dispelled any lingering trace of bipartisan consensus' (Downes and Morgan 1997 p93) that had prevailed for several decades (Windlesham 1993 p139).

The end of the post-war consensus in relation to crime and its treatment, which would have a profound effect on probation, can be further illustrated by the different perspectives associated with Labour and Conservative. Old Labour, contrasted with the phenomenon of New Labour that emerged in the 1990s and consolidated in government from 1997, understood crime within a wider framework of social conditions that needed to be ameliorated; in part, a social policy approach that acknowledged that social conditions needed to be addressed by a positive welfare approach in conjunction with a rehabilitative perspective towards the individual and the family. This approach is neatly captured by Raynor and Vanstone when they say that 'for much of the twentieth century "penological modernism", underpinned by the belief that crime was at least partly caused by socio-economic factors, formed the basis of criminal justice and social welfare practice aimed at rehabilitation' (2002 p68). By contrast, after 1979 the Conservatives distanced themselves from this explanatory framework and returned to a more neo-classical view that crime is largely a matter of individual choice rather than linked to or caused by wider socio-economic factors. Therefore, instead of the themes of welfare, positive help, treatment and rehabilitation, the approach to crime becomes more orientated towards discipline and punishment because the individual is perceived to be responsible for his own behaviour, which is of course an overly simplistic yet politically convenient proposition to advance. This contrast between the two main parties caricatures the complex reality of what occurred after 1979, but it does capture the general direction in which the criminal justice system and penal policy were moving. In other words, there was a shift of emphasis from care to control, welfare to punishment, treatment to the justice model, positivism to classicism, yet without totally abolishing the former approaches established in these dyads. Therefore, within the context of a strategic shift in criminal justice attitudes, at a political level, we can talk legitimately about discontinuity but also about a qualified continuity with the past (Garland 2001). Of course there is always the temptation to overplay one's hand to prove a particular point, which is why as a corrective to our analysis we should refer to an article by Burnham (1981a, 1981b). He says that despite a shift to the right under the Conservatives there was not a law and order holocaust. Moreover, the 1982 Act was ambivalent because, notwithstanding the introduction of the new 21-day detention centre order, there were criteria established to restrict the use of custody. Importantly, Whitelaw was by no means dismissive of the work of the probation service. We can further illustrate this ambivalence as follows.

Conservative Criminology

In her 1995 autobiographical volume, *The Path To Power*, Mrs Thatcher alludes to an approach to crime influenced by the thinking of two American criminologists, Ernest Van Den Haag and James Q. Wilson (see Brake and Hale 1992). This approach locates the responsibility for offending with the offender; crime is a form of behaviour rationally chosen; there is less emphasis on the causes of crime located in the wider social context; less concern to understand the individual and a greater emphasis on deterrence and harsher punishment through sending more people to prison. This neo-classical attitude was not, of course, helpful for the philosophy of the probation service and, as Mrs

Thatcher so starkly put it, 'the most direct way to act against crime is to make life as difficult as possible for the potential and actual criminal' (1995 p558). In fact, we can with profit draw further attention to James Q. Wilson's 1975 book, *Thinking About Crime*, which was published whilst he was at Harvard University between 1973 and 1987. Andrew Rutherford has said that Wilson was 'in step' (1996 p21) with the shift to the right in American politics and criminal justice policy beginning with the Reagan years during the 1980s. Consequently, symmetry prevailed between America and Britain in their right-wing approach to dealing with offenders. This is in marked contrast to the more positive tenets of the rehabilitative ideal that had been fixed during the 1890s–1970s period (Garland 2001 p34f). Rutherford reminds us that the American criminal justice system gave expression to the penchant for imprisonment advocated by Wilson because between 1975 and 1990 the prison population increased from 240,593 to 774,375; in percentage terms, an increase of 221% (Rutherford 1996 p37). In 2005 the USA prison population was 2 million (Murray 2005).

It is important to recall that William Whitelaw was Home Secretary during the 1979–83 government after which he became leader of the House of Lords, to be replaced at the Home Office by Leon Brittan. On the former the Prime Minister said that 'My views on sentencing in general and immigration are a good deal tougher than his' (1993 p307). Additionally, Windlesham describes Whitelaw as a 'kindly and tolerant man' (1993 p159) whose heart was not in those more extreme manifestations of law and order (such as the introduction of the short, sharp, shock experiment in November 1979 in two detention centres at New Hall, West Yorkshire and Send, Surrey; two more were added to the penal experiment in 1981). On Brittan it may be suggested she disclosed her own instincts when commenting that 'He would have no time for the false sentimentality which surrounds so much discussion on the causes of crime' (1993 p308). This was a political, ideological and criminological position that did not encourage intelligent probation practice, which was more in tune with the comment by Peter Raynor in the mid-1980s when he stated that 'People may be able to choose how they respond to the world, but they do not usually choose the world in which they have to respond' (1985 p181). For an increasing number of people during the period after 1979 life became extremely difficult, in particular the clients of the probation service. It is helpful to include one last point on the role of the Prime Minister before moving on because, once again, it adds a semblance of balance to our story. Windlesham explains that 'Over her eleven-year premiership the only substantial issue of penal policy in which Mrs Thatcher played a decisive part was the privatisation of prisons and remand centres, and the contracting out of certain criminal justice services' (1993 p30).

Furthermore, it was during the early 1980s that the Home Office was, perhaps understandably, operating with a more pessimistic diagnosis of the crime problem. This is hardly surprising given the academic critiques and research findings that questioned the efficacy of rehabilitation and treatment in the 1970s, and even earlier. It was unclear about aetiology and unsure about what to do, notwithstanding the more visceral theorising of the Prime Minister. There is no doubt that this was an increasingly difficult period for the probation service because it was being forced by the weight of critical research away from treatment and individual casework towards a different organisational rationale (as was made clear during the previous chapter). Consequently, the 1980s witnessed the emergence of the justice model with its determinate sentences that made their way into the Criminal Justice Act 1982. The 1980s for probation was a period of affirming the rationale of alternatives to custody, in addition to which Bill McWilliams drew attention to managerial, radical and personalist schools of thought that responded in various ways to the vacuum created by the collapse of rehabilitation (McWilliams 1987). Nevertheless, we have already documented in our historical excavation contained in the previous chapter how managerialism was emerging as a dominant force in probation from the 1960s and has continued ever since (as we shall see). We must be careful not to run too far ahead at this point but it is interesting to observe that, by 1991, Mary Tuck, Head of the Home Office Research and Planning Unit, said that the Home Office is increasingly drawn to a 'managerial model ... based on the insight that crime is inevitable in any society and conceives the task as being more to manage, reduce or even prevent the amount of crime' (rather than the probation task of trying to appreciate, understand, explain and then address positively the offending behaviour of individuals; Rock 1990).

During the 1980s much greater emphasis was placed on individual responsibility (as already mentioned). In fact it may be said to be one of the central tenets of Thatcherism (Seldon and Collings 2000). This approach at the level of political ideology was complemented at the criminological level by the emergence of right realism under whose umbrella we can locate administrative criminology that emerged from within the Home Office, routine activity and rational choice theory

(Walklate 2003). We have already alluded to some of the key features of this neo-classical approach but it is worth emphasising the shift away from explanatory structural factors, welfare and positivist rehabilitation, towards the need for personal discipline, punishment, management control, the needs of the victim, and blaming the offender for resorting to antisocial behaviour. It may be said that this approach juxtaposed quite well with the new-right political agenda in the 1980s that focused upon personal responsibility and managing rather than explaining the crime problem. For, as it has been stated: 'Certainly a focus on the individual absolves governments of responsibility on the one hand and expects greater responsibility of individual citizens on the other' (Walklate 2003 p47). Therefore, it may be argued that during the early 1980s the probation service found itself in a situation where it was being forced to adjust to a less sympathetic political context in relation to the growing crime problem that affected thinking and attitudes; a changing criminal justice system; a less forgiving climate in relation to penal policy and criminological perspectives. It is at this point that we should begin to turn our attention to the Criminal Justice Act 1982. But first a preamble that helps to locate probation work in the new political and criminal justice context.

Background to the Criminal Justice Act 1982

One year after the Probation of Offenders Act 1907 had created the probation system, the Children Act 1908 established separate courts for young offenders and restrictions on imprisonment for children. From 1908 to the 1970s the system for dealing with young offenders oscillated between care and control, punishment and welfare, justice and treatment, understanding, help and condemnation. Had everything proceeded as anticipated during the 1960s – Longford Report (1964); 1965 White Paper on *The Child, Family and Young Offender*; 1968 White Paper, *Children in Trouble*; culminating in the Children and Young Persons Act 1969 – then a juvenile justice system would have been created that was tilted towards welfare rather than punishment. In fact the 1969 Act tried to impose a major shift in policy towards young people that would have had the effect of decriminalising and de-stigmatising the young offender (Pitts 2003). For example:

(a) juvenile offenders would be offered social work help rather than punishment;

(b) services for offenders would be determined at local not national level;

(c) offenders would be helped in the community rather than custody;

(d) if the 1969 Act had been fully implemented it would have:

    (i) raised the age of criminal responsibility from 10 to 14 (section 4);

    (ii) ensured compulsory liaison between police and welfare agencies before prosecution (section 5);

    (iii) raised the age of borstal admission from 15 to 17 (section 7);

    (iv) abolished for juveniles the detention centre and attendance centre (section 7(3).

Approved schools (introduced in the CYPA 1933 to replace the Victorian Industrial and Reformatory Schools to 'save' children who had offended from adult prisons – Radzinowicz and Hood 1990 and specifically Chapters 6 and 7) were to be replaced by community homes with education (section 35) and supervision orders and intermediate treatment orders introduced (sections 11 and 12).

However, what in fact happened was the new welfare system was introduced, albeit to a limited extent, but the old custodial penal system remained intact; in other words, not replacement of one system with another, but the assimilation of two systems (Thorpe et al 1980). The more radical measures were not implemented by the incoming Conservative government in 1970. By the time the Labour Party was returned to power in 1974 it was in no mood to implement what it was proposing during the 1960s. Moreover, upon arriving at the unveiling of the Conservative manifesto of 1979, there were four commitments on law and order that had implications for offenders:

(a) free parliamentary vote on hanging;

(b) tougher regimes in four detention centres (implemented between November 1979 and 1981, but the evaluation demonstrated that the experiment was a failure);

(c) a wider range of sentencing options for young people;

(d) the tightening of immigration rules.

But, it may be asked, why was there such an emphasis on law and order, as opposed to welfare, during the 1970s that manifested itself in the Conservative manifesto of 1979 and then the Criminal Justice

Act 1982? Why such an emphasis when the criminal statistics were notoriously difficult to interpret and when Robert Mark could claim towards the end of the 1970s that 'crime is not even among the most serious of our difficulties'? (1978 p255). Why the emotive language of law and order that has been heard increasingly during the last 25 years? One answer to our question can be found in the work of Stuart Hall and his colleagues (1978) because in Part 1 of *Policing The Crisis* Hall takes us back to the early 1970s when the rise in crime was considered by the police, courts, judiciary and press to be a product of the permissive society of the 1960s, in addition to a relatively lenient pattern of sentencing. In fact, various crimes were conflated to give the impression that there had been a sharp rise in crimes of violence during 1972–73 when the mugging panic was at its height. So how can we explain the phenomenon of mugging?

In *Policing The Crisis* mugging is seen as a symbol of social malaise in the inner city and the mugger becomes the perfect folk devil and scapegoat for social ills created by an unjust and unequal capitalist socio-economic system that produces winners and losers. Due to the breakdown of the post-war consensus (that we have already considered) during the 1970s, and because economic decline bears heaviest on the working class, there is the danger that working class youth in particular will no longer accept the legitimacy of the prevailing political system, the established status quo. Therefore, it is argued that a crisis is *invented* that focuses, for example, on mugging and crime for political and ideological reasons, not supported by facts and evidence, yet which act as a unifying force for all those who are not involved in crime to gather around the theme of law and order. Furthermore, this process can legitimise a more punitive response; it directs attention away from the real structural problems associated with capitalism, inequality, social and criminal injustice, and pushes the problem onto the criminal. Such a process serves to ratchet-up a more punitive penal response directed at the individual, to what is fundamentally a political and social issue. Therefore crime can result in 'good' politics, as Muncie explains: 'The meaning of mugging then has little to do with the escalation of a particular crime, but is more an attempt by the state to isolate deviant populations, manufacture a moral panic about them, and eventually persuade the public to accept more coercive means of social control. Indeed, the construction and career of mugging have played a central part in Britain's drift into a law and order society' (Muncie 1984; Cavadino, Crow and Dignan 1999 p26 on the relationship between economic conditions and crime).

Criminal Justice Act 1982

Consequently, in addition to the political advantage that could be drawn from the winter of discontent during 1978/79, the theme of law and order could be an election winner. In 1980 a White Paper was published on Young Offenders that reflected the views of the Conservative Parliamentary Home Affairs Committee and the Conservative Women's National Advisory Committee, who opposed the philosophy that permeated the abortive welfare-oriented 1969 Act by advocating tougher measures that found their way into the 1982 Act. A great deal had happened between 1969 and 1982, illustrated by the measures contained in the 1982 Act that may be summarised as follows:

- The detention centre that was introduced in the CJA 1948 was retained but with shorter sentences of 21 days to 4 months for 14–20-year-old offenders.

- Borstal, introduced in 1901 as a semi-indeterminate sentence for young offenders, in addition to young persons' sentences, was abolished and replaced with a single determinate youth custody sentence.

- There was to be a probation presence in the newly formatted detention centres but no professional social work service.

- Youth custody replaced the 31 borstal and YP centres. In the latter the probation service had a major responsibility for social work provision.

- The probation officer supervised both detention centre and youth custody licences following release from custody.

- The supervision order and intermediate treatment provision for 14–17-year-olds involved the probation service in their delivery.

- The community service order was made available for 16-year-old offenders for 40–120 hours, operated by probation.

- The probation order could have Schedule 11 conditions included.

- Social enquiry reports remained a major probation task.

Finally section 65 dropped the title 'After-Care' that had been introduced in 1967, so that from now on the organisation was to be called 'The Probation Service'. The sentencing framework for juvenile offenders that involved the probation service in its organisation and implementation following the 1982 Act (in addition to adult courts and sentences, of course) was thus:

- Conditional Discharge
- Financial Penalty
- Attendance Centre Order
- Supervision Order
- Supervision Order and discretionary Intermediate Treatment
- Supervision Order and non-discretionary supervised activity requirement
- Supervision Order and negative requirements
- Community Service Order for 16-year-olds and over
- Care Order
- Residential Care Order
- Detention Centre
- Youth Custody.

We have just alluded to Schedule 11 conditions that were an adjunct to a probation order subsequent to the implementation of the 1982 Act and we need to say more about this condition and its history, particularly against the background of our discussion at the end of Chapter 2. Towards the end of the previous chapter we alluded to some of the contentious issues surrounding care and control during the late 1970s. Against the background of these debates the Kent Probation Control Unit opened in 1980 and probationers were required to attend for six days each week for a period of six months. The facility was established under the Powers of Criminal Courts Act 1973, in which section 4 provided for attendance at a Day Training Centre as a condition of probation, and attendance was limited to 60 days at those centres established in London, Liverpool, Sheffield and Pontypridd. However, section 2 of the 1973 Act stated that 'a probation order may in addition require the offender to comply during the whole or any part of the probation period with such requirements as the court … considers necessary for securing the good conduct of the offender …'(s 2(3)). It was section 2(3) that Kent was claiming as the justification for the Control Unit, which became the focus of the ongoing care and control debate. But then something happened to deal the control lobby a significant blow, albeit only temporarily.

In 1981 a person on probation in North Shields was ordered to attend a Day Centre (not a Day Training Centre) as a condition of a probation order, but it was not a designated centre under the 1973 Act. The probationer was returned to court and breached for non-attendance but appealed against the action taken by the probation service. The process continued through the Divisional Court, which upheld the appeal, as did the House of Lords by finding that the condition was invalid. This is the now famous *Cullen v Rogers* case (House of Lords 1982). Therefore, the legality of certain conditions in probation orders was questioned and Lord Bridge opined that 'a requirement … must not introduce such a custodial or other element as will amount in substance to the imposition of a sentence' (quoted in Raynor 1985 p50), which has been a feature of the Probation Order since 1907. Additionally, there is an interesting subtext to what happened in North Shields: one of the authors of this book co-authored the Whitehead and Thompson (2004) textbook for trainee probation officers and practice development assessors. The significance of this is that Jamie Thompson was the qualified probation officer at the North Shields Day Centre that opened in 1980 and was staffed, in addition to one probation officer, by three ancillaries, some volunteers, and a secretary. Peter Cullen managed the Day Centre in addition to a probation field team. The Centre catered for probationers who attended as a requirement of a probation order from nine to five each day, five days each week for three months. The facility provided a rigorous timetable of cooking, social skills, budgeting help, basic reading and writing skills, in quite a controlled environment as a direct alternative to custody for relatively serious offenders. It is interesting to recall that in those days local practice initiatives were allowed to evolve in probation areas, more often than not as a consequence of a particular team interest or the passion of an individual, sometimes without the knowledge and direction of headquarters let alone the Home Office as the central authority. It appears that the Day Centre in North Shields is a good example of this. But when the probationer in question objected to action being taken against her for non-attendance the initial prosecution proceedings were presented at the Wallsend Magistrates' Court by Jamie Thompson. Therefore it could so easily have been *Thompson v Rogers* rather than *Cullen v Rogers*. Subsequently, the Home Office shaped the Criminal Justice Act 1982 to allow for the making of a requirement to attend a location or participate in a specified activity for not more than 60 days. This was the Schedule 11 requirement that, it may be argued, cast into sharp relief the fundamental differences between care and control, treatment and the demands of justice for more 'punishment'. But for a while the control lobby did not have all its own way, as the *Cullen v Rogers* case demonstrated; and before continuing with this theme we want to say a little more about the day centre model.

The development of day centres provided opportunities for innovation within probation. For example, the Shelton probation office experiment during the early 1970s aimed at providing a safety net for the disaffected and disconnected. It became a drop-in centre for those probationers who were inevitably out of work. Dropping in was not usually part of the statutory requirement of probation but was perceived as a useful adjunct to the more structured format of the supervision process. By the end of the 1970s some day centres had been established that were attempting to offer more than tea and counselling. In fact, the Barbican Centre in Gloucester was at this time at the forefront of day centre developments providing education and vocational training opportunities. Next, the Staffordshire service established the Rainbow day centre in Hanley that was managed by one of the authors of this book from 1982 to 1984. This was largely a voluntary centre that had crime prevention as its *raison d'être*. It was yet another variation on the North Shields, Gloucester and Middlesbrough models of probation practice, making provision for constructive activities, social skills training such as budgeting and problem solving. We have had access to a copy of a day book from the Rainbow centre that was regularly attended by 60–100 people daily. The log makes fascinating reading and is illustrative of the often huge amount of practical and emotional support that attendees received from probation staff. The centre also had a workshop attached to it teaching carpentry skills as part of the Youth Opportunities Programme (YOP) scheme. The Youth Training Scheme (YTS) replaced the YOP in 1983 and the workshop continued but under new arrangements. Probation had clearly demonstrated that, as part of its penchant for creative innovation under changing political, socio-economic conditions, it could also work in partnership with other government departments (responding to social problems they perhaps had helped to create in the first place). However, the day centre experiment with the voluntary and preventative model was not to last as services found it difficult to justify expenditure on what was not a statutory activity. By the mid-1980s most of them had disappeared but the legacy of group activity with offenders could indeed be built on. The commitment to responding to and tackling the effects of unemployment would continue, largely through the development of partnerships with other agencies.

We should also observe by returning to an earlier point that, as a further corrective to the growing emphasis on law and order, the 1982 Act included restrictions on the use of custody for juveniles because statutory criteria had to be applied and met before a custodial sentence could be imposed. Section 1(4) stated that a custodial sentence should only be imposed on a young person when:

(a) he is unwilling or unable to respond to non-custodial penalties;

(b) a custodial sentence is necessary for the protection of the public;

(c) the offence was so serious that a non-custodial sentence cannot be justified.

Moreover, the court must express its reasons when imposing custody and log these in the court register; a social enquiry report must normally be consulted; and the offender must be offered legal representation. Research conducted by one of the authors of this book in one juvenile justice system after the implementation of the 1982 Act clearly demonstrated the problems courts were experiencing in adhering to the new legislative criteria, as in a number of cases the safeguards were not being met and custody was not always being imposed as a last resort (Whitehead and MacMillan 1985).[4]

It is also instructive to turn to an analysis of the 1982 Act provided by Jordan (1983) in which he advanced the view that it signalled a change within probation from constituting an alternative to custody (the philosophy underpinning the Probation of Offenders Act 1907) to an alternative form of the prison system. In other words, the drift towards punishment, containment, control, deterrence, discipline and the enforcement of rules was more reflective of prison than probation in the community, particularly the form of probation envisaged by the 1907 Act. In fact, Jordan goes on to say that the political purpose of the 1982 Act was: (a) a compromise between the urgent need to reduce the custodial population and the demand for deterrence within a new law and order context; (b) greater emphasis on conditions, containment, retribution and deterrence following the *Cullen v Rogers* judgement; (c) emerging closer links between the juvenile justice system and the adult criminal justice system, exemplified by the introduction of community service for 16-year-old offenders. He concludes his analysis by saying something we think is significantly prescient: 'The present government is more pragmatic than many of its critics allow, and more skilful. It has extended and consolidated the mechanisms of central government power in a number of fields, and this is just one of them. In the long run we can expect more of the same' (1983 p87).

Against the background of the changing political context; the emergence of the new-right, the themes of efficiency and law and order, but with certain qualifications, we now turn to consider the significance of the Statement of National Objectives and Priorities (SNOP), published by the Home Office in 1984. By doing so, one of the themes contained within SNOP resonates with the emphasis on efficiency that we addressed within a macro political context at the beginning of the chapter, in addition to which the focus on alternatives to custody became an important feature of criminal justice during the 1980s, culminating in the Criminal Justice Act 1991 (which will be looked at in some detail in the next chapter).

Statement of National Objectives and Priorities 1984

The first point to establish when we turn our attention to SNOP (Home Office 1984) is that the probation service was reviewed and scrutinised on a number of occasions prior to 1984. Chapter 2 has already alluded to those Departmental Committee reports that were published in 1909, 1922, 1936 and 1962. These reports have been succinctly reviewed elsewhere in this text, including, importantly, the way in which they are different from SNOP in relation to the processes at work that produced the various reports: content; underpinning ideology; and the degree of Home Office central control over the service (Whitehead 1988). Additionally, Raynor and Vanstone support our analysis by arguing that what occurred in 1983–84 signalled a new set of priorities for probation within a new political environment because before 1984 the service 'had survived in a relatively benign political and social world' (2002 p77f). The new world is characterised by a rapidly changing culture in probation; a more centrally regulated and prescriptive service with a corresponding loss of local autonomy and control. To some degree (as we saw above) Jordan perceives these tendencies at work, particularly the centralisation of government power, when analysing the Criminal Justice Act 1982. We want to add the national statement to the list.

From 1979 the newly elected Conservative government's approach to the public sector was to question the notion of indefinite growth. Consequently, it was during the 1979–82 period that the Cabinet Office Efficiency Unit was established under Derek Rayner, who was in fact appointed only five days after the general election of May 1979 as a special adviser on efficiency and therefore eliminating waste in the civil service and government departments. In fact, the Prime Minister herself stated the following in the House of Commons in 1980: 'In the past Government have progressively increased the number of tasks that the Civil Service is asked to do without paying sufficient attention to the need for economy and efficiency. Consequently staff members have grown over the years. The present Government are committed both to a reduction in tasks and to better management. We believe that we should now concentrate on simplifying the work and doing it more efficiently. The studies that departments have carried out, including those in conjunction with Sir Derek Rayner, have demonstrated clearly the scope for this. All Ministers in charge of departments will now work out detailed plans for concentrating on essential functions and making operations simpler and more efficient in their departments' (Humphrey 1987 pp10–11).

During the early 1980s government departments – Employment, Education and Science; Health and Social Security; Lord Chancellor's Department – were asked carefully to examine how they managed all aspects of their programmes and by the end of 1983 a total of 155 scrutinies and six government interdepartmental reviews had been conducted with potential savings of £400 million per annum (Humphrey 1987 p91; Fullwood 1984). The Conservatives also published three White Papers on the subject of efficiency in July 1981, September 1982 and September 1983, and Rayner's work is important within this context. These efficiency scrutinies were concerned to promote managerial improvements in government and public sector departments, which helped to shape the Financial Management Initiative (FMI) that was launched on 17th May 1982 and announced in Cmnd 8616 – *Government Observations on the Third Report from the Treasury and Civil Service Select Committee*, Session 1981–82, HC 236 (Butler 1983). The FMI evolved with the overall purpose of improving management in government, but it is interesting to note that it was the Fulton Committee in 1968 (Cmnd 2638) which gave the first impetus to management accountability within the sphere of the civil service (Humphrey 1987). More specifically the aim of the FMI was to promote in each government department a system in which managers at all levels have:

(a) a clear view of their objectives and, wherever possible, the means to assess and measure outputs and therefore performance in relation to objectives;

(b) a clear responsibility for making the best use of resources, including a critical scrutiny of outputs and value for money;

(c) information about costs, the training and access to expert advice that managers need to exercise their responsibilities (Butler 1983).

The FMI has been described as an integrated planning and control system (Tayler and Nuttall 1989) and when applied to the civil service and government departments it saved something like £1 billion of taxpayers' money (Harris 1988). From this point onwards the language of the 3Es (economy, efficiency and effectiveness); performance management; greater accountability; cash limits; value for money; the setting of clear objectives, priorities and targets; management information systems; becomes firmly established within government, the public sector, and of course the probation service was not left untouched. The Statement of National Objectives and Priorities is the document through which the principles of the Financial Management Initiative were given expression in the probation service. The philosophy underlying both documents is elucidated by David Faulkner when he said that 'The principle upon which the present government operates – across the whole field of public expenditure – is that resources must determine the policy and not that the policy can determine the resources. This means that each service or programme is given a budget and is expected to get on and do the best job that can be done with it' (1984 p3). Against the background of the emergence of the FMI it can be argued that the Statement is unique and therefore important when exploring the relationship between central government, the Home Office and the probation service. It is the first centrally imposed definition of what the 56 area services should be doing and what they should have in common, in relation to more centrally determined objectives and priorities. It was the policy framework within which all local probation services were expected to determine their own priorities (as we will see in the next chapter), and it may be claimed that this was the first serious attempt by central government to create a more consistent national probation service (that of course would come to fruition in 2001, but more of this later). It could also be suggested that this is an inchoate example of the Centralisation (Strong State) Critique of Thatcherism (Seldon and Collings 2000 p86) whose thesis is the centralisation of state power in

Number 10; if not Number 10 directly then most certainly the Home Office.

At this point we need to provide the reader with a summary of the Statement, which contained seven main sections. Some of the early sections touch upon locating the service within the wider criminal justice system; the Statement emphasises that the central purpose of probation is to supervise offenders in the community; the principal statutory tasks are affirmed as the provision of social enquiry reports to the courts, the supervision of non-custodial orders including probation and community service, throughcare and aftercare, in addition to civil work. Section 5 describes several specific objectives related to the tasks of the preceding two sections as:

(a) working with courts;

(b) supervision in the community;

(c) through-care;

(d) other work in the community (including civil work).

The final two sections, 6 and 7, delineate service priorities and consider the appropriate allocation of resources to achieve service objectives (Raynor 1984).

One of the important features of SNOP is the way in which it expected that each of the 56 area services must be able to put into effect community orders, particularly where custodial sentences would otherwise be imposed. This resonates with the developing motif of alternatives to custody during the 1980s because of the ongoing concerns about the rising prison population and the level of expenditure (Lloyd 1986 p4). In fact, the 1983 draft Home Office document that preceded SNOP resorted to the language of 'the service's capacity to cope with offenders with comparatively serious records of crime' (Home Office 1983a 5(v)). Subsequently, SNOP proceeded to state that 'The first priority should be to ensure that, wherever possible, offenders can be dealt with by non-custodial measures' (VI(a)). We can also point out that, in addition to SNOP, the objective of alternatives to custody during the 1980s was picked up in a series of papers by Pointing (1986); the Green Paper (Home Office 1988a) that eventually culminated in the Criminal Justice Act 1991 that foreshadowed a central role for probation; the collection of papers by Rees and Williams (1989); and finally a further collection of papers edited by Shaw and Haines (1989). However, and this illustrates the contradictory nature of penal policy with which the probation service has had to contend over many decades now, whilst Leon Brittan agreed with the position of SNOP on alternatives to custody (1984 p16), during his tenure at the Home Office he was also responsible for the building of 14 new prisons, in addition to adversely affecting the possibility of prisoners obtaining parole if they had been sentenced to more than 5 years' imprisonment. We will return to this theme as the book progresses but suffice to say, at this point, it was envisaged that alternatives to custody would be achieved by more targeted reports for courts and the proper use of probation and community service, in addition to the development of additional requirements. In this way the service would become more effective and credible at working with more serious offenders, in addition to protecting the public. Extra conditions, made possible by Schedule 11 to the Criminal Justice Act 1982 (as we saw above), signalled the need to make real demands on offenders linked to appropriate enforcement action for non-compliance, which is what had occurred at the North Shields Day Centre. It is interesting to observe how SNOP, when addressing features of supervision in the community in section VB(v), slips into the language of 'ensuring by clear planning and follow-up action that the supervision, support, advice and guidance available to offenders under probation and supervision orders, through the exercise of social work skills and use of available facilities, are applied as efficiently and effectively as possible in each case so that the risk of offending is reduced, to the benefit of the offender and of the community'.

Therefore, as we move towards the end of this chapter, it is interesting to pick up on the use of the language of social work skills, as well as efficiency, within a more law and order oriented context, which illustrates the presence of certain contradictory tendencies in the approach to offenders. Within a climate when probation is evolving into a more criminal justice oriented rather than social work agency, even the Statement of National Objectives and Priorities makes reference to the need for the probation officer to exercise social work skills. Perhaps, during the early 1980s, there was some common ground between this reference in SNOP and the clear view of NAPO when it stated, in response to the draft of SNOP in 1983, that 'The success of our work depends upon our ability to create and maintain useful relationships with them, to encourage trust and exercise influence. The balance is a delicate one but a great deal will be lost if the service is pressed to adopt a more controlling role, a brusque approach' (Beaumont 1984 p13). Nevertheless, NAPO took issue with the draft and final Home Office documents on the following basis: they failed to provide additional resources; the failure to endorse social work values; and the downgrading of throughcare, aftercare and civil work.

We have already considered the origins of NAPO in the previous chapter and in a different political climate. By the 1980s it is reasonable to claim that the views of the Home Office on one hand and those of NAPO on the other provide us with a good example of the working out of a complex dialectical process, yet without much synthesis of views. At a time when it could be suggested that the service was in danger of being reduced to a narrow range of tasks on the basis of the application of the political principles of economy, efficiency and effectiveness in the post-rehabilitative age, NAPO was desperately trying to preserve and promote what, it can be argued, is the ideal-type probation practice for a number of probation officers: 'advise, assist and befriend'; social work values; a clear view that custody is harmful; and, additionally, the provision of support and help for damaged people who are victims themselves of an unjust and unequal political system; counselling and welfare services; the centrality of a positive relationship with clients. This is the humane, caring and understanding face of the criminal justice system, which finds an echo in the work of Tony Bottoms and Bill McWilliams, Robert Harris, and Peter Raynor, for example. Importantly, NAPO's position was to oppose the Home Office policy of more control, surveillance, containment and extra conditions in probation orders. Therefore, NAPO, the professional organisation, trade union and penal-political pressure group, was assertively defending its professional concerns and liberal-ethical values that are in marked contrast to the new political agenda during the 1980s. In fact, by the mid-1980s the 1986 Annual Report captures NAPO's stance when we read 'The past year has produced no relaxation in the harsh social context in which the probation service works. Continued mass unemployment, new restrictions in social security benefit payments and further cuts in welfare services have left probation officers struggling to offer hope to embittered clients' (Beaumont 1986).

Perhaps it is permissible to indulge ourselves in speculation, prior to concluding this chapter, by considering what would or could have happened if the process that culminated in a national statement for probation had not occurred. We think that prior to 1979 there was an alternative course of action available to government if it felt that the probation service was in need of critical scrutiny. What we mean by this is to make reference once again to the Advisory Council on the

Penal System that was, of course, disbanded as a quango by the Home Office after May 1979 due to financial pressures. But if it had survived in order to review the service in more favourable political circumstances, then the future of probation may have been quite different to the one we are describing in this book. The fact that this process did not occur created the conditions in which more centralising pressures could evolve as the 1980s progressed.

Summary and Conclusion

This chapter has tried to demonstrate that, by the time we arrive at the 1979–1984 period, the political, economic and cultural supports that had promoted the post-war consensus of the welfare state, a commitment to full employment, and of course rehabilitation and treatment, were in the process of being undermined (Garland 2001; Brake and Hale 1992). A combination of interrelated developments during the 1960s and 1970s (that we have already alluded to) eroded social and penal policies that were interventionist in the way they addressed poverty, deprivation, inequality, and those maladjusted individuals and families who came within the orbit of the penal-welfare system (Garland 2001 p77) that had been in existence for many decades. Significantly, the probation service had an important role to play within this intellectual framework of a commitment to post-war welfare and rehabilitation on behalf of the state in the maintenance of order and the control of predominantly working class offenders.

But against a background of rising crime, economic decline, an escalating prison population, disenchantment with welfare, treatment and rehabilitation, a new-right Conservative government was elected in 1979 that contributed to a drift into a more law and order oriented society that signalled the end of the post-war criminal justice consensus. This political shift resulted in the delicate balance of penal-welfare being tilted from care to control, welfare to punishment, treatment to justice, positivism to neo-classicism, to some extent illustrated by the Criminal Justice Act 1982. However, it is not accurate to say that these shifts in political and criminal justice philosophy destroyed all vestiges of welfare and social work attitudes (Whitehead 1988). Nevertheless, what we can say is that the balance was reoriented towards a less sympathetic and understanding approach to offenders that accentuated personal responsibility for one's own actions regardless of the social circumstances in which behaviour should be located, understood and explained. In fact this rebalancing was undertaken by a new-right government committed to cuts in public spending and which perceived welfare as the problem rather than the solution. In the process, a combination of political rhetoric and the media stigmatised the homeless and unemployed so much so that families caught in the poverty trap rose from 120,000 in 1980 to 570,000 in 1988 (Gilmore 1992). The probation service could not escape being affected by these changes.

It was within this changing political and penal context that the probation service was scrutinised during 1983–84 by a confident Conservative government that had been re-elected, and the Statement of National Objectives and Priorities was the result. This was one of the last attempts by central government to create a more consistent, accountable and efficient service by consultation and persuasion. It drew attention to the pressing need for clear policies to address crime, the wider community, and of course to provide alternatives to custody to reduce reliance on the prison, in a much more managerial environment. From autonomous area fiefdoms that had been characterised for many years by individual probation officers exercising a considerable degree of professional autonomy and discretion with offenders; to the elevation of policies, objectives and priorities within a national framework of economy, efficiency and effectiveness; value for money; the disciplines of financial management. This was the effect of the national statement that began to change the organisational dynamics of probation, a consequence of central government intervening more decisively in local area services. So, as we arrive at the publication of SNOP in 1984, it can be said that it raised certain questions for the service to answer. For example: How will area services respond to the guidance provided by the national statement? Will they fall into line with the will of central government or offer resistance? Will they engage constructively with central government's concerns about crime and custody, or pretend that the changes being advocated will evaporate in the not too distant future? How will the service respond to the new political and managerial landscape being created from the mid-1980s? These are some of the questions that appear pertinent as we continue with our story in the next chapter.

NOTES – Chapter 3

1 It is important to distinguish between (a) 'Mrs Thatcher's social mission was equally clear cut: roll back excessive state activity and bureaucracy and let individuals stand on their own two feet' (Seldon and Collings 2000 p70); and (b) what Seldon and Collings refer to as the Centralisation ('Strong State') Critique of Thatcherism (p86) that describes the centralisation of state power in Number 10. In other words, it is the difference between economic liberalism and social authoritarianism.

2 In Mrs Thatcher's 1993 autobiographical volume she explains why she resorted to the words of St Francis of Assisi. 'I quoted the famous prayer attributed to St Francis of Assisi, beginning "where there is discord may we bring harmony". Afterwards a good deal of sarcasm was expended on this choice, but the rest of the quotation is often forgotten ... The forces of error, doubt and despair were so firmly entrenched in British society, as the 'winter of discontent' had just powerfully illustrated, that overcoming them would not be possible without some measure of discord' (Thatcher 1993 p19).

3 It is interesting to recall some of the changes that occurred during the 1970s: the Yom Kippur/Arab–Israeli war in 1973 followed by the oil crisis; recession during 1973–75; economic problems of 1976 that culminated in spending cuts and the International Monetary Fund team arriving in Britain on 1st November 1976. However, by 1978–79 the economy was improving, with a fall in inflation and unemployment (Thatcher 1995 p409), but it was the winter of discontent in 1978/79 that prevented Labour winning the 1979 election after being in office since 1974.

4 Where the statutory criteria that are intended to restrict the use of custody are concerned in section 1(4) of the CJA 1982, the Criminal Justice Act 1988 amended s 1(4) by the words: the offence must be 'so serious that a non-custodial sentence for it cannot be justified'. Furthermore, statutory criteria were extended to all ages in the CJA 1991 when it used the language of 'so serious' in relation to custody; and 'serious enough' to justify a community sentence.

Chapter 4

PROBATION MOVES CENTRE STAGE: 1985 TO THE CRIMINAL JUSTICE ACT 1991

'There are great opportunities for the probation service. In the short term, no other existing service or organisation is better placed to take responsibility for supervising punishment in the community.' *(Home Office 1988a)*

Introduction: Responses to the Home Office's National Statement

As early as May 1983, one month prior to the Conservative party being re-elected on 9th June, the 56 area probation services were aware they were being reviewed by the Home Office. By August 1983 a draft was published (Home Office 1983a and 1983b) that culminated in the SNOP document by April 1984. At this time a letter was sent by David Faulkner to all Chief Probation Officers, accompanying the national statement. In the letter the view was expressed that the new Home Secretary, Leon Brittan, hoped that all chiefs, in conjunction with their committees, would seriously consider the national statement when formulating their local objectives and priorities. The process that evolved in one probation area was researched (Whitehead 1988) and is an example of the local dynamics that elicited a response to the national statement. In fact this process, in the one area just cited, continued throughout 1985 and into January 1986, yet not without certain problems along the way between NAPO representatives and senior management.

Notwithstanding these local difficulties, the point to emphasise is that the centre, in the form of the Home Office, expected local area services to make a positive response to SNOP by articulating clearly how it would be put into effect. We should not underestimate how much this process created shockwaves within local probation areas, each one hitherto operating in a way which reflected the traditions and dynamics of the local culture. On the whole, services had managed in a reactive manner to work demands and legislative change. There had also been a flexible approach to funding and, consequently, as we described earlier, some areas had little experience of financial restraint. SNOP and the subsequent local exercises were the progeny of a government determined to control the public sector, even if it meant cutting services. Politically, probation could no longer claim to be a popular concept and would not be in a strong position to compete on equal terms against other public sector demands. Additionally, local statements in the post-SNOP period had to be translated into an everyday tool of management so that scarce resources were directed towards the most important areas of work. At first sight the issue appears straightforward but convincing staff was sometimes tortuous for managers who were uncomfortable with the political message and role they were being asked to perform. Traditionally probation was structured as teams of officers working in geographical patches. Within this framework senior probation officers were distributors of work and enablers of performance. Prior to the 1980s, many had been used to a working environment that left them largely untouched by the gaze of senior managers and the expectations of the external political world. Equally, probation officers had a fairly free rein in the way they supervised offenders, developing the academic inputs of their training into a personalised and sometimes idiosyncratic working style. Within neither group was there any great enthusiasm for the perceived constraints of Home Office policies, objectives and targets demanded after SNOP. With these preliminary thoughts in mind, it was during this period that the Association of Chief Officers of Probation (ACOP) commissioned a study of local statements that were collated and analysed during the final months of 1985 at the Cambridge Institute of Criminology (Lloyd 1986). The analysis of these statements reveals a rich diversity of opinions in the different area services and helps to account for subsequent developments.

First of all, we saw in the previous chapter how section VB of SNOP focused on the supervision of offenders in the community. Specifically, section VB(iv) repairs to the language of 'maintaining a range of facilities', which could be interpreted to mean the development, for example, of day care facilities under the provisions contained in Schedule 11 to the Criminal Justice Act 1982. Lloyd discovered, when undertaking his research, that of the 32 probation areas that described the setting up of special facilities to deal with offenders as an alternative to custody, 10 areas referred to the requirements contained in Schedule 11. By contrast, 3 areas did not resort to requirements, ostensibly on the basis that extra conditions could adversely affect the flexibility inherent within the probation order (p14). Therefore, once again we stray into the contentious zone of the care-control debate and the legitimacy of probation services when exercising control over offenders on probation. For as Lloyd found: 'Areas are divided in their approach to the issue of control; some are keen to take on more serious offenders and develop more coercive practices, while others are less so.'

Secondly, the subject matter of the national statement's priorities elicited a variety of responses from probation areas (p56f) in that few areas produced a list of priorities that compared with the national blueprint. It is helpful, therefore, to recapitulate on what these priorities were, specifically in relation to the allocation of resources. Section VI(a) of the Home Office statement stated that the first priority of the service must be the supervision of as many offenders as possible in the community, especially in circumstances where custody is a real possibility. Consequently, social enquiry reports should be prepared more selectively (VI (b)) and only sufficient resources allocated to throughcare in order for the service to fulfil its statutory obligations (VI(c)). Moreover, sufficient resources should be allocated to community work and civil work (VI(d) and (e)). But section VII of the statement clarified that priority VI (a) will demand a larger proportion of an area's total resources, which will involve a reappraisal of those sections that deal with reports, throughcare, aftercare and civil work. Therefore, there were real concerns expressed in the service about de-prioritising certain areas of probation work. Of the 51 areas analysed by Lloyd, 28 failed to include a list of priorities in their local statement; 6 areas duplicated the priorities contained in the national statement; 5 resorted to a different order of priorities; leaving 12 to adopt a different form of priorities to SNOP which was, from a Home Office perspective, hardly the desired outcome (which clearly was to achieve greater consistency throughout area services by the imposition of more central control).

Thirdly, the question of local area services shaping their priorities to conform to a Home Office driven initiative touched on the sometimes vexed question of values. For many probation officers this was an issue of some importance as we have already alluded to above when illustrating the different agendas of the Home Office and NAPO which, it may be argued, can be reduced to a clash of values, ethical perspectives and priorities when working with offenders. This area of concern was given an airing by Lloyd when he said that: 'The implication of any process of prioritisation is that some tasks are more important than others and as a result should receive more resources. To many people involved in the service, all the work done is important and none can be given up, due to the fact that people will suffer as a result' (p62). Therefore, this finding neatly encapsulates a clash of cultures, political priorities and values because, on the one hand, we have a more centrally directed, administrative, bureaucratic and financially determined policy located in SNOP that classifies areas of work into a scale of priorities; on the other, a rich tradition within the service of social work values, relationships with people, and response to the needs of individuals. This is a conflict between a politically driven policy determined by the principles of economy, efficiency and effectiveness, and one driven by the moral values of a people oriented profession that works with individuals rather than categories determined by economics. It is therefore interesting that in Lloyd's survey 30 out of 51 services mentioned social work ethics; and one-third did not refer to the Financial Management Initiative. As one service stated: 'Given the need to provide a cost effective service it would be well to acknowledge that human values cannot be assessed by financial methods of accounting alone' (Lloyd p63).

The strategic future of probation areas was the clear responsibility of chief officers and their senior management teams. It was their responsibility to plan the future of local services within a rapidly shifting climate making political demands. For senior management teams that responded to the challenge of defining a more strategic future for local services, the latter half of the 1980s became an exercise in cultural change. There were few that were entirely comfortable with the process of relentless challenge from the centre, combined with sceptical and resistant staff, that was wearing for those who were acquiring an insightful grasp of the new leadership role. In the political and social context of the late 1980s the cohesiveness of staff was essential in delivering a local service strategy, without which there was little chance of success. What was clear then and during the next few years was that there was no guarantee that even senior management teams were corporate, as deeply ingrained individualism remained a stronger force than the requirement of collective responsibility.

We should also add that, in addition to the draft, national and local statements that covered the period 1983–86, the Probation Inspectorate carried out a review of the translation of the national statement into local statements in 20 areas during 1986–1987. A further 22 areas were more selectively inspected. Her Majesty's Inspectorate of Probation found that most areas had produced local statements that reflected the priorities contained in SNOP. Additionally, HMIP discovered that only about one-half had measurable objectives and detailed statements at an operational level, and only a minority of areas had identified improvements in local management practices stemming directly from the implementation of the national statement. The Inspectorate also found that information systems, fundamental to the proper monitoring of activities, were at different stages of development (referred to in National Audit Office 1989 paragraph 2.10). Subsequently, the Home Office encouraged the production of a second generation of statements that were to be informed by better management information systems and measurable objectives (for example, the Cleveland probation service produced a Future Directions Mark 2 document in the summer of 1989: Whitehead 1988).

After summarising an important period in the history of the probation service during the mid-1980s that witnessed the varied responses of area services to the national statement, our next step is to operate at two levels of discourse. These two levels, despite the fact that they are of course inextricably connected, should be dealt with separately, simply to organise our material coherently (to ease its digestion by the reader). Therefore, the first level we want to pursue is to some degree indebted to the researches of Lord Windlesham who, in the second volume of his four-volume work on *Responses to Crime* (1993), provides us with an informed and rich source of material that illuminates probation developments during the 1980s and early 1990s.

From Law and Order to Punishment in the Community

Shortly after the general election of 11th June 1987 that signalled the third consecutive general election victory for the Conservatives since May 1979, a one-day seminar for Home Office ministers and officials was held at Leeds Castle in Kent on 28th September 1987. It was attended by Douglas Hurd, who was Home Secretary from 2nd September 1985 to 26th October 1989; John Patten as Junior Home Office minister; the Earl of Caithness, who was responsible for the prison department; Tim Renton and Douglas Hogg; in addition to six Deputy Secretaries, one of whom was David Faulkner. Finally, Mary Tuck from the research and statistics department attended (Windlesham 1993 p215). Lord Windlesham says that the seminar addressed three main issues: the Safer Cities initiatives; sentencing policy and probation; young people and the criminal justice system. We want to focus primarily on the second of these agenda items.

'Cautious and pragmatic rather than visionary in outlook, but aware of the dangers of floating on the tide, Hurd, like Butler and Jenkins before him, had a gift for spotting openings' (Windlesham 1993 p210), and it may be suggested that the event at Leeds Castle and what subsequently transpired can be interpreted as one of Windlesham's 'openings'. By September 1987 the prison population had reached what was considered to be an alarming 50,000, when it had been 43,109 in 1980. New prisons had been built during the 1980s yet the statistical projections were for an increase to 60,000 prisoners in the foreseeable future, but with the possibility of a staggering and unimaginable rise to 70,000 by 2000. 'If there was any single moment at Leeds Castle when opinions changed, it was at this point. Ministers and officials were united in their reaction that such a situation would be intolerable and must not be allowed to happen' (Windlesham 1993 pp238–239) which, it can be said, is not an attitude that is consistent with an unqualified law and order attitude.[1]

There were concerns about the political implications of overcrowding in prisons as well as the strain on the public finances, given the political commitment to economy and efficiency. It was also considered unnecessary that so many offenders should be imprisoned, which helps to explain the context within which the twin-track approach to sentencing emerged towards the end of the 1980s, culminating in the Criminal Justice Act 1991. This approach was clear in the sense that custodial sentences should be reserved for the most serious offenders (sex and violence predominantly), leaving non-custodial sentences for other offenders. However, to make such a policy work the Home Office reasoned that it had to find a way of making community sentences more credible so that magistrates and judges could have confidence in using them. It was during this period that, coincidentally, one of the authors was involved in empirical research in one probation area in the North-East of England that quantitatively and qualitatively focused on the probation order. Part of this research involved talking to magistrates and judges and some of the findings are replicated here to illustrate some of the problems that were being addressed at Leeds Castle (Whitehead 1988).

The third and final stage of this empirical research built on quantitative research already completed that involved drawing attention to 35 cases in which a custodial sentence had been imposed by local courts when a probation order had been recommended in the social enquiry report prepared by probation officers. Even though one of the judges interviewed stated that 'You should not worry about the figures you produced; they are not unreasonable and you should not think that the judge can comply with your recommendations in one hundred percent of cases'. Nevertheless, as we have seen over recent pages, by this stage the Home Office had produced the national statement that had made it clear to area probation services that its mandate was to deal with more serious offenders in the community. After explaining some of the more important features of these 35 cases to a group of sentencers, the question posed at the beginning of the interviews was: 'Are there any further provisions the Cleveland probation service can develop to make the probation order a more credible and effective alternative to custody for the more serious offender?' Therefore, how was the probation order perceived by the people being interviewed during the early months of 1988, only three to four months after the Leeds Castle event? A few examples can be provided that will illustrate the problem the probation service was facing when attempting to achieve one of the central objectives of SNOP.

It should be elucidated that 15 out of the 35 offenders committed to custody were charged with dwelling house burglary offences and a further 11 offenders were charged with other burglary matters. This resulted in one magistrate saying that 'These 35 cases where they had been before the courts about 5.8 times previously and graduated through the system and probation, in their context a probation order does not seem relevant; it seems like a let off for them.' Another magistrate went on to comment that 'The public feeling is that a probation order is not required or appropriate (for dwelling house burglary offences) because they want offenders to get prison. The public feel that the punishment does not fit the crime in such cases.' A third magistrate appeared to speak on behalf of many of his colleagues when he said that 'In the public's eye probation is a cop out because they are not getting punished ... For dwelling house burglary the sentence is punishment. Probation does not appear to be punishment.' Next it is interesting to hear comment from a judge who reflected on the offence of dwelling house burglary that is quite pertinent. 'The Home Office is telling you one thing [for example, in the SNOP document] and someone is telling us something else and we are not receiving the same message. We get directives that dwelling house burglars should receive prison, so there is conflict between what the Home Office wants us to do and what it wants you to do ... For people under stress a probation order might be helpful, but for a repeat criminal then it is difficult.' Another judge stated that 'The problem really is the feeling of the public. Since becoming a judge I have become rapidly aware of the views of what we call the public. Probation is still a soft option for the public.' Finally, one of the magistrates interviewed made the telling comment that 'Magistrates perceive the probation service providing help and support rather than punishment', which is an interesting insight at a time when the Home Office was talking about the concept of punishment in the community to address the lack of credibility being experienced by the probation order as perceived by sentencers, clearly illustrated by these research findings.

Therefore it was being reasoned at Leeds Castle that in order to give effect to a policy of reducing the prison population, sentencers needed some persuading if they were to place their confidence in existing community disposals and, by implication, what was on offer by the probation service. In fact it was being rightly questioned whether the probation service was in a position to do this because of its prevailing culture of care rather than control, the language of social work help rather than punishment, an emphasis on the individual client rather than offender, and an ongoing philosophical and ethical commitment to advise, assist and befriend that had deep roots in the Probation of Offenders Act 1907. Nevertheless, what emerged after September 1987 can be summarised as the publication of the government's Green Paper on *Punishment, Custody and The Community* in 1988; next, the 1990 White Paper, *Crime, Justice and Protecting The Public*. These two documents culminated in the Criminal Justice Bill published on 9th November 1990, and the end of this lengthy legislative process produced the Criminal Justice Act 1991, which was implemented on 1st October 1992. It is clear that the 1991 Act constituted, to some degree, a restructuring of the rationale of the probation order that had been introduced in 1907 around the notion of punishment in the community (expanded upon later in this chapter).

Windlesham (1993) reminds us that to deliver punishment in the community, and therefore reduce the number of offenders being committed to custody, Home Office politicians and officials present at Leeds Castle had to be mindful of three constituencies: the conservative parliamentary party; a powerful and independent judiciary; and of course the probation service. For a number of individual probation officers, in addition to NAPO as the trade union, the language of punishment in the community was anathema. There would be little contentious debate between the Home Office and NAPO concerning the central sentencing objective of government, which was to deal with as many offenders as possible in the community to prevent the prison population escalating to 60,000–70,000 as predicted and feared (a financial and ethical argument combining to achieve a desirable objective). Rather, it was the *modus operandi* for achieving this objective that caused not a little disquiet in the service and of which the Home Office was mindful, of course, at the Leeds Castle seminar. Those present knew that its proposals would offend deeply held ethical principles and values, which is why both John Patten as the Junior

Home Office minister, and David Faulkner as senior civil servant responsible for probation, embarked upon a charm offensive with chief officers and the wider criminal justice system to support a more pragmatic approach to managing crime beyond the moral claims of welfare. The Home Office also established a Special Conferences Unit that created a constructive mechanism for dialogue within the criminal justice system with a view to producing a consensus on approaches to crime and sentencing.

However, it can be claimed that to survive in the changing political and criminal justice climate being created by government, the probation service was being challenged to assimilate radically new thinking, attitudes and approaches, within a different organisational culture shaped by a new language. Would it adapt or would the Home Office need to consider creating or finding another organisation to deliver its new proposals for sentencing and criminal justice? Would the Home Office seriously consider the existence of two organisations: one to provide a social work–welfare oriented service for those in need (the probation service) and another to deliver punishment in the community without the complexity of adhering to certain moral values and social work sensibilities? We do not think this suggestion, which mirrors the proposal of Robert Harris alluded to towards the end of Chapter 2, was a serious political contender for the future development of the service. There is no way that such an argument could have any political or economic cogency by the late 1980s.

Traditionally, as we have explained already, yet it bears repetition, although this somewhat ideal-type representation must be subject to certain qualifications, the probation service was associated with a set of ideas and values expressed in the language of social work help for individual offenders who were themselves often victims of circumstances, in addition to constructive methods of working using positive relationships. In fact, the relationship between officer and client was the essential dynamic of the work. Of course (and here come some of the qualifications) the service has always been associated with a vestige of authority, control and regulation, in undertaking a specific role on behalf of the state (Garland 1985). Moreover, we should not forget that the service had assimilated more conditions attached to probation orders, albeit reluctantly in some quarters, following the Criminal Justice Act 1982; some probation officers were known to recommend custody for offenders in their court reports; officers returned offenders to court in breach proceedings who could then be committed to custody for failing to comply. Furthermore, the service had been living with the care–control debates for a number of years that resulted in lively exchanges between probation staff with differing values working for the same service. Nevertheless, the critical change by the end of the 1980s, we would argue, was a concerted political manoeuvre to restructure probation services in the direction of more control and punishment, to promote credible community sentences that would result in much greater confidence amongst magistrates and judges. This would involve more restrictions on offenders and Windlesham draws attention to the crucial issue for the probation service as it was perceived in a paper prepared for the Leeds Castle seminar: 'The extent to which the probation service can be used to divert more serious offenders from custody, is dependent upon persuading the courts of the service's ability to hold and control serious offenders. An important issue for future consideration is whether more could and should be done to encourage the courts to have greater confidence in the service and the extent to which this might require a change in the probation service's attitude to offenders away from advising, assisting and befriending towards controlling' (1993 pp225–226). Again there is an echo of the concerns of the magistrates and judges considered in the research referred to earlier in this statement.

Probation Officers and the Courts

We should pause for a moment at this juncture to reflect upon what had been going on from within the service itself and over which it had some control. We have already discussed (in Chapter 2) the process by which, perhaps inadvertently and unwittingly, a number of probation officers over the years (from the 1930s to the 1960s) became semi-detached from the influence and oversight of the court due to the creation of a probation hierarchy consisting of: main grade officer; senior probation officer; assistant principal; principal officer. This evolving hierarchical structure eventually supplanted the oversight of the probation committee. Furthermore, the expansion of the service in the 1960s; its closer association with the penal system; the evolution of management whose supervision of staff, amongst other things, eventually replaced judicial oversight; the creation of specialisms because of an expanding service (for example, probation court teams that resulted in an increasing number of probation officers not being required to attend court any more); a changing political situation, from the 1970s, that was moving towards a more punitive and controlling response to offenders in the post-rehabilitative era. In other words, the crime problem and the probation service were becoming politicised and all those factors just alluded to helped to create a situation in which the courts had less contact with its probation officers and, concomitantly, it can be argued, the service suffered declining credibility. The bonds of confidence had to some extent been broken, a situation for which the probation service itself must accept some responsibility over recent years. Once again, the empirical research referred to earlier in this chapter (Whitehead 1988) illustrates this area of concern for which the service itself had primary responsibility (and to which we now briefly turn).

As we continue with the themes of probation service credibility and the confidence of sentencers introduced above by considering the professional responsibility of probation officers attending court with their social enquiry reports, one of the magistrates said that 'Before we give custody a great deal of thought is given. Custody is not imposed lightly. Therefore you should explain what you feel, but in the end the decision is made by the bench.' At the meeting where this comment was expressed, a probation officer who was present wanted to know if the court was positively influenced by the *attendance* of the report writer to support the recommendation. The reply by one of the magistrate's was 'Yes, some reports are good, but some are awful. If you feel strongly about a case, come to court and tell us. And if the officer cannot attend personally, please put forward your views to the court officer who can pass them on to us.' It was also felt quite strongly by two magistrates at a probation liaison committee meeting that, in those cases where an offender was in danger of receiving a custodial sentence but had nevertheless been placed on probation, the commitment to provide a periodic assessment of an offender's progress to the court could dispose sentencers to take a risk by imposing a probation order. One of these two magistrates reminded the meeting that 'In years past the probation case committee received information on clients under supervision. In future could we have feedback on clients so that we have more faith in the system?' The other magistrate added 'Yes that is a very good point for it would increase the credibility of the service.' The point being emphasised here, in conjunction with the way in which the Home Office was gestating its own plans to enhance credibility and confidence by developing punishment in the community, is the suggestion that the service itself was culpable because of the way some area services had weakened those important working relationships between individual officers and the sentencing courts through specialisation, probably on the grounds of efficiency facilitated by, for example, the national statement. Looking back, the attenuation of the links between probation officers and magistrates and local courts was not conducive to the promotion of credibility and confidence. Before turning our attention to the second level of discourse referred to at the beginning of this chapter, we need to refer to a number of documents that were in circulation between 1987 and 1991, in addition to describing the role of ACOP.

A Joint Statement in 1987

In July 1987 a joint statement was published by the Association of Chief Officers of Probation, the Central Council of Probation Committees and the National Association of Probation Officers, called 'Probation – the next five years'. It was clarified that the 'aim of this briefing document is to recommend ways in which the probation service could operate more effectively in assisting the government in restricting the increase in crime and at the same time reducing the use of custodial sentences' (p1). It states clearly and confidently that the probation service can perform an enhanced role in curtailing the use of custody against a background of some success over recent years. For example, between 1979 and the mid-1980s there was an increase of 48% in the use of probation orders; the proportion of probationers with no previous convictions fell from 26% to 18%, thus indicating that the service was dealing with more heavily convicted offenders in the community. There had also been a 137% increase in the use of community service orders. Therefore, the question being posed was: what about the next five years? The document quite properly acknowledged the adverse social conditions since 1979 that had militated against the rehabilitative objectives of the probation service: for example, unemployment amongst young people, low incomes, offenders with an impoverished education and therefore restricted opportunities, and ongoing accommodation problems. Furthermore, any new developments must be 'consistent with the main values underlying probation work – a respect for the worth of each individual; a belief in the freedom of the individual and the capacity for individuals to change for the better; a belief that lasting change can only be developed from within, not imposed from without; a commitment to the minimum necessary intervention and to constructive, humanitarian approaches' (p3).

So, what were the main recommendations? First, more community involvement that focused on victim support and crime prevention. Secondly, increase the use of non-custodial disposals. It was pointed out that 50% of prison sentences were for less than six months and that more focused probation intervention could make inroads into these sentencing practices through probation orders and community service.

Thirdly, improve services to courts. We have already alluded to this area of practice as perhaps a missed opportunity by the service over recent years. This document reinforces our position by saying that court work is important and that probation officers should attend court with their reports, which would undoubtedly increase their credibility. Fourthly, there should be an improved service to civil courts, a recommendation that was certainly in conflict with the national statement's position that fewer resources should be given to this area of probation practice. Finally, the service should not forget its responsibilities for the throughcare of prisoners and resettlement work. There was much in this document to commend itself to a wide range of staff within the probation service. However, we cannot help reflecting on the fact that its emphasis on developing the probation order *without* specifically considering the scope for additional requirements missed an opportunity to be more politically astute with Home Office ministers and officials prior to the publication of the Green Paper the following year.

The Association of Chief Officers of Probation (1988) produced its own document, 'More Demanding Than Prison', which was an attempt to reduce custodial sentences by proposing a new sentence, once again designed to address the issue of the confidence of sentencers and the credibility of the service. It was suggested that a new sentence would need to be tough and demanding to replace custodial sentences of up to 30 months that would, of course, include a proportion of violence and burglary offences. Consequently, the Community Restitution Order would have four main components: making restitution for damage inflicted or loss incurred; social training to confront offending behaviour; problem solving; addressing accommodation. Interestingly, this proposal takes ACOP beyond its position of the previous year when NAPO, ACOP and CCPC (1987) produced their joint document that advocated developing existing disposals rather than introducing new ones.

The Green Paper 1988

A few weeks after the publication of ACOP's contribution to the debate the Home Office published the Green Paper on *Punishment, Custody and the Community* (Home Office 1988a) against the background of the deliberations at Leeds Castle the previous September. The Green Paper confirmed that custodial sentences should only be used for serious offenders and, if a financial penalty or conditional discharge, for example, are not appropriate, then a community sentence should:

restrict the freedom of the offender as punishment; take action to reduce re-offending; and ensure reparation to the community and compensation to the victim. Consequently, these factors would constitute the three main elements of punishment in the community. As such it was optimistically stated that 'Punishment in the community would encourage offenders to grow out of crime and to develop into responsible and law-abiding citizens' (Home Office 1988 paragraph 1.1). Additionally, there were references to curfew orders (paragraph 3.19), electronic monitoring and tagging (paragraphs 3.20 and 3.21) and intermittent custody (paragraph 3.22), as well as the possibility of a new sentence that would include restrictions, compulsory activities and positive and voluntary elements. This was the proposal for a Supervision and Restriction Order. What is of particular interest is the way in which the Green Paper raised the possibility of a new organisation 'to organise punishment in the community. It would not itself supervise offenders or provide facilities directly, but would contract with other services and organisations to do so' (paragraph 4.4). We should also draw attention to Part II of the Green Paper that focused on 17–20-year-old young adult offenders.

Subsequently, John Patten, an influential Home Office minister at this time, who was present at Leeds Castle and a committed advocate of the principles underlying punishment in the community, was interviewed by Nigel Stone of the *Probation Journal* (Patten 1988). The service was undoubtedly disquieted at the thought that it could be replaced by another organisation to deliver community punishment. In this interview Patten expressed the hope that the probation service would not become an irrelevance, but the idea of the possibility of a rival organisation had to be floated. He readily acknowledged that the skills of probation officers and culture of the organisation did not make it an obvious candidate to deliver punishment. Nevertheless, the message seemed to be do or die; adapt or atrophy from the person who handled much of the interface work between the Home Office and area services. Additionally, David Garland (1989) expressed the view in a collection of papers that debated the implications of the Green Paper that, notwithstanding problems with the underlying concept of community punishment, it appealed to two important audiences. On one hand, it had a certain resonance for law and order supporters who were viscerally attached to punishment. On the other hand, it could appeal to reformers and liberals who could support a reduction in custodial sentences. In other words, it appealed to the political right and left – which was some achievement.[2]

By December 1988, NAPO made its response to the Green Paper and argued that punishment in the community would not be effective at reducing custodial sentences. It was stated that the Home Office document ignored the causes of crime and NAPO rejected the proposal for a new sentence but acknowledged that better use could be made of existing disposals such as the probation order and community service order. In fact, during 1989 ACOP's response echoed the position of NAPO in arguing for the strengthening of existing disposals rather than experimenting with a new one. However, this view appears to be in conflict with its suggestion for a Community Restitution Order the previous year. Also during the early part of 1989, area services were trying to formulate their responses to Part II of the Green Paper expanded in a separate document: *Tackling Offending – An Action Plan* (Home Office 1988b). This document was linked to the Green Paper in that it required area services to prepare an action plan to specify how more intensive forms of probation supervision could be used to reduce custodial sentences for young adult offenders aged between 17 and 20. *Tackling Offending* drew attention to the fact that 25% of all people convicted of an indictable offence were aged between 17 and 20 and that only 5% of offenders committed 70% of all detected crime. Significantly, 30% of 17–20-year-old offenders were receiving a custodial sentence with two or fewer previous convictions, a specific concern because they were receiving this sanction too early. Consequently, selected areas introduced intensive probation programmes to increase confidence in community sentences.

ACOP: Politics, Management and Social Policy in the 1980s

We need to expand on the role of the Association of Chief Officers of Probation (ACOP). By the 1980s the association of service managers was building national and regional networks that it used to develop probation policies and respond to government initiatives. Notwithstanding managerial developments within probation over recent years, it is difficult to sustain the view that there was a strong managerial culture at any level. This is why some chief officers were encouraged to attend business schools, encouraged and paid for by the Home Office. In addition to learning about management, assimilating and making a response to the new politics of probation, ACOP was also contributing to the social policy debates of the 1980s. For example, a snapshot of unemployment in the North-East in 1987 yielded an indictment of government policy because, whilst unemployment figures published by the Department of Employment for July 1987 specified rates of 14.4% in the North and 11.7% in Yorkshire and Humberside, research revealed that across probation areas in the North-East the rate of unemployment of probation caseloads ranged from 61.1% to 81.2%, an average of 71.5%. These figures were of great concern for those of us within probation, as an illustration of how a government's social policies could impact upon society's most vulnerable offenders (Brake and Hale 1992). Consequently, ACOP concluded that an effective welfare rights strategy was required to help individuals and families deal with poverty. Additionally, more Manpower Service Commission places should be made available to offenders, who should have greater access to educational and leisure facilities (Association of Chief Officers of Probation 1987). It should be made plain that the preoccupation of many probation staff with the presenting problems of poverty and deprivation inevitably coloured political attitudes within the service. How was it possible to support a government that manifestly pursued policies that exacerbated the position of the most disadvantaged and therefore militated against the objective of helping offenders to grow out of crime? The service's antipathy to the Conservative administration was clearly heard in many of its public utterances. ACOP to its credit recognised the importance of the wider debate about social conditions within which to locate human behaviour by commissioning research through Lancaster University. *Surviving Poverty* was published in 1989 and highlighted the problems of young offenders and the impact of the Social Fund (ACOP 1989), which can be seen as an antidote to Conservative criminology (Brake and Hale 1992).

Notwithstanding its contribution to the social policy debate of the 1980s and beyond (also see next chapter), ACOP became ensnared by the philosophical angst that focused on values, rather than promoting strategic leadership. We would argue that leadership was one of the major issues confronting area services, which lacked a cohesive approach to government policy, thus diluting its potential to shape the future agenda being driven by politicians and civil servants. As we survey the post-SNOP years we think that the mid-to-late 1980s was an important time for probation, though few appreciated this at the time. Probation remained a compelling environment in which to earn one's living and who could deny the ethical importance of working with disaffected people who turned to crime. By contrast, there was also a swelling sense of discomfort amongst managers and operational staff because tough questions were being posed about individual and service performance. In fact, the questioning of performance, seen as part of the process of determining future priorities within a context of managing scarce resources, was greeted with scepticism. When such exercises revealed the possibility that some staff might be underperforming, this was unnerving within an occupational culture unused to such scrutiny. Consequently, the theme of effective performance was located on the probation agenda that, by the late 1990s, would culminate in the evolution of *What Works?* The Green and White Papers of 1988 (Home Office 1988a) and 1990 (Home Office 1990a) respectively were pushed through the familiar consultation process that enabled the major players, ACOP, CCPC and NAPO, to respond. As always interminable meetings diligently pondered the meaning of language, but any sense of urgency seemed to be absent. Interestingly, in 1991 ACOP did in fact consider closer links with the CCPC but both organisations retreated. Also of interest is the way ACOP, towards the end of 1991, moved its secretariat into a converted flat in the Whitechapel Methodist Mission. Whilst the move had a certain resonance with religious sensibilities that would have impressed police court missionaries, it did not transmit appropriate political messages. It must be said that the offices were an unflattering combination of the shambolic and cramped, and august meetings were lightened only by the stage whispers of 'winos' arguing outside and falling over dustbins.

The period towards the end of the 1980s was busy, perhaps too busy. In September 1989 a two-day conference was held at Ditchley Park in Oxfordshire (Windlesham 1993) that was attended by Douglas Hurd just before he was replaced by David Waddington as Home Secretary on 26th October 1989; the Chancellor; the Attorney General; the Lord Chief Justice; and members of the judiciary. The purpose of the conference was to undertake a review of government thinking on the criminal justice system and sentencing, and to make plans for the future in anticipation of those proposals that would become the Criminal Justice Act 1991. Moreover, the appointment of David Waddington as Home Secretary signalled that dialogue between probation and ministers was going to become less comfortable, a situation reinforced by successive Home Secretaries during the 1990s, as we shall see later.

The 1990 White Paper

The White Paper, *Crime, Justice and Protecting The Public* (Home Office 1990a), presages the introduction of a new legislative framework based upon just deserts. In other words, the sentence of the court, from fines and conditional discharges through to probation and then custody, should be commensurate with and proportionate to the level of seriousness contained within the offence. The government's position was that many property offences could be punished adequately by fines and discharges but, when these were not appropriate, punishment should restrict the liberty of the offender either in the community or custody. Where community sentences are concerned, they should be more demanding and realistic; the courts would have the power to combine probation with community service; the courts would also have the power to impose a curfew which might be enforced by electronic monitoring. One significant change introduced by the White Paper was the proposal to make the probation order a sentence of the court so that it could be combined with other penalties. It is worth pausing for a moment to consider this development by reminding ourselves that under the terms of the 1907 Act the imposition of a probation order was an alternative to sentencing the offender; it was not a punishment and it required the consent of the prospective probationer. In 1990 it was to become a sentence in its own right because it was primarily no longer being used for first or trivial offenders, but rather aimed at persistent and more serious offenders as an alternative to custody. Furthermore, the balance was being shifted from an order to provide advice, assistance and friendship, to a punishment in the community to enhance its credibility to magistrates and judges. By doing so it also reflected the political changes that had occurred during the previous decade in relation to crime, which is away from treatment and rehabilitation towards a more demanding and punitive political response to the crime problem. The White Paper considered issues as diverse as the role of the court, custody, parole, and young offenders, but its proposals for community penalties in addition to parole should be understood in relation to three key components, which were: public protection; the prevention of re-offending; and the reintegration of offenders into their communities. One important development was the proposal for national standards[3] for court reports and supervision to achieve greater consistency and to ensure minimum standards. Finally, the section on resources and costs acknowledged that the present annual cost of the criminal justice system was a staggering £7 billion. The proposed changes, specifically to the rationale of community sentences, would hopefully save money because fewer people would be committed to prison. Therefore, an attempt was being made by the politicians, and others, to create a more coherent sentencing framework within which probation had a central role (see Rees and Williams 1989 for different views).

It should be emphasised that the White Paper referred to the Carlisle Committee on parole and the government's response. According to these proposals all prisoners would now spend at least half their sentence in prison instead of the previous minimum of one-third. There would be a selective system of parole for prisoners sentenced to four years and over and all prisoners sentenced to twelve months or more would be supervised on release. Therefore, it was expected that the new system would result in the probation service being responsible for more offenders being released on licence. (This system was to remain in place until the proposals contained in the Criminal Justice Act 2003, which will be addressed later.)

Supervision and Punishment in the Community

Alongside the 1990 White Paper, the Home Office published another Green Paper, *Supervision and Punishment in the Community: A Framework for Action* (Home Office 1990b). This is a highly significant document because its rationale was to give effect to the White Paper by clarifying for probation how government expected it to achieve its reformulated objectives. It provided further impetus in the re-balancing of the service towards more discipline and control, yet it also acknowledged the role of help and care. Additionally, it drew attention to the importance of national standards; the relationship between probation, the courts and the wider criminal justice system if it was going to deliver punishment in the community; victims; and it precedes our discussion on probation training in the next chapter.

The probation service was being told without a vestige of ambiguity that it was a criminal justice not social work agency; it must devote itself to public protection and think about victims; it had a professional duty to challenge and confront offending behaviour; it must work closely with partners in the criminal justice system and the voluntary and private sectors in the fight against crime; and it must have credible products to offer the courts and deliver quality reports. 'At its best, the probation service has shown itself to be creative, innovative and responsive to a rapidly changing environment' (p9) but it had weaknesses too and certain changes would have to be considered. For example, government was increasingly perturbed because it provided 80% of the resources required by area services (taxpayers' money) yet had little control over how it was spent due to the autonomy of area services, chiefs and committees. Hence the reference to a system of cash limits, which will be considered later. Furthermore, this Green Paper proceeded in a searching manner to anticipate the evolution of probation committees into boards; developments within the Inspectorate; changes to probation training (the Coleman Report had been published in 1989); and the notion of contracting out services. Where the latter was concerned, it was stated that 'The Government believes that the disciplines of the market place can often serve as an effective guarantee of quality and value for money in the provision of public services' (p37). Not only was this a tenet of Thatcherism; New Labour was also captured by this approach after 1997, as we shall see (Seldon 2004).

Significantly, the 1990 Green Paper alluded to the possibility of a national service, just as Morison did in 1962. Again the idea was floated before being sunk (but not without trace). It was suggested that a national service could be necessary to deliver government's objectives for the probation service as it progressed beyond 1990 because such a structure could: result in more effective funding arrangements; better target resources; create clearer lines of accountability; enable good practice to be shared more easily; and promote economy, efficiency and effectiveness. It would also facilitate, we might add, greater central, political and financial control, particularly if a grant of 100% by central government under a new cash limits formula was introduced. On the other hand, it was thought that a national service would probably be disruptive for staff, adversely affect morale, and incur additional costs. Importantly, it was acknowledged that the loss of local identity could be damaging and it posed the question of how a national service would be organised.

In 1991, prior to the introduction of the 1991 Act, the Home Office followed up the 1990 Green Paper just considered with *Organising Supervision and Punishment in the Community*. This document reflected the fact that the Home Office had digested some 160 responses to the 1990 document and, importantly, the arguments to persist with locally based services were accepted but 'within a centrally determined framework of objectives and accountability' (p2). Consequently, the shift towards more central control demanded by SNOP in 1984 was taken a step further by the early 1990s. Furthermore, this document anticipated the need to revise SNOP because it raised the possibility of producing a three-year plan for the probation service.

Prior to concluding this chapter by turning to our second level of discourse, in addition to drawing attention to some of the main points of the Criminal Justice Act 1991 and their implications for probation, for the sake of completeness we should briefly make reference to certain legislative developments during the mid-to-late 1980s, as follows.

Relevant Legislation

The Police and Criminal Evidence Act 1984 began its life as a Royal Commission during 1978 under a Labour government but given birth by the Conservatives. It was concerned with modernising the law which governed the investigation of crime. To civil libertarians it constituted a challenge to the rights of the individual suspected of committing an offence (Windlesham 1993 p185f). Secondly, the Prosecution of Offences Act 1985 created the Crown Prosecution Service whose duty it is to prosecute crimes in the magistrates' courts that until this point had been a function undertaken by the police. Next we must make reference to the Public Order Act 1986 and the following offences: riot (s 1); violent disorder (s 2); affray (s 3); fear of provocation or violence (s 4); harassment, alarm or distress (s 5). We point the reader to Windlesham (1993 p192f) for the political context within which this legislation emerged. Finally, the Criminal Justice Act 1988 was published in the same year as the Green Paper. One of the important changes introduced was the conflation of the detention centre and youth custody sentences into a single young offender institution sentence. It also reinforced the criteria established in the Criminal Justice Act 1982 that restricted the use of custody for young offenders, shortly to be extended to adults in the Criminal Justice Act 1991; but more of this below.

Further Developments from the Centre: Grimsey and HMIP

Alongside significant changes affecting probation from the mid-1980s within a criminal justice system being politically restructured to deliver punishment in the community, in addition to legislative developments, we now turn to our second level of discourse. This second level, for want of a better expression, continues to reflect on the next stage in our story but with particular weight being given to managerial developments and their linkage with the political and criminal justice developments just considered. We begin this section with changes to Her Majesty's Inspectorate of Probation during the second half of the 1980s.

On 16th October 1986 E.J. Grimsey was appointed to examine the role and operation of Her Majesty's Inspectorate of Probation (HMIP). The terms of reference were to review the objectives, powers and responsibilities of the Inspectorate and to make recommendations to maximise:

(a) the Inspectorate's contribution to the economy, efficiency and effectiveness of the probation service;

(b) the Inspectorate's contribution to the formulation of the department's policies for the probation service and for an effective response to crime.

We saw in the last chapter how, during the early part of the 1980s, the probation service was being pushed in the direction of providing value for money that was primarily manifested in the national statement of 1984. It is specifically within this context that the work of the Inspectorate was being reviewed to assist area services after 1986/87 to achieve national objectives and to ensure that areas were using their resources efficiently. The Inspectorate was created in 1936 (see Chapter 2) and one of its tasks initially was to provide assurance to the Home Secretary that probation services were operating efficiently. Furthermore, it was to provide advice and encouragement to the service and professional advice to the Home Office on probation matters. Fifty years after the creation of the Inspectorate the theme of efficiency was one of Grimsey's main concerns because, when she published her report (1987), it was clearly stated that one of the essential functions of the Inspectorate should be to 'inspect area services in terms of their efficiency and effectiveness ... and to promote efficiency and effectiveness' (1987 p13).

Grimsey articulated the view that in the past the Inspectorate had not operated with clear criteria when assessing the performance of the service, which was considered to be an obvious deficiency. She therefore proposed that from 1988/89 there should be two types of inspection. First, there would be an efficiency and effectiveness inspection primarily to satisfy the Home Secretary that area services were providing value for money. This would be achieved by a desk-top inspection each year that would be supplemented by a visit every four years by two or three inspectors to provide a comprehensive review of area performance. Importantly, to measure performance it was proposed that a matrix of key performance indicators should be developed and used by the Inspectorate. Secondly, there should be a thematic inspection every few years. We can provide an example of these new arrangements because the Cleveland probation service received the results of its first desk-top efficiency and effectiveness inspection on 25th April 1989. The Cleveland service was compared with four other areas – Leicestershire, Derbyshire, South West London, Hereford and Worcestershire – and at this stage the inspection was based upon the application of what were referred to as initial performance indicators, about which more will be said shortly. Moreover, in March 1989 the Cleveland service was given notice concerning its first thematic inspection on Day Provision for Young Offenders aged 17 to 20, which was to take place in the week beginning 5th June 1989.[4] Prior to moving on, an anecdote is illustrative at this point. One of the authors recalls a chance meeting with a retired principal probation officer, George Chesters, in Hanley in 1976. During a challenging first inspection of community service, he proffered comforting words by saying that the Home Office did not really count for much, so in a sense the inspection was to be endured and then it would go away. This charmingly old-fashioned view, reassuring at the time, still reflected the position of some chiefs ten years later when Grimsey gave the inspectorate a new sense of purpose.

Performance Indicators

One of Grimsey's recommendations was to establish a working party within four months of the completion of her report in February 1987 to undertake work on the development of performance indicators that were defined as 'a tool which illuminates the effects of the actions or achievements of an organisation'. This is indeed what occurred because a working party was created and met six times between June 1987 and March 1988 comprising members of the Inspectorate, C6 Division, M Division, the Research and Planning Unit, Association of Chief Probation Officers, Central Council of Probation Committees, and the National Association of Probation Officers. Its terms of reference included: to identify aspects of performance which enable the Inspectorate to assess the effectiveness of area probation services; to identify those aspects of performance not covered by existing information and to consider what additional information should be collected; and to take account of work already underway on what was known as the FMIS – Financial Management Information System. Furthermore, performance indicators should be concerned with three things:

(a) the outputs and effectiveness of the service;

(b) the inputs or resources used to obtain outputs: for example, the degree of economy in the use of resources;

(c) the relationship between (a) and (b).

In order to develop the innovative system of performance indicators, the working party dismantled the Statement of National Objectives and Priorities clause by clause in relation to the five task areas: working with the courts; supervision in the community; throughcare; community work; and civil work. In total over 100 indicators were developed but it should be acknowledged that a system of performance indicators depends upon appropriate information systems being available in area services. Accordingly, three types of indicators are mentioned by the working party: first, initial indicators are based upon data already being collected and currently in use; secondly, interim indicators will require additional data; thirdly, preferred indicators are the ideal type which will require further development.

To illustrate these developments it could be helpful to remind ourselves what performance indicators actually look like by referring to task area one of SNOP, working with the courts. The central objective in the first task area is to ensure that offenders can be dealt with by non-custodial sentences thus implying that area services must be able to assess whether this objective has been achieved. Therefore:

P1.1 is the contribution of the service in cases where an immediate or suspended custodial sentence was imposed. The preferred indicator would be the number and proportion of cases in which an immediate or suspended custodial sentence was passed, broken down by type of court, sex, age, risk of custody, and the social enquiry report recommendation.

P1.2 is the contribution of the service in cases where a supervisory disposal was imposed (probation, community service, and juvenile supervision) and the use of these disposals for offenders who might otherwise have received a custodial sentence. The preferred indicator would be the number and proportion of cases in which a supervisory disposal was made, broken down by type of court, sex, age, risk of custody and social enquiry report recommendation.

P1.3 concerns the contribution of the probation service in cases other than a custodial or supervisory disposal, broken down by the same variables.

P1.4 is the contribution of the probation service to those sentenced to custody, financial penalties and other default.

We think we have probably said enough about the somewhat arid topic of performance indicators to provide the reader with what was a significant managerial development during this period.

Nevertheless, it should be clarified that the round of efficiency and effectiveness desk-top inspections during 1988/89 were based upon a system of initial indicators, and that further work leading up to the creation of preferred indicators would depend upon the successful outcome of applying initial indicators. The working party made it clear that 'Performance Indicators are not ends in themselves; their merits lie in the investigations and reviews they generate. Performance Indicators can assist in: disclosing variations between areas; suggesting reasons for variations; evaluating progress towards aims; developing appropriate targets; examining management effectiveness; examining resource utilisation and requirements; demonstrating cost effectiveness and inspecting information systems' (HMIP 1988 pp13–14). Consequently, when considering the inspection process within a probation area envisaged by Grimsey and developed by the performance indicators working party, the inspector would receive an annual area profile based upon performance indicators and additional background information, which would be used to undertake the annual desk-top inspection.

Better Financial Management

Whilst pursuing the development of performance indicators, the Home Office was also working on an accompanying Financial Management Information System that was primarily concerned with resource management. The first attempt to create such a system in 1982 failed after three years because of its complexity. However, in 1986 the Home Office commissioned a team of consultants, Deloitte, Haskins and Sells, to create an FMIS for the probation service to ensure that the taxpayer was getting value for money and that services complied with the principles of economy, efficiency and effectiveness. To ensure an FMIS worked it was envisaged that information gleaned from (1) local authority budgets and (2) probation caseload and report data stored in the then probation computer system called PROBIS (Probation Information System) would be loaded into FMIS computer software to produce numerous reports which would help to determine whether an area service was performing efficiently. By September 1989 the FMIS project team produced its first report on 'Producing A Functional Specification', which dealt with the issue of how the team proposed to tackle the task of producing an FMIS (Home Office 1989a, 1989b). The second report, which examined the objectives and content of the FMIS was produced in January 1989, and by March 1989 a third report was published. Given that the second report contained the objectives of the proposed FMIS, we think it is worth recording these in full as follows:

(a) to enable area management and probation committees to monitor performance against area objectives and priorities;

(b) to give managers the information to ensure that they are utilising resources economically;

(c) to provide information which helps all staff to monitor and control resources by enabling inputs (resources needed to produce results, for example equipment, labour and materials) to be related to expected and actual outcomes, so that appropriate responses can be made when plans and reality part company;

(d) to provide information in accordance with (c) to enable devolution of responsibility and accountability to staff at all levels;

(e) to provide information to HM Inspectorate and C6 Division to monitor resource use and area effectiveness;

(f) to enable the Home Office accurately to cost specific probation activities;

(g) to facilitate at various levels later evaluation of the usefulness of the effectiveness measures implied in (c) (Home Office 1989a, 1989b).

By June 1989 a report on stage 3A was published which reinforced the rationale of the entire project by stating that an FMIS should provide integrated financial, activity and staff information in order to give probation committees and managers within an area the information needed to support policy planning and related budget development; to monitor performance against objectives and priorities; to provide information to ensure that resources are utilised in an effective, efficient and economic manner; to facilitate the development of delegated budgets; and to enable specific probation service activities to be costed. At this particular juncture it was estimated that, despite the intentions of the Home Office towards the end of the 1980s, it was being envisaged that the computer software to take advantage of the proposed system would not be available until at least 1992.

The Audit Commission

There are three other significant documents that we need to mention before concluding this chapter with a summary of the Criminal Justice

Act 1991. The first is the Audit Commission Report on the Probation Service: *Promoting Value for Money* (1989). The Audit Commission is the agency that appoints and supervises the auditors of the service and therefore has a role in monitoring the value for money it provides. It is the body responsible for local government audits. In the first part of this report the Commission examined the role of the service in the wider criminal justice system and reinforced the 1988 Green Paper on targeting more serious offenders for community supervision. Part 2 proceeded to argue that probation officers must begin to supervise high risk offenders more effectively. To do this they had to acquire the necessary skills and interventions had to be properly assessed. The final part of the report stated that better management systems were required to facilitate probation skills and methods of working with offenders. Accordingly, further progress was required by probation managers in six key areas, which were: demonstrating the effectiveness of its work with offenders; spreading good practice from one area service to another; developing management information systems, which should be simple, flexible and tuned to local targets and objectives; furthermore, clarifying lines of accountability in relation to the organisational and financial structure of the service; the development of skills in a multi-disciplinary service; and working with other agencies in the wider criminal justice system. It was the intention of the Commission to undertake a further review of managerial and financial arrangements and conduct audits of the economy, efficiency and effectiveness of all area services at a later date. Finally, the Audit Commission found that the service as a whole was not delivering value for money.

A Residential Conference in Cambridge, 1989

In July 1989 a residential conference was held in Cambridge that resulted in the publication of a number of papers (Shaw and Haines 1989), one of which was by David Faulkner. It was said that the Conservative government acknowledged that the probation service was built on social work foundations, but that by 1989 this was not enough to justify its existence. The service had moved on or, to put it more accurately, had been moved on to become an integral component of the criminal justice system that must be concerned about the effects of crime, victims and, of course, punishment in the community. Additionally, as we have just explained, the historical juncture has been reached when the service cannot eschew performance issues, managerial developments, and the language of outputs and service delivery. In fact, Faulkner summarised the position in his paper to the conference by saying that 'The service has come a long way fast (through the process of SNOP and local responses in the mid-1980s) and in some ways feeling the strain, but there is still more to be done in developing coherent management systems which include the setting of both corporate and individual objectives, measuring their achievement, identifying target groups, guaranteeing the delivery of services and maintaining their quality, holding individuals to account, and handling the service's increasingly complicated external relationships' (Faulkner 1989 p5).

The National Audit Office

The year 1989 was busy for probation because we must consider yet another report, this time by the National Audit Office (NAO): *Home Office: Control and Management of Probation Services in England and Wales* (1989). The NAO is independent of government and its job is to certify the accounts of all central government departments and a number of public sector bodies. It reports to Parliament on the economy, efficiency and effectiveness of both government departments and public bodies, and it should be acknowledged that this report was written concurrently with the Audit Commission report. The NAO report concentrated on three main issues: first, whether the performance of the probation service was monitored against predetermined objectives and priorities; secondly, whether satisfactory arrangements existed to allocate funds to and control spending by area services; and finally, what was being done to promote an efficient and effective organisation. Accordingly, the report discussed the objectives and priorities of the service; future funding, control and financial management/monitoring information systems; and future training, inspections and performance indicators. The report emphasised the central role of management, whose task was to ensure that resources were being used efficiently, to set objectives, priorities and targets, and also to ensure the highest possible standards of performance. Unfortunately, argued the report, management skills had not kept pace with a rapidly changing, developing and expanding service. Interestingly, the NAO report echoed the findings of the Audit Commission when it stated that the service had weaknesses in the area of management uncertainty about its objectives and doubts about its effectiveness. In fact, both the Audit Commission and National Audit Office reports perceived a pressing need for more effective management, better targeting of resources, management information systems and more efficient use of resources provided by the taxpayer and distributed by government.

Therefore we can argue, beginning with the Statement of National

Objectives and Priorities during 1983/84 (discussed in Chapter 3), we have witnessed a discernible shift towards more central political direction and political-managerial control over the service. This process continued during the latter stages of the 1980s, illustrated by a changing role for the Inspectorate, complemented by the Audit Commission and National Audit Office reports that draw attention to the need for quantitative measures of performance in the guise of performance indicators.

Criminal Justice Act 1991

To conclude this chapter we must turn to the Criminal Justice Act 1991 and consider some of its main implications for the probation service. Undoubtedly, the probation organisation had a central role under the 1991 Act to deliver punishment in the community and produce effective pre-sentence reports (which replaced social enquiry reports) to address three main areas: current offence, the offender, leading to a conclusion for the court to consider. By doing this the pre-sentence report would contribute to the new sentencing framework by assisting courts to formulate a judgment about the seriousness of the offence. Community punishments had to be rigorous and demanding and a new combination order was introduced that for the first time combined probation and community service. Importantly, consent was still required for probation that, as we saw earlier, became a sentence of the court. The Act also introduced national standards for court reports and community sentences, although we need to reiterate that national standards were first introduced in 1988 for community service. Section 29 of the Act stated that the current offence before the court is not made more serious because the offender has previous convictions or due to the fact that there was a failure to respond to previous sentences. We should also refer to section 94, which introduced the notion of cash limits that was to have far-reaching consequences during the next few years.

It is important to draw attention to the rationale of the revised sentencing framework that was based upon just deserts. This means that the punishment determined by the sentencing court must fit the crime, which critically depends upon an evaluation of seriousness. The 1991 Act did not define the meaning of *seriousness* and yet the concept was used to differentiate between those offences that were suitable for a community sentence and those that should result in custody (envisaged as predominantly sex and violence offences, thus endorsing the principle of bifurcation). Furthermore, the 1991 Act introduced a number of thresholds that would determine whether or not the offender would be located in one of three sentencing bands that relied upon the court's judgment on offence seriousness. Consequently, the court should not impose a community sentence unless it has made the judgment that the offence, together with one associated offence, is *serious enough* to warrant such a sentence (s 6(1)).

Where custody is concerned, the court should not impose this form of sentence unless the offence, together with one associated offence, is *so serious* that only custody can be justified; or that the offence is a violent or sexual offence and that only such a sentence is appropriate to protect the public from serious harm (s 1(2)). A custodial sentence can be imposed when the offender refuses to consent to the imposition of a community sentence (s 1(3)). The court's adjudication on offence seriousness is of paramount importance and of equal importance is the professional responsibility of the probation officer to contribute to the court's sentencing decision through the preparation of the pre-sentence report. In other words, the report will help the court to come to a view on the most suitable sentence that is proportionate to, and commensurate with, the level of seriousness contained within the offence by providing all relevant information about the offence and offender, including aggravating and mitigating factors. However, it should be noted that the 1991 Act placed more emphasis on the current offences than the biographical details of the offender, thus promoting a justice rather than treatment model orientation. As a result of this, court reports became impoverished for a period by concentrating too much on *what* the offender had done rather than *why*, which in turn affected the quality of the probation officer's assessment of the individual. In other words, there was less emphasis on aetiology. However, this position was corrected with the introduction of national standards for reports during the 1990s, even though the sentencing framework remained the same until the introduction of the Criminal Justice Act 2003. At this point the Criminal Justice Act 1991 can be further illustrated by presenting information on available sentences and the threshold between one sentencing band and another.

Level 3 – Custodial Sentences
The custody threshold specifies that the offence must be 'so serious' that only a custodial sentence can be justified. This criterion had to be satisfied by the court in relation to:

Imprisonment (21 and over)
Suspended sentence (21 and over)

Detention in a Young Offender Institution (18–20)
Suspended Sentence Supervision Order (21 and over)

Level 2 – Community Sentences
The community sentence threshold specifies that the offence must be 'serious enough' to warrant such a sentence:

Probation Order with and without requirements (16 and over)
Community Service Order (16 and over)
Combination Order (16 and over)
Curfew (10 and over)
Supervision Order (10–17)
Attendance Centre Order (10–20)

Level 1 – Other Orders
Fines (10 and over)
Compensation (10 and over)
Absolute Discharge (10 and over)
Conditional Discharge (10 and over)
Deferred Sentence (10 and over).

These were the available sentences following the 1991 Act and we have presented succinct details of the revised sentencing framework within which the probation service had to find its niche. In light of what we have already discussed, it should be reinforced that at the beginning of the 1990s there was a clear policy of aspiring to reduce the number of custodial sentences by making community sentences more credible. Such a policy does not support the assertion that the 1991 Act is the manifestation of a tough law and order approach, mainly because of the restrictions on resorting to custody. Even though the probation service had been challenged to amend its thinking on the nature of probation supervision by engaging with punishment in the community, nevertheless it was presented with certain opportunities to keep more offenders out of custody by becoming centre stage in the delivery of the new legislation that had been gestating for the last three to four years. Our final task is to summarise what may be considered to be the main points of this legislation:

(a) three sentencing bands and corresponding thresholds;

(b) criteria governing custody and community sentences based upon an assessment of 'seriousness';

(c) more severe sentences for sex and violent offences to meet the requirement of public protection;

(d) more limited use of previous convictions;

(e) unit fines;

(f) the new combination order;

(g) curfew and electronic tagging;

(h) abolition of partly suspended sentences and the more limited use of the suspended sentence;

(i) creation of the Youth Court.

Summary and Conclusion

We have tried to demonstrate that the years 1985 to 1991 are dominated by a number of interrelated developments, beginning with the differential way in which area probation services responded to SNOP (Lloyd 1986). Furthermore, the Hurd, Patten and Faulkner era developed the politically necessary yet professionally contentious notion of punishment in the community (depending, of course, on your point of view). Writing during the month of the Leeds Castle seminar, Harry Fletcher, Assistant General Secretary of NAPO, generously commented that 'Douglas Hurd is not unsympathetic to the work and values of the probation service' (1987 p83). By contrast, he thought that many of his colleagues were 'hostile'. Douglas Hurd welcomed the joint statement, 'Probation – the next five years' (NAPO, ACOP and CCPC 1987), although his memoirs provide few clues about his preoccupations as Home Secretary beyond concerns with the prison population (Hurd 2003).

We refer to Harry Fletcher because he draws attention to the ongoing conflict between NAPO and the Home Office that centres on values. It would be churlish if we did not acknowledge the fact that NAPO continued to promote social work values. On the other hand, David Faulkner was making it clear that for the service to survive it had to be premised on something more than its traditional values. In the political climate of the 1980s it had to embrace the developing managerial ethos of policy, objectives and targets, in addition to working out the implications of punishment in the community (Faulkner 1989). We should be clear that anti-management perspectives were also a feature of this period, most notably encapsulated in the writings of Bill McWilliams (1987, 1992). His views had a certain cachet within the probation world, yet despite the attractiveness of this thinking it was stranded within a political culture that starved it of longevity. In the

course of this chapter, we have referred to the politics of making community sentences more credible to boost the confidence of sentencers in the probation service in pursuit of a strategy of alternatives to custody that dominated the 1980s. All these developments were occurring within a context of rising crime; an expanding prison population; Conservative new-right politics; the restructuring of probation from welfare to punishment to work with more serious offenders; and the new sentencing framework of the Criminal Justice Act 1991 that emphasised deeds rather than offender needs.

We have already touched upon the emergence of management during the 1960s and 1970s (towards the end of Chapter 2). We built on this in Chapter 3 when exploring the SNOP document in 1984. In this chapter we have taken managerial developments to the next level by excavating the creation of a financial management information system; national standards from 1988; changes to the Inspectorate after Grimsey; and the ongoing political preoccupation with efficiency and value for money. Furthermore, we have addressed the emergence of performance indicators; alluded to the language of policies, priorities, objectives and targets; touched on the Audit Commission and National Audit Office reports; all within a political and managerial framework concerned with inputs, outputs, outcomes, practice guidelines, minimum standards, consistency, competence and accountability. In other words, we have drawn attention to some of the political control mechanisms intended to promote more effective management within the probation service, increasingly understood in terms of measurable objectives. Furthermore, similar developments were occurring in the civil service and other government departments, the health service, local authorities, the police, prisons and schools (Whittington 1988 p205; Humphrey 1987 p23). These control mechanisms evolved in the shadow of cash limits as the service moved into the 1990s.

The new political priorities for probation that began to emerge with the FMI and SNOP influenced the development of management during the 1980s. This facilitated notions of performance and effectiveness in terms of objectively, statistically and therefore quantifiably measuring probation service activities. It has been obsessed with measuring things ever since. Humphrey, Pease and Carter (1993) researched managerial changes in four area services and field work was undertaken between April 1990 and June 1991. It is a magical mystery tour of performance assessment and accountable management, including the mechanisms that emerged to achieve this. They draw attention to the Audit Commission report (1989) that emphasised measurable targets. To some degree this had been facilitated by Gilpin-Black, a firm of private consultants imposing ideas from the private sector on probation through the language of corporate performance, organisational excellence, managerial styles, effectiveness, planning and control, and key output areas.

However, we have a problem with this approach, primarily because of what it omits in a people-based organisation like probation (but also teaching, health service and social work organisations). Mechanisms of political/financial control linked to complementary managerial developments understood in terms of quantifiable measurable objectives and targets, are indicative of codification. Such a process of codification, we would argue, attempts to impose a semblance of order and control by determining clear organisational parameters. But in so doing there is the danger of reducing and limiting the totality of work being undertaken to the objectively measurable that, by definition, omits moral and ineffable dimensions. The concept of the ineffable in probation is to acknowledge that there are areas of practice that are difficult to define and quantifiably measure with precision, yet are fundamentally necessary in an organisation that works with people. The ineffable dimension of probation practice includes: insight, awareness, intuition, a deep understanding of the person, appreciation, passion, empathy and artistry through reflection. These are some of the critical qualitative features which establish the foundation of effective interviewing, assessment and intervention skills. We raise this as a matter of concern at the end of this chapter (with a view to expansion later) because it illustrates an escalating tension between politicians, managers and practitioners.

Our last point for emphasis is leadership. If there had been any doubt about the position of leadership within probation in the political climate at the end of the 1980s, the demands were clear by the beginning of the 1990s. The discomfort with the concept of management was palpable in many of the utterances of its leaders and few chief probation officers in managing their areas saw themselves as leaders in a business sense. Where this book is concerned, this is a perspective that must be reinforced. Leaders in probation were uncomfortable with perceiving themselves as managers because it could be interpreted as a betrayal of those people-oriented values that brought them into the service as main grade probation officers in the 1950s and 1960s. However, this discomfort masked a complacency which surrounded the service in its belief that the right-wing political climate could not possibly challenge the moral high ground of their sincerely held compassion for offenders and liberal values that underpinned practice. Yet the political world and its values were being changed, with the result that probation and its allies failed to win the argument linking crime to social deprivation, despite the evidence to the contrary. It may be said that probation was becoming unpopular and a future Home Secretary was prepared to endorse this view. Furthermore, the era of civil servants as a 'metropolitan elite' (Ryan 2003 p16) supportive of the service was also coming to an end, with the result that there would be no effective buffer between the punitive views of politicians and the service; the old order was giving way to something quite different that would persist under New Labour after 1997. There were some who tried to provide alternative thinking. A paper by Statham (1990) attempted to inject some reality into ongoing debates by redefining management roles, and thus create a culture of managerialism that could withstand the perceived external threats to the service's monopoly position in the community supervision of offenders. The desire for social markets in the public sector was already impacting upon health and education, and it was inconceivable that probation would not be faced with further challenges. But few were listening and it is tempting, albeit regrettably, to end this chapter on a somewhat pessimistic note. The next part of our story will look at the Major and Howard years from 1992 to 1997, which are hardly likely to lighten the mood of the reader.

NOTES – Chapter 4

[1] It should be acknowledged that 21 new prisons were built between 1980 and 1995 at a cost of £1.2 billion.

[2] This is a helpful collection of papers edited by Rees and Williams, the result of a seminar held at the London School of Economics during April 1989. In addition to the critical reflections of David Garland on the Green Paper, there are also contributions from: Bill Beaumont of NAPO; the late Graham Smith; and David Downes.

[3] National standards to improve performance and achieve greater consistency across area services and between individual probation officers were first introduced into community service in 1988. They were subsequently expanded to incorporate other areas of practice, such as all community penalties and court reports in 1992; then revised in 1995, 2000 and 2002. At the time of writing (2005), national standards are once again being revised, but this time to reflect the changes introduced by the Criminal Justice Act 2003. If we return to the late 1980s, it should be acknowledged that national standards were linked to cultural change in probation. For example, the Action Plan for the Cleveland Probation Service for the period 1989/90 contained a target for level of contact with offenders and a target of eight face-to-face contacts in the first three months of an order was agreed after discussion between managers, staff, and probation committee. In fact, this was a compromise position because the chief officer wanted twelve contacts in order for the service to be seen as a credible supervisory organisation of offenders. This was a development that was vehemently opposed by some, perhaps for various reasons: prevailing anti-management culture; a fear of performance exposure; a sense of discomfort in handling discretion.

[4] In 2004 the Inspectorate clarified that it was given statutory authority by the Criminal Justice Act 1991. The Criminal Justice and Court Services Act 2000 renamed HMIP as Her Majesty's Inspectorate of the National Probation Service for England and Wales, funded by the Home Office and reporting directly to the Home Secretary. Its role is defined as follows:

'Report to the Home Secretary on the extent to which the National Probation Service for England and Wales is fulfilling its statutory duties, contributing to the achievement of Home Office and Criminal Justice Aims and meeting performance and efficiency targets as required.

Demonstrate that inspections contribute to improved performance in the National Probation Service.

Contribute to sound policy and effective service delivery by providing advice and disseminating good practice, based on inspection findings, to Ministers, Home Office and National Probation Service staff and Probation Boards/areas.

Promote actively race equality and wider diversity issues in the National Probation Service.

Promote the overall effectiveness of the criminal justice system.'

Chapter 5

THE CENTRE CANNOT HOLD: DIFFICULT YEARS FROM 1992 TO 1997

'All this adds up to clear evidence that the Government believes in the work of the Service and is committed to enabling it to expand that work ... I personally think the Service has a great future in both its criminal and its civil work.' *(Philippa Drew, Head of the Probation Division, Home Office (1992))*

'With his distrust of orthodoxy he was happy with the idea that I expected him to work closely with me and with my Policy Unit to raise the profile of our fight against crime ... By October 1993 Michael was able to use the party conference platform to signal a radical break with the past consensus on criminal justice.' *(John Major (2000) on Michael Howard)*

Introduction

We concluded the last chapter on a justifiably sombre note. However, there was another tune being played, which we can reprise by tuning into the perceptions of someone associated with central government. After occupying the position of Head of the Probation Division at the Home Office for over four years, Philippa Drew's valedictory comment was that the service was in good shape (1992 p93). To justify this positive view she referred to: probation and community sentences located at the heart of the Criminal Justice Act 1991; increased resources during the 1980s; a commitment to raise the quality of pre-qualifying and in-service training; and an expanded programme of research. She concluded that 'this adds up to clear evidence that the Government believes in the work of the Service and is committed to enabling it to expand that work' (p93). She refers to recent successes such as the expansion of bail information schemes during the 1980s; a reduction of custodial sentences for young offenders following *Tackling Offending: An Action Plan* (Home Office 1988b). Furthermore, the service had seen the introduction of national standards; effective work with parolees and life licences had been achieved; there were committed staff who believed that offenders can change; and it had a proud history of experimentation and innovation. We should also add that, during the previous decade, the service had been involved in intensive probation programmes in eight services from April 1990 (Mair

1996b): crime prevention and community work; mediation, reparation and conciliation schemes; assessment schemes for mentally disordered offenders; risk of custody and re-conviction tools (Mair 1989; 1996a for a succinct review of probation developments between 1984 and 1993). Ms Drew takes a swipe at those within the service who had overly negative perceptions of probation and were reluctant to embrace change. Nevertheless, she concluded by stating that, in her opinion, the service had a great future (whatever that might mean). With these up-beat thoughts in mind we can begin to explore the 1992–97 period by first of all reflecting on the wider political situation within which to locate probation developments.

The Major and Howard Axis

On 28th November 1990 John Major replaced Margaret Thatcher as Prime Minister. Subsequently, on 9th April 1992 he received his own mandate to govern from the electorate when the Conservatives were once again re-elected, for the fourth consecutive time since May 1979. It was also to be the last time for a while because New Labour was in the ascendancy during the 1990s that, by 1997, would bring to an end 18 years of Conservative governments. We should also remind the reader that David Waddington, having replaced Douglas Hurd, was the last Home Secretary appointed by Mrs Thatcher (26th October 1989 to 30th November 1990). Subsequently, Kenneth Baker was the first Home Secretary under Mr Major (30th November 1990 to 11th April 1992), followed by Kenneth Clarke (11th April 1992 to 27th May 1993) and then Michael Howard (27th May 1993 to 1st May 1997).

When the political parties were preparing for the general election that was held in April 1992, John Major, in his acclaimed autobiography, reminds us that the country was attempting to recover from yet another recession. After the difficult years of the early 1980s (see Chapter 3), followed by more favourable economic conditions under Nigel Lawson (but only for some rather than all), once again there were economic concerns. Even though inflation was only 3%, unemployment was 2.5 million and a number of people had their homes repossessed (Major 2000 p295). Despite a vestige of optimism at the beginning of 1992, just before the election, by the summer there were fears about economic recovery as unemployment continued to rise. These fears were more than realised by 7.30 on the evening of 16th September 1992 when Norman Lamont, Chancellor, announced the suspension of membership of the Exchange Rate Mechanism that devalued the currency. To the Prime Minister this was 'a political and economic calamity ... and it changed the political landscape of Britain' (2000 p312). In fact, John Sargeant comments that joining the ERM was the greatest mistake of John Major's political life (Sargeant 2005 p98). We think it is important to refer to the political, social and economic circumstances that prevailed during the early 1990s because of the implications for the tone of penal policy in general and probation in particular.

We have already touched upon the work of David Garland (1985, 2001) who persuasively argues that, beginning with late Victorian society, wider political and economic circumstances structure the conditions that shape penal policy and the treatment of offenders (he refers to the concepts of 'surface of emergence' and 'conditions of existence'). This position is supported, for example, by the work of Cavadino and Dignan (2002), Cavadino, Crow and Dignan (1999). The latter text is of interest because it draws attention to changes in penal policy since 1979, taking account of changing economic conditions. It is, of course, necessary to guard against an overly simplistic analysis of the vagaries of penal policy but during the recession of the early 1980s there was an emphasis on law and order; from the mid-1980s the Lawson–Thatcher economic boom moderated law and order for punishment in the community under Douglas Hurd; but the early 1990s, particularly the period after 1992, reveal a return to a more punitive law and order approach during economic difficulties. Therefore, Cavadino, Crow and Dignan suggest an association between politics, economic circumstances and penal policy by saying that, when societies feel stressed because of economic misfortune, they can become more punitive and look for scapegoats. One factor at play within this line of reasoning (already encountered in Chapter 3) (Hall et al 1978), is the way in which governments 'seek to distract attention from their economic failures and court popularity by promising to attack the criminal enemy within' (1999 p26). Cavadino, Crow and Dignan consider that John Major's government was an 'outstanding example' of this process. In other words, it is the 'let's play the law and order game' approach to divert attention from those political and economic factors that are the real cause of people's problems, particularly the population the probation service comes into contact with on a daily basis.

It was within this context that Mr Major resorted to the language of back to basics, which was pejoratively interpreted for its unseemly and sanctimonious tones in the press. According to the Prime Minister, the phrase was shorthand for confronting a set of permissive and misguided ideas that had, in his judgment, invited policies down blind alleys on crime, health, education and social work (2000 p387). Interestingly, where crime is concerned there is some evidence in his autobiography to indicate a balanced and insightful approach. At one point he writes about the adverse effects of crime on victims with a measure of understanding distilled from his own difficult upbringing that led him away from the harsh view that the individual is solely responsible for criminal behaviour. In other words, human behaviour should not be disconnected from 'those personal, educational and social difficulties which are linked to crime' (2000 p387). This is promising because it has the makings of a liberal and balanced approach that the probation ideal could warm to, in opposition to more traditional conservative criminology (Brake and Hale 1992). But he then proceeds to claim that everyone, regardless of their background, can be honest. If not, those who break the law must be punished and go to prison. It may be suggested that he is appealing to two different audiences in this contradictory language: on one hand, an approach that would find favour with liberals and probation officers; on the other, the conservative right in his own party, for whom criminals deserve little sympathy and even less understanding. And it is easy not to understand or be sympathetic towards the plight of certain sections of the community if you come from a propitious background with a stake in society, belong to a good family, had educational opportunities which have provided a decent job, living wage and some prospects for the future.

By 1993 the political context for the criminal justice system, but specifically probation, was disconcertingly deteriorating, because of an escalation in the harsh rhetoric of punishment, law and order. Moreover, other events were making their impact upon an already fragile situation, considered at this point because it helps us to appreciate the climate within which probation had to survive between 1993 and 1997. On 12th February 1993 Jon Venables and Robert Thompson, two ten-year-old boys, abducted and killed two-year-old Jamie Bulger in Liverpool. The body of the child was discovered on the 14th February (Morrison 1997). Then on 22nd April 1993 Stephen Lawrence was murdered in a racist attack in London. In addition to these two events that rightly troubled the nation's psyche, there were wider concerns about crime: recorded crime in England and Wales was 2.38 million offences in 1979; by 1992, 5.38 million (Benyon 1994 p13). There were specific concerns about juvenile crime (Benyon

1994 p16) and disorder on the streets of Shrewsbury, Birmingham and Rugby. It was in this situation that the Home Secretary, Kenneth Clarke, was replaced by Michael Howard in May 1993.[1]

It is also possible to detect a different approach to crime in the mind of Mr Major compared to the elements of a more balanced one recounted earlier. This is because in February 1993 he talked of condemning more and understanding less (Major 1993). Additionally, on 12th November 1993 it is reported he stated that it was in fact the individual and not society that was responsible for crime, at a crime prevention meeting in London (Benyon 1994 p76). And by appointing Michael Howard as Home Secretary he had someone who 'was able to use the party platform [on 6th October 1993] to signal a radical break with the past consensus on criminal justice' by announcing a 27-point plan on law and order. Some of these points are:

- Abolish the right to silence.

- Tougher laws against squatters.

- Give the police new powers to stop trespassers and hunt saboteurs.

- Build six new prisons.

- Secure training order/centres for persistent 12–14-year-old offenders.

- Double the maximum YOI sentence to two years for 15–16-year-olds.

- Make community service orders more punitive.

- Review community sentences.[2]

We need to make it clear that the Howard years were some of the most difficult for the probation service. As Home Secretary, his daily rhetoric and general demeanour left no one in any doubt that rehabilitation was not the first word in his vocabulary when thinking about probation. The most astonishing and disturbing change that was initiated by the conference speech was to reverse the penal policy that underpinned the Criminal Justice Act 1991, introduced on 1st October 1992. We need to make it clear that a policy of reducing custodial sentences, which had been developing from 1985 to 1991, experienced a remarkable *volte-face* as Michael Howard propounded the view that 'prison works', sending a shudder of alarm throughout the service. This reversed the policy that had been assiduously pursued by Douglas Hurd, John Patten and David Faulkner. If this was not bad enough, by 1993 certain features of the 1991 Act were beginning to unravel. At this point we will clarify the significance of these changes.

Criminal Justice Act 1993

Sections 65 and 66 of the Criminal Justice Act 1993 made important changes to three features of the Criminal Justice Act 1991: the criteria for justifying custodial sentences; s 29 of the 1991 Act on the offender's previous record; and the fine. Let us focus on the last two features, beginning with s 29(1) of the 1991 Act, which stated that the court may not conclude that the offence it is considering is made more serious because of previous convictions or failure to respond to previous sentences. However, s 29(2) proceeded to say that any aggravating factors of the current offence revealed by the circumstances of other offences may be taken into account in making decisions about seriousness. We think that these two subsections were always problematic for report writers because we struggled with their precise meaning. It was the intention of the politics underpinning the 1991 Act to prohibit courts from placing too much emphasis upon an offender's previous convictions and response to previous sentences when formulating a view on sentencing for the current offences. In other words, the emphasis should be located upon the current offences, which had implications for probation officers thinking differently about the information being provided in their reports to magistrates and judges.

Benyon's survey of the state of the criminal justice system during 1993 (1994 p39) reminds us that aspects of the 1991 Act, namely previous convictions and fines, caused not a little consternation. A survey of magistrates during April 1993 revealed that 94% were not content with certain aspects of the new legislation to such an extent that some had resigned in protest. To make matters worse, the Lord Chief Justice, Lord Taylor, was critical. If concerns were expressed about the status of previous convictions, disquiet surrounding unit fines can be illustrated by recounting that a man was fined £1,250 for dropping litter, a disproportionate amount (cited in Benyon 1994 pp70–71). Therefore, changes to the unit fine were implemented on 20th September 1993; and the new criteria for custodial sentences, in addition to allowing courts to consider an offender's previous record and response to previous sentences before passing sentence, were implemented on 16th August 1993. By imposing this legislative change it was expected that custodial sentences would begin to rise. Cavadino and Dignan (2002) remind us that, following the implementation of the 1991 Act, the prison population actually fell from 45,835 in September to 40,606 in December 1992. However, due to Mr Howard's and Mr Major's *volte-face* that emphasised incapacitation in prison, by 1993 it was 44,566; rising in 1995 to 51,047; and by 1997 it was 61,114. Therefore, we can establish the point that the penal policy *Zeitgeist* between 1992 and 1997 was different by being less favourable for the probation service compared to the Hurd era in that there were fewer qualms about sending people to prison. At this point we want to continue to explore some of these differences by reflecting upon other features of this period.

The First Three-Year Plan
In November 1992 the Home Office published the first of its three-year plans for the probation service. This document covered the period 1993–96 and was intended to supersede SNOP, published eight years earlier in 1984 (Home Office 1992). This three-year plan clarified the main responsibilities of the probation service as:

- To prepare reports for the courts.

- To implement community sentences.

- To provide effective programmes for offenders.

- Pre- and post-release prison work.

- Crime prevention and concern for victims.

- Civil work.

- Partnerships (probation working alongside other agencies).

Like SNOP, the plan was a statement produced by central government then published by the Home Office; area services were expected to make decisions, set budgets, and to plan for the future, within the parameters established by the plan. Importantly, it was stated that 'future plans are likely to see a shift more towards quantified objectives of desired impact', the implications of which we started to ponder in the last chapter (Home Office 1992 p1). Therefore, clear expectations were being made upon area services by central government; local objectives should be measurable and therefore targets quantifiable; and the Inspectorate would assess services against this plan. By the time the statement was published, the 1991 Act had just been implemented but it was to pose certain problems as we have just seen. Furthermore, the 1992 version of National Standards had clarified the probation task in relation to pre-sentence reports, probation orders, supervision orders, community service, combination orders, hostels, pre- and post-release work. A resource management information system was beginning to replace the financial management information system. In fact, it is worth reminding ourselves that the latter system had been in the process of being developed since 1986 in pursuit of economy, efficiency and effectiveness, in addition to value for money, but was now being refined. Importantly, a system of cash limits came into force in April 1991 that we need to consider in more detail because this was a significant step within probation's governance arrangements.

Cash Limits

Roger Tarling, Head of the Home Office Research and Planning Unit (Field and Hough 1993) explains that it was a decision by the Conservative government in November 1989 to cash limit the grant paid to the local authorities towards expenditure on probation that resulted in a new financial system being imposed in April 1991. Prior to this, as we have already considered in Chapter 2, central government since the 1970s had paid 80% towards the cost of the 55 area services to local authority treasurers. Under this somewhat open-ended financial system, central government did not have much control over public expenditure because the money would be stumped up to meet the costs of staff recruited and appointed by probation committees and their chief officers. So the bolder committees and chiefs were, the more resources they could attract to their area – which helps to explain how services could grow at differential rates. However, the down side to this, particularly from a Home Office and Treasury perspective, was that spending was not subject to tight control.

Earlier in the book we described some of the dynamics that influenced the funding of area services and associated budgeting processes. Local authorities acted as bankers to probation areas, receiving the government grant of 80% of their area's budget and adding their own 20% from a levy on local ratepayers. The central grant arrived in area coffers in quarterly payments which might have created cash flow problems had the local authorities not provided probation areas with other financial services like payroll and account payments. Consequently, and over time, not only had probation financial systems become inextricably linked with local authority systems, they had in effect become dependent on the cushioning effect they could provide. In such a climate, if the local authority was sympathetic to the probation cause, in addition to imaginative chief probation officers and committees, then area services had no difficulty in expanding their budgets, thus developing provision to offenders. But this sometimes cosy arrangement, in some areas at least, was about to change because Conservative governments since 1979, with their monetarist approach, had developed a challenging attitude to public expenditure. Whilst promoting the new right politics of anti-welfare and self-help, they were also espousing a market philosophy in the delivery of public services. A significant feature of this strategy was to impose strict controls over public expenditure; and restricting local authority expenditure was central to this approach. These political and economic dynamics caught up with probation rather later than in other areas of public service, but in November 1989 the government announced that it was going to cash limit the grant to probation areas, a measure that would be introduced at the beginning of the financial year in April 1991.

This measure had far-reaching consequences for all area services because it imposed strict limits on operational expenditure. Instantaneously, it added new meaning to the concept of priorities; and for the first time in its history the probation service was faced with the uncomfortable prospect of redundancies. Furthermore, cash limits constituted a personal challenge for chief officers. The need to assess their impact on local operations became critical, as were the longer-term implications for both workloads and capacity. Indubitably these were uncomfortable times for those chiefs who had enjoyed a measure of protection from local authority structures, and those areas that had been able to expand their budgets in a relatively unfettered way for a considerable period of time.

Since 1988, work on new funding arrangements had been underway that involved the Home Office developing a cash limits formula based upon *needs* and *workload*. This approach mirrored other devices used to determine the level of government grant and was to gain new levels of sophistication as it developed. The needs component that accounted for two-thirds of an area's budget allocation comprised four variables:

(a) the number of persons found guilty or cautioned;

(b) the number of people aged between 15 and 29;

(c) the number of unemployed males between 15 and 24;

(d) the number of overcrowded households.

The workload component accounted for the remaining one-third and comprised another four variables:

(a) probation order commencements;

(b) number of pre-sentence reports prepared;

(c) throughcare services;

(d) community service order commencements.

In whatever way the cash limit was to be devised, there was an almost inevitable sense of arbitrariness about the process and outcome. Whilst one reaction was to promote the case for increasing the national budget, or the size of the cake, the size of the different slices and the various reflections on the permutations of the cash limit budget created frisson. What the emerging process revealed, in a clearer way than ever before, were disparities between comparative levels of funding, which in some ways were magnified by workload levels. What was exposed was the possibility for an area to be both underfunded and overworked or, by contrast, comparatively well funded and with more manageable workloads. At a single stroke, the cash limits approach revealed anomalies created by years of differential approaches to funding (discussed in an earlier chapter). However, it was recognised that these anomalies, if indeed they were anomalies, could not be put right in a single exercise. Therefore, a system of 'damping' was adopted which meant that small adjustments up or down would be made to each area's budget year by year, until hypothetical parity was achieved. This made sense because, whilst some areas spotted the possibility of growing their services, albeit modestly, others were faced with the possibility of enforcing staff redundancies in addition to increasing the size of workloads – never a popular outcome amongst hard-pressed staff in historically hard-pressed areas.

The picture that emerged was that areas with comparatively high levels of deprivation (for example, Derbyshire, Lancashire, South Glamorgan and Teesside) were underfunded; more affluent areas (such as Surrey) were not. The newly created metropolitan areas, although covering populations with high needs, were not placed too badly by cash limits, largely because they had slightly different financial structures and their own in-house treasurers who had brought a new level of financial acumen to their area services. Nevertheless, the budget process had now become a dynamic one for every area service, with potential fluctuations in both the workloads and needs components of the formula that were factors to be considered alongside the actual mechanisms of the formula. Some prescient chief officers soon began to anticipate potential fluctuations and to challenge data being inputted into the formula. Others argued for additional factors such as population scarcity to be included in the variables. All could agree that there were concerns about the pressure on national levels of funding and some of the bureaucratic ideas central government seemed to favour.

So what did all these somewhat abstruse issues mean in practical terms? By using Teesside (formerly Cleveland) as a ready source of data, we can explain that a series of initiatives began which ultimately changed the governance arrangements of the service. When it became clear in 1989 that cash limits were closing in, every effort was made to grow the service over the next two years. It should be stated that Teesside had never been generously resourced and had to cope with relatively high caseloads in circumstances of a high crime rate and social deprivation that deteriorated during the 1980s.[3] The arguments for a better resourced service existed but historically the energy to promote the arguments in the interests of the needs of the service was missing. However, towards the end of the 1980s a new senior management regime was more responsive to the burdens of its probation officers and became more energetic in its struggle to prosecute Teesside's cause. It should also be said that there were other areas throughout the country that were similarly galvanised into action. Consequently, the probation committee on Teesside set budgets between 1989 and 1991 that strengthened the staffing complement, a totally justifiable course of action in light of high workloads and a history of underfunding. The local authority, as was its right within existing governance arrangements, could refuse to support the proposal for an expanded budget and force the probation committee and chief officer to go to 'determination'. Determination was the name given to a process of budget scrutiny which was undertaken by the Home Office in order to examine the rationale for the budget proposed by the committee. The outcome of this process, which seemed generally to be acceptable, was binding upon the probation committee and local authority, but we should be reminded that the Home Office had an 80% stake in the outcome of its deliberations.

What the events of 1989–91 revealed was that, whilst the elected representatives of the then Cleveland County Council were sympathetic to the work of the probation service, they were not prepared to agree to incurring any additional costs in order to subsidise the aspirations of a Conservative government. Nevertheless, the probation committee was largely successful in both years of going to determination, exemplified by a perusal of staffing figures during this period. The staffing figures in terms of full-time equivalents were 191.7 on 31st March 1989; 210.8 on 31st March 1990; and then 212.3 on 31st March 1991. Staffing costs amounted to approximately 85% of the total budget of any probation area. Other area services have their own stories to tell about the impact of cash limits within a framework of new national dynamics. Cash limits had become a significant part of changing governance arrangements and probation committees would no longer set their local budget based on local need, a truly significant shift in what is a people-based organisation.

The advent of cash limits and the somewhat convoluted dynamics between central government, local authority and local service, prompted a closer examination of the precise ways in which financial regulations and accounting systems functioned. Again using Teesside to illustrate this point, we can say that, before cash limits, probation areas were effectively the customers of their local authorities. On the whole, the system worked well and, as we have suggested, provided a measure of comfort in some areas. However, as every penny of the budget was becoming important, it was necessary to enquire into how much a probation area was being charged for services being provided by the local authority in what was a monopoly situation. Local authorities provided a range of services – secretariat, legal, banking, budgeting, handling debtors and creditors, personnel etc. – that had to be paid for. They added these 'on costs' to the budget for area probation services then sent the bill to the Home Office for 80% of the total bill. Therefore, the probation service was something of a 'cash cow'. Prior to cash limits no one had seriously questioned either the processes or costs that we are describing here. However, when forced to examine them, they did not always provide value for money. Consequently, Teesside began to explore the possibility of new governance arrangements that resulted in historically provided local authority services being brought in-house. This transpired to be a significant exercise that required the oversight of financial consultants and the agreement of the Home Office and Audit Commission. The cost-benefits of the proposed changes were considerable, as well as improving performance in terms of area budgeting, where the newly created commitment accounting systems were crucial in managing a cash limited budget. A simple and practical consequence of this strategy was to ensure that the staffing complement could be maintained at the highest possible level. This was vital to meet the challenges of the most difficult work of the service and keep probation workloads as manageable as possible. The world of probation was changing fast at so many different levels and with a degree of complexity that few front-line staff or academic commentators could appreciate. Strategic leadership of the kind that might normally be associated with industrial or commercial organisations was arguably essential in maintaining the credibility of probation services in the new political and economic circumstances. Furthermore, the level of discomfort created by these changes was palpable, even amongst chief officers. Before moving on, it is of interest to note that cash limits began to bite in probation by 1992, in addition to magistrates' courts; the police were also subject to this system by 1995.

More Three-Year Plans

We alluded earlier to the first three-year plan that superseded SNOP in 1992 (Home Office 1992). After our cash limits interlude, we now continue with this theme a little longer by considering subsequent plans during the 1990s to see how they began to develop. It is a little puzzling to observe that the first of its so-called three-year plans did not in fact last for three years but only one year because by December 1993 the Home Office had produced its second plan, which covered the period 1994–97. The second plan reinforced Home Office terminology of objectives, measurable outcomes and targets. Importantly, by this stage, as a consequence of a working party comprising ACOP, CCPC and HMIP, the Home Office had produced a set of Key Performance Indicators (KPIs) that built upon those performance indicators that were already being utilised by the Inspectorate in their scrutiny of area services. Therefore, the KPIs enumerated in 1993 were:

1. Predicted and actual reconviction rates.

2. Community orders satisfactorily completed – no breaches.

3. Prison licences.

4. The cost of pre-sentence reports and welfare reports.

5. Average numbers of days to produce reports for criminal courts.

6. Number of welfare reports completed within 12 weeks.

7. Number of occupied bed spaces in hostels.

8. Number of hostel residents.

9. Measure court satisfaction with probation work (Home Office 1993 p14).

By the third three-year plan, published in 1994 for the period 1995–98, a statement of values was included that did not feature in the first two documents. It is stated that:

'The service is committed to:

– treating all people fairly, openly and with respect

– challenging attitudes and behaviour which result in crime and cause distress to victims

– working at all times to bring out the best in people

– reconciling offenders and communities and recognising the obligations of both.' *(Home Office 1994 p4)*

For some of us within the service this was an anaemic and tokenistic expression of values, as will shortly be explained. A second innovation in this plan was a list of what are referred to as Supporting Management Information Needs (or SMINs). Finally, when we arrive at the fifth of these rolling three-year plans (Home Office 1997) we are provided with information on KPIs and targets, an example of which we can now provide by looking at Key Performance Indicator 2:

KPI 2: Number of community orders completed without early termination for breach or a further offence/total number of orders completed for:

Probation Order
Community Service Order
Supervision Order
Combination Order

1996–97 Targets
To achieve the following completion rates:

Probation Order – 82% or more
CSO – 71% or more
Supervision Order – 80% or more
Combination Order – 73% or more

Progress

Targets are being exceeded in respect of all four types of orders. However, it remains of concern that these high levels of completion may be the result of lax enforcement which does not meet the requirements of revised National Standards (Home Office 1995).

1997–98 Targets

To achieve the following completion rates within the framework of the enforcement requirements of National Standards:

Probation Order – 82%
CSO – 80%
Supervision Order – 80%
Combination Order – 80%

Probation under Pressure

Due to the creation of a more right-wing oriented political climate since 1979 (Brake and Hale 1992 for the Thatcher period), but specifically after 1992 (the period we are concentrating on in this chapter), it can be argued that it was a difficult time for the probation service in its work with offenders. Nor should we underestimate the difficulties for senior managers who were burdened with trying to make sense of and manage services under difficult circumstances induced by political imperatives. Increasingly since the early 1980s, Conservative new-right philosophy had been less inclined to demonstrate an approach towards offenders characterised by understanding and sympathy for their plight. Within a philosophical and ideological climate oriented towards a strong (Hobbesian Leviathan) state characterised by law and order, punishment and deterrence, as a bulwark against rising crime to keep predominantly working class people who were also offenders in check, probation services were under pressure (Broad 1991). Of course, there never was an all-out campaign against probation (although it certainly felt like this between 1993 and 1997 with the emphasis upon prison works and other developments afoot, discussed later in this chapter) but rather significant attempts to reshape and rebalance: law and order during the early 1980s; punishment in the community by the early 1990s; the focus on prison and incapacitation by the mid-1990s rather than rehabilitation in the community with probation centre stage as promised; and making community sentences even more robust. By this stage there is a new level of toughness that the service had to contend with, which emphasised management, containment, punishment and control over social work and welfare approaches.

One of our major problems and acute contradictions with the penal policy context, politically inspired between 1992 and 1997, is that it militated against what we consider to be insightful, intelligent and understanding probation practice. The essence of good practice – and we are conscious of making this point on more than one occasion in the book, but it bears the weight of repetition – does not collude with, condone, attempt to justify or excuse offending. Behaviour that causes problems for and inflicts harm upon other people, particularly innocent victims not wanting or asking for trouble, is not acceptable in any society with aspirations to be civilised. But good probation work is curious about people and starts from the premise that behaviour needs to be understood, appreciated, and put into an explanatory context, with a view to addressing it constructively in the community and reducing the likelihood of it happening again, rather than incapacitation in the prison system. Thoughtful probation officers know from their own experiences that offending behaviour is associated with many factors such as the individual's temperament, predispositions, family background, environmental factors, social circumstances, educational and employment opportunities, relative deprivation and poverty, lack of attachment and bonds to conventional society. But increasingly, since 1979, there have been political pressures at work to undermine this approach to probation practice by disconnecting behaviour from wider social factors that must be taken into consideration when making sense of people's lives. Attitudes have hardened; sentencers and sentences have become tougher; the probation approach undermined under the weight of pressure to punish, control and manage rather than constructively help. We have no wish to condone offending episodes; nor do we wish to be associated with a mindless approach to offending behaviour that suggests that factors outside the individual, including social circumstances, do not matter because it is plain that they do. In order to summon support for our position we turn to a number of studies that demand we locate human behaviour, and therefore probation practice, within a specific context of understanding. This is the approach advocated by, for example, Millar and Buchanan, who correctly state that an individual's circumstances are not simply a matter of choice, but also associated with social conditions (1995 p198).

Further Social Policy Issues

We have already alluded to social policy issues in previous chapters but we want to expand upon them here because of the political situation for probation during the mid-1990s. First, it is of interest to begin with a Durham University study in 1962–63 because it showed that unemployment rates amongst probation officer caseloads were higher than in the population as a whole, ranging from 20.1% to 32.6% compared with 4.0% to 9.1% (in Davies 1969 p65). Secondly, the research study conducted by Martin Davies (1969) found that, of 502 men in his study, 204 (40.6%) were unemployed.

Next, if we move into the 1990s we can refer to a significant report published by ACOP based upon research undertaken by a team of Lancaster University researchers (Stewart and Stewart 1993). When this research was underway the probation service in England and Wales had approximately 141,500 men and women under supervision. It describes the lifestyles of 1,389 young people aged 17–23 years who were being supervised by probation officers at the beginning of 1991 in Avon, London and the South, in addition to the North-East of England. This research provides an important insight into the world of probation after 12 years of Conservative governments, and shortly before the Howard reforms to the criminal justice system after 1993. Some of the main findings are:

- 36% of the 23-year-olds had experienced marriage/relationship breakdown.

- Accommodation problems emerged as an important issue, coupled with uncertainty for young people at a time in life when they needed parental guidance, thus making it more difficult to make the transition from being a teenager to adult status.

- When the national unemployment average rate was 6.7%, 20% of this sample was in waged employment; 9% on government schemes; 7% had caring responsibilities; but 64% were unemployed.

- Applying the EEC measure of poverty – that is, having less than 50% of the average income of a particular group – 72% were in poverty.

- 80% had left school with no qualifications.

- There were links between alcohol, drugs and offending.

- Financial motives were a factor in offending behaviour.

Therefore it was concluded that both social background and current social circumstances play a part in offending behaviour. In other words, if we are serious about understanding and explaining in order to address offending, we are forced to look beyond the notion of blaming the individual.

Then Mair and May (1997) had their research on *Offenders on Probation* published (N=1,213 comprising offenders on probation, combination orders, and some subject to separate probation and community service orders). They found that:

• Only 1 in 5 was employed compared to 60% of the general population.

• One fifth had been in a residential children's home.

• 70% were in rented accommodation.

• Two thirds were on benefit.

• About 50% had health problems.

• Again drink and drugs characterised the sample.

The most commonly discussed subject at the last supervision session between the probation officer and client was employment, yet the value of probation was to have someone to talk to so that probation was seen as quite useful. Furthermore, offending was perceived to be linked to peer pressure, money, boredom, unemployment, problems at home and lack of thought. Even though Mair and May add the caveat that those most critical of probation were not included in the survey, nevertheless the service was viewed favourably and relationships between probation officers and clients were generally positive. When reviewing the characteristics of the sample Mair and May conclude with a telling comment: 'In general, probationers appear to have a variety of needs and problems. Their characteristics are, on the whole, similar to those in custody – with both groups being very different from the overall population. Irrespective of how these characteristics are related to offending, the poverty and deprivation exhibited by those on probation is an important factor which is likely to have implications for supervision and should not be forgotten or dismissed' (1997 p30).

We can round off this discussion by including other material that the reader is invited to consider. Lord Scarman, when reporting on the Brixton disorders of 10th–12th April 1981, concluded that unemployment was a major factor underlying problems for black and white (Home Office 1981 p107). After considering a number of research studies, Steven Box (1987) comes to the conclusion that there are grounds for affirming a link between unemployment and crime, and between income inequality and property offences. David Downes (1997) also draws attention to the association between unemployment and crime. He qualifies the relationship by saying that we should not simply assume unemployment is a major cause of crime but rather that employment opportunities are important for reducing crime. The reader is also pointed in the direction of Brake and Hale who provide us with pertinent material (1992 pp111–115). Last of all we refer to Benyon (1994), encountered several times in this chapter already. When reflecting on the year 1993 he said that 'The real reasons for the current difficulties are, of course, to be found in the deep fractures and fissures in British society as a result of the policies and ideology of recent years under the Thatcher and Major governments. A fragmented society will have higher levels of crime and disorder than a consensual, less divided one. When people have despaired, little to hope for, and low levels of investment in society, crime is likely to increase' (1994 pp66–68).

By thinking about the social circumstances of offenders or, to put it another way, the totality of their lives as the context within which to explain offending behaviour, these research studies have implications for the response of government and of course probation services. In other words, confronted with research data on unemployment, accommodation, relationships, drugs, alcohol and other addictions, in addition to the knowledge and experience gleaned from working as probation officers with a specific client group, we think it is futile to base one's penal policy upon an approach replete with the emotive language of law, order, discipline, punishment, condemnation and incremental toughness. We are not sure how to confront or punish people into conformity by a stiff dose of something unpleasant. We understand the politics behind the rhetoric but it creates the conditions for thoughtless probation practice. Yet this was the situation for area services during the 1990s, explained by looking at a number of related areas.

Strengthening Punishment in the Community and Revised National Standards 1995

Only two-and-a-half years after the implementation of the Criminal Justice Act 1991 in October 1992, the Home Office published a Green Paper on *Strengthening Punishment in the Community* (Home Office 1995c). By this time it was being reasoned that 'Probation supervision is still widely regarded as a soft option' (p11) despite the repositioning of the service over recent years, even though it is acknowledged that this could be a misplaced perception. Nevertheless, government proposed a new integrated community sentence that would effect certain changes to how sentences are determined, by giving courts more control over the content of community sentences and greater flexibility that would result in more certainty of purpose and credibility. In other words, the proposal is for a single integrated sentence that would incorporate but also extend the existing range of community orders. Offenders would no longer be sentenced to a probation or community service order but 'the community sentence' that would have three main elements: reparation, restriction of liberty and the prevention of re-offending. The court would select from a range of options – a pick-and-mix approach from a menu of possibilities including:

- Supervision up to three years.

- Probation centre attendance.

- Community service.

- Specified activities.

- Compensation to the victim.

- Curfew.

- Ban on attending specified places.

- Ban on undertaking specified activities. *(Home Office 1995c p47)*

In each case the court would decide the extent of reparation, restriction of liberty and the prevention of re-offending commensurate with the seriousness of the offence. Furthermore, prior to the probation service preparing a pre-sentence report on an offender, the court would provide a steer to the report writer by indicating its preliminary indications concerning the purpose of sentence. Importantly, the new sentence would not require consent that had been a feature of the probation order since 1907 and subsequently other community orders.

We should also reinforce that the 1995 Green Paper makes several references to national standards that, following their appearance in 1992, were reviewed and revised between January and June 1994. According to Worrall, 'National Standards must also be seen as the government's attempt to make individual probation officers more accountable to management and management more accountable to government' (Worrall 1997 p72). The revised standards were introduced on 9th March 1995 and included, for example, an outline supervision plan in pre-sentence reports; 12 contacts in the first 3 months for probation orders; enforcement procedures that specified breach action after two unacceptable absences within a 12-month period (that is, two final warnings prior to intention to breach). Whilst *Strengthening Punishment in the Community* acknowledged that the 1995 standards had tightened up on the 1992 standards where enforcement practice is concerned, it proceeded to state the following at paragraph 10.6: 'Consideration has also been given to the possibility of enhancing enforcement procedures more directly by extending the powers of the supervising probation officer, so that the courts could authorise the supervising officer to punish early or minor failures to comply with a community sentence with an additional limited and clearly defined penalty. The argument for this option is that it would create a graduated response to encourage offenders to complete community sentences while preserving rigorous standards of enforcement and relieving the courts of the initial stages of the enforcement burden' (Home Office 1995c p40). We should make it clear at this point that the new form of sentencing proposed in the Green Paper was not introduced by government, nor were probation officers given further punitive powers to enforce orders. However, it may be observed that the Criminal Justice Act 2003 has in fact legislated for a new generic (pick-and-mix) community order that came into force in April 2005 and to which we turn in Chapter 7.

Before looking at the response to government's proposals for strengthening punishment in the community, Michael Howard's conference speech at Blackpool during the autumn of 1995 drew attention to the need to put honesty back into sentencing. This meant that the time served in prison was closer to the sentence passed by the court. Furthermore, he alluded to victim issues; longer sentences for sexual, violent and burglary offences, in addition to a call for minimum sentences for burglars and drug dealers that would culminate in the Crime (Sentences) Act 1997, popularly known as the 'two and three' strikes legislation. We will return to important items of legislation prior to concluding this chapter.

Preparing the Ground for Two Demonstration Projects

Coincidentally, as far as we are aware, a National Probation Conference was held in March 1995, organised by ACOP and the Central Probation

Council. The conference was inevitably captured by the Green Paper on *Strengthening Punishment in the Community*. It was the theme of advocating the significantly stronger involvement of sentencers in proposing the ingredients of a single integrated community sentence that exercised those who attended (Association of Chief Officers of Probation 2001). The ACOP review of the conference, published in 2001, suggested that Michael Howard was persuaded to take up the idea for a non-legislative route to strengthening punishment in the community, which culminated in two Demonstration Projects. Two further important conferences, one involving the judiciary and one the magistracy, were organised to test the strength of support for the non-legislative route. These initiatives seem to have tapped into a rich seam of resistance to yet more legislation and the feelings of sentencers were influenced by Mr Justice Garland, at this time President of the Central Council of Probation Committees. In his speech launching the Teesside Demonstration Project on 16th April 1997, he articulated the view that 'The genesis of the project lies in the 1995 Green Paper which was generally regarded as having gone too far by proposing that Sentencers could, when imposing a Community Sentence, in effect select a Chinese menu of restrictions and compulsions to achieve a preferred takeaway of restrictions of liberty, reparation and prevention of re-offending which they would then require the probation service to deliver … If we need a sound-bite it is "dialogue not dictation" when the Court is asking for a pre-sentence report and considering with the Probation Service what form of Community Sentence could be appropriate for the offender … A most encouraging aspect of the planning has been the breadth of consultation – something that has not always happened in the past and which was not conspicuous in the changes to Probation Officer training or in the origins of the Crime (Sentences) Act 1997, now in general election suspended animation' (Garland 1997; full text of speech in Teesside Probation Archive).

These carefully crafted comments were designed to be openly critical of the political processes that had made fundamental changes without genuine consultation. Whilst Mr Justice Garland, as President of the Central Council of Probation Committees, was close to the probation service, he was also reflecting widespread disquiet about certain attitudes associated with Home Secretary Howard. He also reinforced another important point in his speech when emphasising that sentencing should evolve from a dialogue between sentencers and the probation service. In doing so he was reinforcing a principle that can be traced back to some of the earliest thinking about the role of probation officers in court. Perhaps even more importantly, he was flexing the judicial muscle in reminding politicians that judges were unhappy with too much prescription from the centre.

Michael Howard deserves credit for listening to the views expressed in the 1995 conferences, and at the end of the consultation period in June of the same year the Home Office began to engage with the feedback they had received. By May 1996 they were able to produce a briefing paper: 'Community Sentence Demonstration Projects' (Teesside Probation Archive). This document was sent to one of the authors on 20th May 1996; it included an appendix on a research specification produced by the Home Office Research and Statistics Directorate in January of that year. The briefing paper explained the aims of the Demonstration Project, which were to work within the scope of existing legislation and offer sentencers more information, choice and flexibility, in order to tune sentences more closely to the wishes of sentencers in cooperation with probation. The other aim of the project, from which it gained its name, was to demonstrate changes in approach by sentencers and probation services which could be evaluated. Consequently, the Home Office Research and Statistics Directorate were involved from the outset and were ever present contributors to the many meetings that were to follow.

The reasons for the decision to choose Cleveland (Teesside) and Shropshire remain shrouded in mystery but in terms of geography, culture and crime profiles they were very different and therefore, it could be argued, offer important points of contrast. The Demonstration Project was established as a national initiative and after the first two meetings, at the Home Office, the National Demonstration Project Group was chaired by a judge, Sir Rhys Davies, from 17th July 1996. Effective networking by the Home Office had secured the support of all major players and the project was remarkable in bringing together government, probation and the judiciary in pursuit of a common purpose. The following bodies were represented on the National Steering Group of the Demonstration Project: The Home Office; Lord Chancellor's Department; Her Majesty's Inspectorate of Probation: the Magistrates' Association; the Justices' Clerks Society and the Law Society; Central Council of Probation Committees; the Association of Chief Officers of Probation; and the Probation Managers' Association. Although invited to participate NAPO decided not to support the Demonstration Project because they opposed the 1995 Green Paper (Letter from NAPO to the Home Office, 22nd May 1996; copy in Teesside Probation Archive).

Parallel to the above national arrangements, in Teesside and Shropshire local steering groups were created, each chaired by a senior judge. The local groups were, in effect, accountable to the national steering group, but the structure preserved a local flavour for each of the projects and this was discernible from the outset. They too were established with the intention of achieving inclusivity, reflected in their membership: Chairs of Benches; Clerks to the Justices; Chief Probation Officers; Chairs of the Probation Committees/Shadow Boards. A Home Office Probation Division representative also attended local steering groups alongside a representative from the Home Office Research Unit. The local groups had the responsibility to develop the project with the judge and Chief Probation Officer, with Home Office representatives attending the National Steering group meetings to report on progress. This structure cemented a high level of commitment signalled initially by the Home Secretary embracing the idea and the national group critically monitored progress of each of the local schemes, recognising the potential of a wider application of the scheme in due course.

It is not an exaggeration to say that the success of the scheme was dependent on commitment and enthusiasm in the local projects. The inclusive nature of the Steering Group structure promoted a free exchange of views (as one of the authors is able to provide personal testimony) so that, as the projects began, there was a sense in which the probation service was on the back foot. The clear message being promoted was that probation had to be more persuasive about the efficacy of community penalties, perhaps even to produce something innovative if it was going to be convincing (an echo here of research findings from ten years earlier; Whitehead 1988). From a probation perspective these were not unreasonable challenges, as many services had for quite some time recognised that in applying modern business-style thinking the courts were the customers of the probation service. Consequently, many services had invested heavily in what can only be described as public relations exercises, as a means of ensuring all sentencers were aware of all dimensions of community penalties. What the Demonstration Projects achieved was to challenge the 'silo' mentality that epitomised the workings of the criminal justice system. Exposure to a constant stream of repeat offenders and growing disrespect for the law had impacted on both sentencers and their legal advisers, therefore cynicism was understandable. The project now provided the opportunity for probation to spell out its approaches and sentencers were obliged to engage in a mutually educational dialogue.

Historically speaking, links can be forged here because what emerged was a return to the exchanges in courts between those early probation officers and justices as they too struggled to determine the most appropriate sentence for offenders and whether probation was suitable.

The idea emerged from the outset that sentencers should provide clearer sentencing expectations when commissioning pre-sentence reports, considered as influential documents (Hedderman et al 1999). This issue became the focus for some innovative thinking on Teesside and required a new process in court. It was agreed that the Bench would ask questions of the defendant and their legal representative to ascertain some basic information, which would facilitate the preparation of the report. As part of this process a questionnaire, or preliminary indications document, was to be completed by the commissioning bench which would be available to the sentencing bench, to build continuity into the sentencing process that would transcend changes to the personnel of the bench as the process unfolded. After completing the questionnaire the Bench would commission a report clarifying, as far as they could, the sentencing options they wished the probation service to comment on. This would be based on a non-binding initial view of seriousness and some early thinking about the key elements of restriction of liberty, reparation, and prevention of re-offending which had been proposed in the Green Paper. Similar arrangements were devised for use in Crown Courts, though it was recognised that in practice they were dealing with a different level of crime that would have an impact on the feasibility of community penalties. At the point of sentencing it was recognised that PSR proposals would have to be weighed against the expectations at the earlier commissioning stage. It was acknowledged that the emerging picture of an offender's lifestyle might be quite different from that envisaged at the commissioning stage because of information subsequently disclosed to the probation officer. Therefore, a second stage dialogue at the point of sentence, between the Bench and the officer presenting the report, including the defendant and counsel, was accepted as an important mechanism. This stage of the process also reflected the transient nature of modern court life and left the probation service with the responsibility of ensuring that if the reporting officer was not available to discuss matters with the Bench, then a suitable substitute would be briefed and available. As the questionnaire completed by the Bench commissioning the PSR was to be made available at the point of sentence, the sentencing Bench would also be able to weigh the initial thinking of its colleagues in determining the level of seriousness of the offence, a critical task within the sentencing framework created by the Criminal Justice Act 1991.

After developing this approach to sentencing, the local steering group established a process to ensure appropriate levels of training for all involved within the criminal justice system including sentencers, courts and probation. The training sessions were delivered by joint teams comprising court and probation staff. The development of this more structured and collaborative approach to sentencing placed an important responsibility on probation to ensure that the courts were fully informed of all features of community penalties. This resulted in the publication of a booklet to coincide with the launch of the Demonstration project on Teesside ('Strengthening Punishment in the Community: Community Demonstration Project', Teesside Probation Service, 1st April 1997). This booklet not only provided details of all community supervision programmes that had been developed and made available to the courts by the Teesside service over recent years; it also redefined the characteristics of the probation order in a way that reflected both good practice and the recently published National Standards. In both Shropshire and Teesside the projects were launched with a commitment (from all involved) to better communication throughout the whole of the sentencing process. This aspiration was sustained remarkably well throughout the entirety of the project, a factor reflected in the comments made to the National Steering Group.

There was also significant wider interest in the Demonstration Projects, illustrated by members of the Home Affairs Committee who were conducting an inquiry into alternatives to prison sentences because they visited Teesside on 31st March 1998. The Home Affairs Committee met members of the local project as well as taking the opportunity to look at some aspects of the local probation service's operations. The national and local steering groups continued to meet after the launch of the projects in Shropshire and Teesside, monitoring and commenting on developments and reinforcing the widespread commitment to the project. The final meeting of the national steering group took place on 15th February 1999 and was devoted to a discussion of the draft of the soon to be published Home Office research document (Hedderman et al 1999). The discussions were significant in that they appeared to influence a change to the final sentence in the conclusion. Originally it read: 'However, the projects also showed that simply encouraging sentencers, especially magistrates, to make more use of community sentences is unlikely to have a desirable impact on sentencing or to be cost effective, without stipulating that this should be in place of custody'. In the final version this was changed to: 'Whilst this (i.e. better communication between sentencers and probation) is undoubtedly an important first step in promoting community sentences, the results of the study suggest that this does not, by itself, lead to a significant increase in community penalties and the question of whether new legislation is required must be revisited' (Hedderman et al 1999 p69). We take the view that the subtleties here were significant. Just what was the desirable impact, and in whose terms? The final version of the research seems to have settled for simply posing the question as to whether or not new legislation was required. Perhaps most significantly, however, in the Foreword of the research document, the Head of the Offenders and Corrections Unit in the Home Office stated, 'The projects were successful in that they showed that more effective communication between the probation service and sentencers did lead to improved understanding. However, the projects also showed that simply encouraging sentencers to make more use of community sentences does not lead to significant changes in sentencing behaviour. The results suggest these changes require legislation' (piii).

By 1997 a new government was elected and the question may therefore be posed: What were the allegiances of the new government to the Green Paper (Home Office 1995) and in what way might they use the research? The growth in the prison population, a reflection of Michael Howard's 'prison works' philosophy, was clearly having an impact; it was also costly. But whatever the cost, the newly elected Labour government was no less determined to be tough on crime as the Conservatives and were probably as committed to spending whatever was needed to win the law and order debate. To us, two things are important here: first, both governments were determined to impose greater controls on sentencers; secondly, by the time the research was published New Labour had established a corrections unit in the Home Office and were prepared to use the Demonstration Project to promote their own aspirations. What is also significant is the way intelligence is absorbed and used by governments of different political persuasions to achieve their own objectives. The comments we have drawn attention to above, as the defined outcomes of the Demonstration Project, are in a sense sitting there to be used at some point. Just how they might be used is not clear, but for a government such as New Labour that initially appeared committed to use research to inform its decisions (the 'What Works' agenda), the potential to use the Demonstration Project for imposing greater control over sentencers and sentencing may be irresistible. These are themes to which we will return.

Having perused the Teesside archive on the Demonstration Project, we make a number of further observations before we conclude a lengthy yet important section in this chapter. It is important to acknowledge some of the differences between Shropshire and Teesside. At the start of the project the unemployment rate on Teesside was 14% compared to 7% in Shropshire; the national average was 8%. The recorded crime rate for Teesside was 14,058 per 100,000 population and for Shropshire 7,115, compared with a national average of 9,719. These statistics yield an insight into the different cultures of these two areas; whilst Shropshire has its pockets of serious deprivation, Teesside has greater social problems. The relationship between the probation services and their local sentencers was also different, with Teesside sentencers having a more sceptical approach to community penalties. It is against this background that we draw further conclusions. As a result of careful implementation of the project and efforts made to improve sentencers' appreciation of the real nature of community supervision, there was a 20% increase in the number of Teesside magistrates who thought that a probation order, without extra conditions, could contribute to the prevention of re-offending. There was a 50% increase in the number of magistrates who considered that the supervision of such orders was satisfactory. There were also marked improvements in the perceptions of Shropshire sentencers, significant because they started with higher levels of confidence.

These findings clearly indicate that better communication could improve understanding of the role of community supervision and what probation was attempting to achieve. The booklet published by the Teesside service took the opportunity to spell out the purposes of supervision in a way that could be expected to fulfil the expectations of sentencers. Supervision was quite properly portrayed as a proactive and challenging process, with clear expectations about levels of contact with offenders and breach action, reflecting both local developments and National Standards. Enforcement policy was explicit and sentencers could believe that Teesside probation officers would not collude with offenders if appointments were missed. The way in which the supervisory relationship challenged behaviour was put into the context of risk assessment and the way in which lifestyle issues, in other words wider social circumstances, might trigger re-offending. The nature of the training for the Demonstration Project provided sentencers with an opportunity to explore these issues and to judge for themselves the value of community supervision.

We would argue that the combination of written material and the training process shifted the opinion of sentencers whose exposure to the Teesside culture had made them a sceptical and sometimes harsh audience. Our own experience of the project also reinforced the view that there was a more negative perception of probation at the outset, as if probation alone was responsible for the behaviour of individuals who continued to commit offences. The results of the project underlined the potential of improved communication between the service and sentencers and the consequent development of insights into both the mechanisms of criminal justice and dynamics of human behaviour. The project also challenged the perceptions of the Justices Clerks' department, powerful people in the sentencing culture of magistrates' courts. These exchanges provided a foundation for the building of local confidence in the operation of the local criminal justice system. That had been a laudable aspiration at the birth of the project in 1995, but now the message was clear that this was no longer enough. Successive governments since 1979 had so politicised crime that the solution to the problem was a prize which only they alone could be seen capable of delivering. Success in future elections may depend on it. Consequently, there was a tension at the heart of the Demonstration Project and any pretext that the traditions of a local sentencing culture had value was now lost. What had started out as a joint exercise in an attempt to avoid further legislation in two local areas in April 1997 was eventually sacrificed to political expediency and new laws to control the process of sentencing. The Demonstration Project had set out to show whether or not better targeted community penalties and changes in sentencing practice could lead to more effective sentencing within existing legislation and resources. We believe the project achieved this objective and so are concerned that it was not more widely promoted; perversely, it was used to demonstrate that there was need for more legislation.

We conclude by referring to a helpful meeting (during April 2005) with the senior representative of the judiciary and now Recorder of Middlesbrough, Judge Peter Fox QC. He championed the Demonstration Project on Teesside and had a beneficial perception of it. He was also disappointed that it only lasted for one year on the grounds that it did not allow sufficient time to turn around a sentencing culture in the direction of increasing the use of community sentences as an alternative to custody. In his view this was short-sighted because the first year simply established solid foundations. It is lamentable that the Home Office required instant gratification within a political culture demanding quick results. If only the project could have been supported for another two years, is Judge Fox's regret.

Probation Training in Flux

Even though we can trace the origins of probation work to the religiously motivated police court missionaries in 1876, the system had to wait until 1930 for the first Home Office Training Scheme. By 1970 the Central Council for the Education and Training in Social Work (CCETSW) was created and became responsible for social work training of local authority social services, health service, education and probation (for a summary of the history of training in probation see Whitehead and Thompson 2004). In 1989 Dr David Coleman of Linacre College, Oxford, recommended that Home Office sponsorship should be removed from those probation courses deemed to be substandard in the provision of training for prospective probation officers. In other words, substandard courses were those that did not pay sufficient attention to the changing needs of a criminal justice rather than social work oriented organisation. In fact, more emphasis was required on legislation for probation officers, the penal system, criminology and sentencing. Following the Coleman Report (1989) the Home Office established a review of probation officer training in 1994, followed by government decisions about the future of recruitment and training on 2nd October 1995. By the autumn of 1995 it was decided that, in future, probation officers would not be required to hold a social work qualification. It was acknowledged that probation officers would continue to require some social work knowledge, along with other social workers. However, more emphasis was being placed on robust skills to change and correct offenders, in addition to enforcing orders. Moreover, government was not convinced that probation training needed to incorporate an academic qualification awarded by the universities. Rather, it was more appropriate for new recruits to undertake in-service, on the job training; practical experience rather than academic work; distance learning; and the incorporation of a National Vocational Qualification. It was envisaged that the new form of training being proposed would attract more mature students who would not need to attend university because they would bring relevant knowledge and experience to the job from the University of Life.

As one would have expected, concerns were expressed about cuts in sponsorship and detaching probation training from social work and higher education. To Ward and Spencer (1994) government proposals amounted to an attempt 'to cut costs and increase central control' (p97) and they cogently argued for probation training to remain part of social work education. Millar and Buchanan became quite exercised by what was going on and said that 'Probation officers are currently reeling from the latest Government directives which appear to confirm the intention to rip the social work heart out of probation practice' (1995 p195). Two years later they argued for the preservation of probation's social work identity (Buchanan and Millar 1997) on the grounds that probation officers work with disaffected and damaged people who are the victims of a harsh social climate. In such circumstances social work values and skills are required to engage with people and do the job effectively.

When the consultation period came to an end on 26th May 1995 the government had received almost 500 responses and two main concerns were: detaching training from social work and a university education; and, correspondingly, a decline in quality. Consequently, the debates over the future of probation training that had emerged during the 1980s, but were now more acute in the 1990s, reflected a significant tension between, on the one hand, the political agenda that was not conducive to probation being understood as a social work agency and, on the other hand, a probation sensibility that was historically oriented to an approach to practice grounded in welfare, social work values and skills. Notwithstanding these tensions and disquiet about the proposals, it was decided that Home Office sponsorship of the Diploma in Social Work would cease after the 1995/96 intake so that no new students would be sponsored from the autumn of 1996.

When Jack Straw became Home Secretary under a new Labour government, he announced his plans for probation service training on 29th July 1997 by stating that he wanted to establish a Diploma in Probation Studies that would be located in higher education after all (Home Office 1999). The new two-year training course would have three main elements: an academic component leading to a degree in community justice; on the job training; and an NVQ in community justice. He confirmed that the award would no longer be linked to social work education which had prevailed under the CQSW arrangements since the 1970s (Whitehead and Thompson 2004). The main focus of the training, and therefore probation work more generally, was public protection, reducing crime, and effective work with offenders that had a more criminal justice than social work orientation. The first intake of trainee probation officers under the new training arrangements was during the autumn of 1998, which meant that the service did not attract any newly qualified recruits from the universities between 1996 and 2000, a period of four years.[4] This hiatus in training was not helpful to the probation service; it did not contribute to probation's ability to achieve government objectives of preventing re-offending. It is interesting to speculate on what would have happened to probation training and the service as a whole if the Conservatives had been re-elected yet again in 1997. Furthermore, it may be argued that if you want to change the culture of an organisation you need to change the staff within it. Again we speculate on the degree to which this has occurred since 1998 because, by 2005, approximately 50% of probation officers in England and Wales had been trained by the Diploma in Probation Studies rather than the Diploma in Social Work regime. In 1997 Buchanan and Millar made a plea for probation to preserve its social work identity and therefore social work values. Therefore, we turn to an exploration of values prior to clarifying important legislative developments between 1992 and 1997 that have implications for probation.

Probation Service Values

From time to time in this book we allude to probation values. At this point we give this theme closer attention not only because the subject is important in its own right, but also because it became the focus of academic debate in the mid-1990s. We begin this more detailed examination by arguing that values have always been important in probation because the service has been preoccupied with people who offend, and with whom relationships must be established, rather than inanimate objects. A statement of values is inherent within the Probation of Offenders Act 1907 in its reference to 'advise, assist and befriend'. This can be interpreted as probation officers relating to probationers in terms of help and friendship rather than punishment, an important feature of supervision for many decades. Even though the Home Office did not abandon the notion of social work values in 1984 with SNOP, it is clear that the document had the potential to undermine the value base of probation because of the implication that some tasks were more important than others; political and economic priorities transcending the needs of individuals.

There is a strain of thinking in probation that has expatiated on values in the sense that offenders, as people, have intrinsic moral worth; ends and not means; they should be treated with decency and humanity. These values have been given practical expression in the attitude of care, concern, respect for persons, help and support, empathy and a deep understanding of the human condition. In fact it can be suggested that for many years the adage 'advise, assist and befriend' was a succinct expression of important values and attitudes in probation practice that practitioners shared with other branches of social work. Therefore, what we are underlining here is a core of professional ethics that has helped to motivate probation officers to do a difficult job and also sustain them during many years of service. Some of us would claim the existence of a moral imperative at the heart of probation practice in the sense that it is morally right that a group of people exist – that an organisation exists – to work with people whom we label as offenders within an ethical framework shaped by clear values. These values should not be understood solely in terms of their instrumental utility, as a means to an end, the 'end' being to prevent re-offending. Nevertheless, we rejoice when this is the outcome of our intervention. Rather, these values are an end in themselves because they have a moral claim upon practitioners that transcends their instrumental efficacy, quite simply because of the people-based nature of the profession. We should remind ourselves that in the wake of the disquiet posed by SNOP, values were important for area services, as Lloyd discovered in his research: 'Given the need to provide a cost effective service it would be well to acknowledge that human values cannot be assessed by financial methods of accounting alone' (1986 p63). Moreover, 'If practice does not fit comfortably with these values, then it is the practice which should be reviewed' rather than the values (p68).

Over the years, social work values have been defended and promoted by NAPO to its credit. We have also seen how the Joint Statement by NAPO, ACOP and the CCPC in 1987 included a statement of values when it referred to respect for persons, a belief in the freedom of individuals, a capacity to change, and humanitarian approaches to offenders, at a time when the politicians were developing punishment in the community. Also in 1987, Bill McWilliams articulated the features of the personalist school of probation work, contrasted with the radical and managerial schools, that finds an echo in the work of Hugman, who says that 'My general thesis is that action or service of any kind, whether by social workers … or whoever, has integrity and value only if it has regard to and respect for the unique capacities and talents of individuals' (1977 p14). Let us not forget that Robert Harris (1977) floated the idea that, if care and control were separated, then the probation service could provide a caring social work service to all offenders in need. It should be acknowledged that a number of probation officers, during the last 25 years, have tried to maintain a commitment to the doctrine of personalism when working with offenders. These values help to explain why we were attracted to probation work in the first place in that we wanted to earn our living working with people, who were also offenders, within a specific ethical framework. These values, we would argue, have both motivated and sustained; they have also underpinned a commitment to criminal and social justice. They have also animated and induced a passion for work with disadvantaged people, as well as making it clear that certain forms of behaviour are not acceptable. Therefore, there is nothing sentimental in our approach to probation values.

According to the story we have so far recounted, particularly during the years after 1984, it has been increasingly difficult to justify probation services to offenders solely on the basis of social work values (although the organisation has never been based solely upon social work values, as discussed in Chapter 1). This is because changes at different levels pressed themselves upon probation and have threatened these values, namely:

- A neo-right political culture less sympathetic to the plight of offenders after 1979.

- The centralising tendencies of SNOP prioritised certain categories of offenders for economic reasons.

- Neo-classical criminology emphasised individual responsibility for offending behaviour rather than the social context.

- The disenchantment with rehabilitation, treatment and social work.

- Accentuating the language of law and order, punishment in the community, deterrence, incapacitation and 'prison works', thus creating a harsher sentencing climate.

- The political message that something *more* than social work is required in probation from the mid-1980s which encouraged a tougher approach.

The Major–Howard axis from 1993 to 1997 was not conducive to social work values because of the emphasis on punishment and prison. We can also mention the politicisation of probation in the fight against crime that resulted in perceiving offenders as categories of risk to be managed, rather than people to be understood and helped.

These factors have combined to put social work values and the accompanying personalist approach within probation practice under considerable strain. In fact, their relevance and credibility have been questioned during the 1990s. It was within this context that the *Howard Journal* played host to a debate on probation values between academics, initiated by Mike Nellis (1995), quickly followed by rejoinders from Spencer (1995), James (1995), and then Masters (1997). We begin with Nellis's paper.

Mike Nellis (1995) pondered whether social work values, with their welfare orientation to advise, assist and befriend, had any relevance in the probation service of the 1980s and 1990s, with its new political, criminal justice and managerial culture. He develops the argument for three alternative values within the contemporary criminal justice system that he calls anti-custodialism, restorative justice and community safety, rather than the language of social work and welfare. This redefines probation as a criminal justice agency and penal reform lobby campaigning for change, as opposed to a social work agency. Spencer (1995) in his reply to Nellis argues that the service must continue to focus on the individual offender; express care and concern; see people as ends and not means; and in a humane manner provide help, maintain respect for persons and work for change with individuals. There are real dangers (as we have hinted at already) in the service being reshaped into 'a servant of increasingly authoritarian governments' (Spencer 1995); emphasising discipline, management, containment and control; depersonalising the job into something that is primarily engaged in surveillance through electronic tagging; a focus on law, order and punishment; thus constituting a range of emotive responses that are not particularly effective at crime control but simply expressive of vengeance at an emotional level. Moreover, the emphasis upon key performance indicators, revised national standards, objectives and quantitative targets, within a more bureaucratic and routinised service, has the potential to reduce staff to technicians based upon computations of various degrees of danger and risk. In such circumstances the value base of the service is no longer important because the person becomes lost in a mass of procedures and systems.

For some of us the social work values we inculcated during training have been undermined by political priorities for criminal justice since 1979, but also challenged by those clients we have worked with who have caused harm to others because of domestic burglary, violence and sexual offences. Paradoxically they have also been reinforced during the difficult years of the 1980s and 1990s when faced with the professional necessity to establish positive working relationships with people to promote rehabilitation. We must continue to asseverate that the heart of probation work is people, often difficult and damaged people, with whom we have to establish relationships. Both research and experience inform us that the quality of these relationships should be characterised by genuineness, warmth, acceptance, encouragement and approval, empathy, responsivity and sensitivity (Lishman 1994). Furthermore, the insights of Traux and Carkhuff (1967), alluded to and confirmed by David Smith (2004), affirm that the quality of the relationship between worker and client is of great importance, in fact as important as the content of supervision. To reiterate, this quality is defined by non-possessive warmth, concern and respect for persons (see also Biestek 1961). This is the value framework that can be expanded to include reasonableness, fairness, attention to tone and manner, thus providing the worker with moral legitimacy. In other words, clients are prepared to accept a direct approach and the use of authority, and will consent to such an approach provided it is exercised fairly. This is also conducive to promoting compliance, which will have positive benefits for all concerned in the process of supervision (Rex 1997).

Therefore, there is evidence to support the contention that social work values have an important role to play in probation practice, which suggests that practitioners should spend as much time thinking and learning about *how* to do the job, as learning about *what* to do (Whitehead and Thompson 2004 p207). Governments will continue to feel the political, ideological and electoral need to behave in a punitive manner towards offenders. By contrast, it is an inescapable fact that probation staff work with people within professional relationships, and it is the nature of these relationships that demands careful thinking about the nature of professional ethics and values; the promotion of criminal and social justice, including the moral claim of the offender on the worker. There is little doubt that the political climate of the 1993–97 period was unfavourable to social work values. Nevertheless, it is difficult for us to understand how an approach to offenders based upon punishment, an absence of understanding and empathy, and a tough approach to enforcement, could possibly be conducive to promoting compliance, the moral legitimacy of the worker, and rehabilitation. It may well be the case that the legislators and probation officers at the beginning of the probation system in 1907, by the way in which they resorted to the language of 'advise, assist and befriend', understood something important that has been threatened but not completely destroyed over recent years (Oldfield 2002). Probation officers require a clear value base to enable them to formulate intelligent and balanced judgements and make decisions in complex situations. This is the value base that facilitates care for individual offenders but also the victims of crime and public protection (Ward and Spencer 1994). Additionally, an appreciation of the social circumstances of offenders we considered above, as one of the subjects of probation training, should result in an attitude of care and compassion because offenders can be victims too (Millar and Buchanan 1995). We return to this theme in the final chapter as we explore the nature of the probation ideal.

Legislation

So far in this chapter we have referred to the Criminal Justice Acts of 1991 and revisions of 1993. We should also give an airing to other legislation. The Criminal Justice and Public Order Act 1994 (CJPOA 1994) introduced Secure Training Orders for 12–14-year-olds; revised bail law; and redefined the right to silence. It also gave police forces the powers to deal with hunt saboteurs, raves and new age travellers (alluded to in Michael Howard's conference speech in 1993), which alarmed civil liberties groups. Previously the 1991 Act included provision for the introduction of the curfew order supported by electronic monitoring. The CJPOA 1994 enabled the curfew order to be implemented and pilots were conducted during 1995. Importantly, and to repeat, the 1991 Act anticipated an increase in the volume of pre-sentence reports, with obvious implications for probation resources. In fact, the 1991 Act made it mandatory for courts to obtain a report prior to imposing a custodial and community sentence. However, paragraph 40 of Schedule 9 to the CJPOA 1994 gave the courts more discretion to dispense with the requirement to request a report from the probation service on offenders aged 18 and over. Andrew Rutherford makes it clear that the 'Criminal Justice Act 1993, which amended core sections of the 1991 legislation and the Criminal Justice and Public Order Act 1994, put the statutory seal' on the dramatic change of direction that occurred under Mr Major and Mr Howard (1996 p128).

In 1997 we see the appearance of the Protection from Harassment Act, in addition to the aforementioned Crime (Sentences) Act 1997 (C(S)A 1997). We should say a little more about the latter. The Crime (Sentences) Act 1997, with its commitment to mandatory minimum sentences, advocated life imprisonment for a second violent or sexual offence; seven years for a third offence of trafficking Class A drugs; and three years for a third offence of dwelling house burglary. This is the American-inspired two and three strikes legislation. These ideas surfaced at the Conservative party conference during the autumn of 1995 and New Labour did not demur. Windlesham makes the telling comment that the 1997 legislation had more to do with electoral considerations than carefully considered, thought through, and dispassionate law-making (2001 p51) based upon wide-ranging consultation. New Labour probably did not oppose it for the same reasons (Cavadino and Dignan 2002 p106). By contrast, the judiciary did not want this mandatory sentencing framework because of restrictions imposed on the principle of judicial independence. Importantly, s 38 of the C(S)A 1997 made the principle of consent, in existence since 1907 where the probation order is concerned, irrelevant prior to imposing a community sentence. So the proposal found in the 1995 Green Paper was at last put into effect by 1997. Finally, the Sex Offender Act 1997 established a sex offender register to keep track of sex offenders.

Summary and Conclusion

Developments surveyed in this chapter take their bearing from the Major–Howard political/penal axis that overturned the anti-custodial approach of Douglas Hurd, David Faulkner and John Patten, notwithstanding the bothersome rhetoric of punishment in the community. In fact, the measured, fundamentally decent and humane approach pursued by David Faulkner, was no longer *de rigueur* and he left the Home Office (joined in 1959) to continue his career at Oxford University in 1992. The years 1992–97 were allowed to become a punishment frenzy of escalating imprisonment that shows no sign of abating as we complete this book in 2005. It could have been so different if the 1991 Act had been given a chance but the combined weight of the police; judicial anxiety; senior politicians; and government's need to counter the 'progress' being made by Labour on law and order; meant that its original intentions were compromised (Rutherford 1996 p127).

Within this deteriorating penal policy context, the first probation three-year plan in 1992 superseded the SNOP document of 1984, so there was no let-up in the shaping of the future by the centre, as cash limits cogently illustrates. Further developments in the form of key performance indicators, in addition to the language of measurable objectives and targets, demonstrated that the service was increasingly understood from a bureaucratic-business rather than people-based perspective. We have discussed the important social policy context of probation work and reflected on the nature of values. Finally, we have alluded to the importance of the Demonstration Project and the disastrous implications of not training new recruits for a period of four years. Consequently, by this stage we can identify a number of recurring themes that have resonance in this book. These include changing governance structures; a harsher penal climate; social policy issues; and the inexorable march of centrally determined managerial, bureaucratic and quantitative systems of measurement and control. On the latter point, the last two chapters make it clear that probation work was being reduced to a narrow range of evaluative criteria to measure its activities. Unfortunately this approach does not sit well with the people-focused nature of the job, which must find a place for qualitative, ethical and ineffable features that cannot easily be measured. However, at long last the increasingly difficult years that began in 1979 were at an end because the Conservatives were voted out of office after 18 years in 1997. Therefore, our next chapter looks at the period of New Labour, initially with some relief and optimism.

NOTES – Chapter 5

[1] John Major's assessment of Kenneth Clarke and Michael Howard are instructive. First, 'Kenneth Clarke, the new Home Secretary, was a bruiser well able to meet the challenges of one of the toughest jobs in government. A liberal by instinct, he could be totally blood-minded, which was ideal for the hard-headed reforms to the justice system that I wanted to implement' (Major 2000 p308). Where Michael Howard is concerned he said that 'For me, Michael's contrasting qualities made him the right candidate for the HO – an ambitious, able politician who knew his way around the criminal justice system and who relished an argument. With his distrust of orthodoxy he was happy with the idea that I expected him to work closely with me and with my Policy Unit to raise the profile of our fight against crime ... By October 1993 Michael was able to use the party conference platform to signal a radical break with the past consensus on criminal justice' (Major 2000 p389).

[2] Mr Howard's 27 points on law and order in the autumn of 1993 were:
1. Abolishing the right to silence without adverse court comments.
2. Allowing the police to take DNA samples from all offenders.
3. Creating a Criminal Cases Review Authority to investigate possible miscarriages of justice.
4. Extending Attorney General's right of appeal against lenient sentences.
5. Removing judges' mandatory warnings about evidence in rape trials.
6. Introducing a new offence of witness intimidation.
7. Creating a system of parish constables.
8. Clarifying police powers to set up road blocks to deter terrorists.
9. Tougher laws against squatters.
10. Issuing guidelines to limit repeat cautioning.
11. Improving help for victims and witnesses.
12. Cutting back of police paperwork.
13. Restoring police powers to set bail conditions.
14. Stopping the presumption of bail for people alleged to have offended on bail.
15. Prohibiting bail for people charged with homicide or rape if they have previous convictions for such offences.
16. Introducing new offence of gathering information to assist terrorism.
17. Excluding from jury service people remanded on bail.
18. Granting courts the power to revoke bail if new information emerges.
19. Allowing retrials where juries have been 'nobbled'.
20. Establishing new offence of suspicion of possessing items for terrorism.
21. Giving the police new powers to stop trespassers and hunt saboteurs.
22. Building six new private prisons.
23. Introducing urine testing in prisons to test for drug use.
24. Setting up secure training centres for persistent 12–14-year-old offenders.
25. Doubling of maximum sentence to two years for 15–16-year-old offenders in young offender institutions.

26. Tightening community service orders to ensure they represent proper punishment.
27. Undertaking review of community sentences in 1994.

3   In 1990 the rate of unemployment in Cleveland was 13%, more than twice the national average (Martin 1989). Furthermore, there were acute divisions within Cleveland in relation to unemployment, ill-health, mortality, poverty and other forms of disadvantage. In fact, half the county was affluent and half disadvantaged. Changes initiated by the Social Security Act 1988 had an adverse impact on many people in Cleveland and some of us in probation provided evidence to support the view that clients were suffering from poverty and inequality. Finally, by relating the location of probation caseloads with areas of disadvantage in Cleveland, Whitehead (1992) discovered that whilst 36.6% of the Cleveland population lived in areas of very high, high and medium disadvantage in 1990, by contrast 81.6% of clients (N=1,781) known to the Cleveland Probation Service lived in these areas of disadvantage.

4   The following comments by David Downes are worth including: 'Basic to the whole strategy of decarceration was a much enhanced role for probation, community service, mediation, reparation and a host of community programmes for training ex-offenders in work skills, anger management and the like. This strategy has been severely damaged by the government's cuts in funding and by the cessation of probation training in the universities' (1997 p9). We might also add, for good measure, the Major–Howard axis and the doctrine of 'prison works' since 1993.

Chapter 6

NEW LABOUR AND PROBATION: 1997 TO THE NATIONAL PROBATION SERVICE 2001

'Like so much in New Labour's modernised public sector, the NPS (National Probation Service) is a quintessentially managerial achievement, shaped far more by contemporary political styles, and the requirements of accountability and cost-effectiveness than criminological theory or research. The Probation Service entered the twenty-first century in a form that would have been unrecognisable, unimaginable to those who developed it in the late nineteenth and early twentieth centuries ...' *(Chui and Nellis 2003 p10)*

'That Labour took the decision to continue Michael Howard's incarceration binge is one of the blackest marks against the government's record on social justice.' *(Kennedy 2005 p283)*

Introduction

Looking back it was unwise to read too much into, and therefore draw political implications from, the unrestrained rejoicing that heralded the election of a reconstructed Labour government on 1st May 1997, particularly from within the probation service. The seeping 'Gradgrind' of cash limits and perniciousness of Michael Howard in abolishing the social work qualification for probation officers, had taken their toll, and the service had acquired a siege mentality. The election of New Labour was seen as an answer to those still holding a torch for liberal ideals, who believed there would be a return to old-style values that included care, compassion and of course social justice. The euphoria, reflected in the new government's massive majority, is difficult to capture retrospectively, partly because it seems like an admission of political naivety. But there was a degree of unrestrained rejoicing promoted by the belief that the service would at last be freed from the negative scrutiny that it had endured for such a long time. The rejoicing was short-lived, however, because the rhetoric about crime did not change and, by July 1997, Jack Straw, the new Labour Home Secretary, announced the Prisons–Probation review, which signalled unease with the probation service. The possibility of perdition remained on the political agenda.

173

Perhaps a more careful reading of New Labour's manifesto and Tony Blair's personal comments about crime would have provided greater insights and therefore better preparation for what was to come. But the probation service had still not developed an acute sense of political awareness. The National Association of Probation Officers had established its own brand of political commentary in pursuit of its aspirations as a campaigning union, but beyond this the service spoke in a fragmented whisper. Part 2 of this book has painted a picture of changing social values, thus suggesting that the 1990s stand out as an era of acute politicisation of the probation service, as crime became a defining electoral issue, reflected in continuous media rhetoric that was often unbalanced. In this unhelpful climate, probation had neither the political acumen nor the sophisticated networks necessary to influence public opinion, which was still being driven by the negative yet populist perceptions created by the Thatcher years, which were to cast a long shadow (Sargeant 2005). It was the election of a Labour government so glaringly short of socialist values that rammed home the fact that the social and moral climate had changed irrevocably. Probation was now swimming against a reactionary tide and was about to be swamped. It was to be a painful drowning.

Our purpose in this chapter is to unravel the impact of the New Labour political agenda on probation through a review of significant events in its first term. Whilst doing this it is important to remember that probation should not be seen as a complete entity (see discussion in Chapter 2); it continued to comprise 54 separate services and a number of representative bodies, all of which were part of a continuous yet fragmented dialogue. This silo-like structure did not facilitate good communication and the problems were exacerbated further by the characteristics of the machinery of government. Before developing a number of themes, we think it is first of all helpful to contrast the notion of Old and New Labour, which will help to ground this chapter.

From Old to New Labour

From 1945 to the mid-1970s there was what has been described as a social democratic consensus between the two main political parties, Conservative and Labour, in relation to public spending; state provision of health, welfare and educational services; social services, housing and social security. Moreover, the state had an important role to play in economic management to achieve full-employment. Chapter 3 made the point that this post-war political consensus extended to crime policy as well. It is worth reminding ourselves that during the 1970s and 1980s old Labour continued to think that crime was associated with poorly socialised and maladjusted individuals and families who, on the whole, needed help rather than punishment. This approach embraced the view that there was a link between wider social circumstances, poverty, deprivation and crime that could be ameliorated by a welfarist, rehabilitative approach. It was Thatcherism during the 1980s that challenged this world view of crime and wider social factors, which resulted in the emergence of a Conservative criminology (Brake and Hale 1992 p5f and 147f). It was against the background of Thatcherism that new rather than old Labour was forced into fashioning a different political response to troublesome offenders. To put it crudely, if the Conservatives were tough on crime and criminals then New Labour must be even tougher.

New Labour won the general election held on 1st May 1997 with a massive majority of 179 seats. However, Anthony Seldon (2004) explains in his comprehensive biography of Blair that before the victory at the polls in 1997 certain issues were becoming important: individual responsibility as well as rights; the market; victims of crime; and modernisation. Consequently, during the 1990s the New Labour leadership modernised its thinking on crime that, to some degree, brought it into line with the Thatcher and Major years, in order to eschew any electoral criticism that they were the offenders' friend. It could be said that the demands of political expediency, rather than principle, forced change. In 1992, after Labour's fourth consecutive election defeat to the Conservatives, Tony Blair was appointed shadow Home Secretary. By 1993 it is reported that John Smith, who was now the leader of the Labour party, was concerned that Mr Blair was too punitive in his approach to crime (Seldon 2004 p180). The politically expedient view was emerging due to pressure being applied by the constituents of Labour members of Parliament that the focus should be on victims of crime rather than the criminal. Furthermore, a shift was required in New Labour thinking from blaming wider social conditions to blaming the individual. Therefore, from 1992 to 1994 as shadow Home Secretary and then between 1994 and the eve of the election in 1997 when Mr Blair was leader, there is some evidence to suggest that a more punitive, moralistic and authoritarian approach emerged from within the New Labour project that was more in tune with new-right and neo-liberal conservatism than the welfare socialist tenets of old Labour (Driver and Martell 1998; Oldfield 2002; Seldon 2004).

Whilst it is possible to compliment New Labour for its investment in public services and commitment to health and education, in addition to its concern with social exclusion, from our point of view it is difficult to be as sanguine when reflecting on its attitude towards the clientele of the probation service. Driver and Martell made a statement and posed a question: 'Labour is less social democratic. And it certainly looks more moralistic and conservative than in the past – but more socially authoritarian?' (1998 p120). This question is intriguing because we will argue below that the phenomenon of New Labour is certainly more punitive and authoritarian compared to old Labour; it has embraced conservative attitudes; it has even proceeded beyond the Conservatives on the continuum of toughness. To some degree this can be readily understood because a tougher and more punitive attitude towards offenders is tantamount to better and more popular electoral politics, but not necessarily more effective probation work. It can be argued that by the 1990s both Conservative and Labour politicians were in a mess of their own making with their similar crime policies, because they had become trapped in a 'cycle of punitiveness' from which they could not extricate themselves. There is a clear pattern of behaviour.

Modernising Probation

Lord Windlesham (2001 p238) says correctly that Labour's modernisation programme as applied to probation had three main elements. First, greater emphasis was placed on enforcement. In fact, it was during the 1998–2001 period that Paul Boateng, as a Home Office minister, repaired to the language of probation as a law enforcement agency by saying 'It is what we are: it is what we do' (Boateng 1999). Consequently, the 2000/02 National Standards tightened up the 1995 standards on breach proceedings. Secondly, the 54 separate areas services were reorganised on 1st April 2001. In fact it is more accurate to say that all the services were nationalised but also rationalised into 42 areas under the control of probation's first national director Eithne Wallis. Thirdly, and also from 1st April 2001, the Family Court Welfare Service that had existed as an integral component of probation became the Children and Family Court Advisory and Support Service (CAFCASS) under the control of the Lord Chancellor's department. Finally, we could go on to mention the creation of Youth Offending Teams from 1999/2000, following the Crime and Disorder Act 1998, which meant that probation services would no longer have responsibility for juvenile offenders (14–17-year-olds); and the creation of 'What Works' modernised probation thinking on rehabilitation. We will expand on some of these themes as this chapter unfolds. Before doing so we need to take our time as we persist with certain reflections on the 1990s.

Further Reflections on the 1990s: Home Office Civil Servants and the Machinery of Government

The Home Office's links with and interests in probation are longstanding and have a structural duality. One facet is the governance arrangements for the probation service, related to the discharging of the government's responsibility for public expenditure. The other facet is through the process of developing penal policy, historically by the work of departmental committees for which the Home Office provided services as a secretariat in addition to civil servants (Rutherford 1996). Our view that the 1990s was a significant decade for probation is reinforced by the way in which Home Office structures and consequently communication changed during this period. In 1990, oversight of probation affairs was being handled by the Home Office through a division of the Criminal Justice and Constitutional Department, headed by an under-secretary of state, a relatively senior civil service appointment. Within this government department existed the Probation Division, which was led by another civil servant who was subordinate to the under-secretary of state. The Division was responsible for the day-to-day oversight of probation and comprised a range of units, each overseen by other civil service staff. Much of the interface between the Home Office, 54 area services, and the representative bodies, was handled by the head of the Probation Division and his staff. The civil servants in the division, operating at a variety of levels and seniority, and in a variety of administration units, also transacted operational matters. The under-secretary had less of an everyday presence but did front what might be described as key events. A feature of these events, and present in the general dialogue, was exposure to the typical constructs of civil service language which couches issues in terms which relate to the wishes of ministers. These attempts to speak the mind of ministers would create a reminder of the television programme 'Yes Minister' and at times it was possible to be transported to this televisual alternative to reality. We recognise that constitutionally there is an obligation for civil servants to carry out the lawful wishes of ministers, which is central to our democratic processes. However, it is worth speculating on the degree to which these constitutional dynamic and, in turn, democratic processes were adversely affected in the Home Office of the 1990s, as the future of the probation service was being politically reshaped.[1]

Ministers, with a desire to control public expenditure on one hand and to get tough with offenders on the other, must have found the probation service both frustrating and tantalisingly beyond their control; in some analysts' terms, irredeemably unaccountable. Whilst the Home Office was investing in a major share of the service's finances and attempting to steer both policy and practice from the centre, constitutionally it was still possible to use a local interpretation of national priorities in defining how the money was spent. Equally, decisions about practice, despite national standards, still had a significant element of local discretion. In the 1970s, as we saw in Chapter 2, community service had been developed in a way which allowed a good deal of local freedom because government recognised that the legislation was a skeleton that required clothes. But the New Labour government in 1997 had a different philosophy and there was an aspiration for centralised control that had not been anticipated but was reinforced by every contact. We were to see a government of unexpected ruthlessness in its desire to stamp its will on the country and, despite anxieties about a second term, which was buoyed and unrestrained by its large majority. As ministers began to articulate tougher messages about their expectations of probation, senior civil servants were effectively a buffer between the contestants.

A more unexpected phenomenon of New Labour was the perceived abandonment of the welfare principle in both social policy and criminal justice. The creation of a Social Exclusion Unit which had a probation representative did not mask the real politik that its political success depended on retaining the goodwill of the tabloid press which represented the values of Thatcherism. Therefore, the idea of probation was under threat. In a gentler age dialogue, debate and even differences were acceptable, but these conventions were changing and with increasing rapidity. The pressure put on civil servants to talk tough to the service in order to persuade or now force it to move into line with the political rhetoric must have been intense. How they coped with this personally would have been through a combination of their own skills as communicators, the perceived conventions of their role and their own personal constructs. A picture emerges of dynamic tension that would be discharged through the many transactions between the Home Office and the probation service over the coming months and years.

Another important issue for probation was that, within the political debate about crime, it had become identified as somehow being responsible for single-handedly failing to prevent individuals from offending. A close analysis of all those factors associated with criminality would suggest there is not one causal factor, as we have indicated in this book, but in the eyes of certain politicians probation was part of the problem rather than the solution. It was this issue that led to the What Works debate and a misguided strategy, largely through the initiative of the Chief Inspector of Probation, to develop intensive supervision programmes. The idea was that such a strategy could deliver a reduction in offending for a fixed investment in the provision of programmes. The research done on this initiative clearly indicated that the programmes in themselves, no matter how close to the protocol they were faithfully delivered, would not be effective without appropriate changes in the social circumstances of those offenders engaged in the programmes. This fundamentally flawed initiative captured the imagination of the politicians and the civil servants in the Treasury whose single *raison d'être* is to put a price on everything.

In attempting to understand these dynamics we need to remember that the Home Office too, like any organisation, has its own culture and norms. These influence the outlook of individuals in their respective roles, not only in terms of behavioural norms but also interpersonal dynamics, in addition to other factors such as personal aspirations for career advancement. Above all, the civil service is an extremely hierarchical organisation, which has a profound impact on every transaction conducted by each single individual drawn from its ranks. This controlling and loyal arm of the government machine was attempting to engage with local probation areas, a disparate range of people who remained both individualistic and deeply sceptical. As a government department, the Home Office was responsible for many aspects of the country's social life, famously including the control of dangerous dogs. A department that has responsibility for dog licences and the licences of dangerous criminals leaving prison has a rich portfolio indeed.

Civil servants had to cope with these issues in an apparently even-handed way and with requisite grace. Many inputs by senior civil servants into the probation arena were indeed graceful, although there were some delightful occasions when the mask was allowed to slip. One under-secretary of state famously told the story that the government of the day was using rats in experiments. However, the story proceeded with the embellishment that the government was also using civil servants in experiments too as there were things that rats would not do! The same individual quoted from Niccolo Machiavelli's renaissance *Prince* (published 1532).[2] Moreover, when pandering to the perceived need for informality at a probation gathering, he sported a rugby jersey over his pinstripe trousers. These rare glimpses of humanity reassured probation that there were attempts within the government machine to balance the politics of crime. Nevertheless, as the 1990s wore on and personnel inevitably changed, there were fewer lighter-hearted moments. There was an undercurrent of how politicised civil servants might become and, indeed, how impartial would they remain; dialogue with the Home Office, both formally and informally, became bleaker. There was a growing sense that probation had few supporters and that the agenda for the future was disconcertingly uncertain. The climate of uncertainty did not facilitate the task of managing local services any easier, and the morale of a hard-working and committed workforce was taken for granted at the centre. The most ironic aspect of all was that none of the civil servants and few ministers had any real experience of managing organisations and their operations. This created a credibility gap with chief probation officers who, in turn, became identified in Home Office culture as 'the un-clubbable'.

Dialogue between Home Office and Probation

Dialogue between area services and the Home Office took many forms. There was a tradition that the Home Secretary attended the Central Council of Probation Committees' AGM, and there was usually a sighting at the ACOP AGM. There was always a likelihood that a junior minister might attend as a substitute, but would be 'on message' with the government's agenda. Junior ministers might also undertake visits to areas and attend conferences and have specific meetings with officers of ACOP or CCPC. The under-secretary and head of division would also attend specific meetings or training events. Invariably, there was also a consultation process about specific issues which would involve civil servants in dialogue with the full range of the services' representative bodies. The written word was also a major form of communication through Home Office Circulars which together with legislation continued to provide the legal framework for operations within areas. This melange of formal and informal communication, open to constant interpretation, misrepresentation and questioning within areas, was the mechanism used for the fundamental changes that lay ahead. It should be acknowledged that this fragmented and increasingly politicised process was far removed from the deliberations and gestations of a departmental committee from 1909 to 1962 (see Chapter 2).

It is tempting to speculate about the personal position of civil servants responsible for the interface with the service whom we imagine were attempting to do their jobs honourably. Even though they were important messengers we speculate upon how effective they were in representing the views of chief officers in touch with the day-to-day operations in areas. But the 'get tougher' messages being received from the government were growing palpably more strident, even if sometimes softened or even obscured by the message-carrying civil servants. Equally, the aspirations of chief officers to persuade the government about the social and operational realities were subject to the same dissembling communication process. Communication between areas and the centre had been particularly difficult during the Howard era, which led some chief probation officers privately to question just how accurately their views were represented through the civil service machinery. It was a time during which suspicion arose and at one point the Probation Division Head was prompted to remark that whilst he may not be the service's best friend, he was the best friend that the service had.

Another change occurred just before the coming to power of New Labour when, in 1996, the traditional Home Office structure that dealt with probation was refined. A Criminal Policy Directorate was created within the Home Office and the Under-Secretary of State was re-designated the Director of this new department. The Probation Division became a Unit retaining a Head who was responsible to the new Director. In 1998 a further role was created in the Home Office structure – Director of Sentencing and Correctional Policy – which was in addition to the Director of the Criminal Policy Directorate. A Prisons–Probation Review Project Board was serviced by the new Directorate and there was support from the Head of the Probation Unit, who also took responsibility for the 'Modernisation Team' when it was established in 1999. The developing climate of mistrust as we moved through the 1990s might have been explained as a manifestation of Conservative negativism, but it was not relieved by the advent of New Labour. Moreover, communications between the Home Office and area services were destined to remain confused, uncertain and tainted by suspicion. The informal messages which suggested that services were under-performing continued unabated, and the implied threat to the service was soon to be realised with the announcement of the Prisons–Probation review.

There were other early indications of the position of New Labour with regard to criminal justice and in the previous chapter we devoted some time to reviewing the Demonstration Project. This particular exercise tantalisingly indicated that the political will of even the most reactionary Home Secretary was still open to influence. However, the Labour Home Secretary from May 1997 was not persuaded that sentencers and local probation services could be trusted to define the sentencing climate. His view was that more legislation was needed to provide a framework for sentencing, an early indication of an aspiration to establish more central control over the sentencing process itself.

Within the Association of Chief Officers of Probation during the 1990s there were stirrings by those who saw power and control shifting to the centre. If probation was to be influenced by its own values and culture then it had to be achieved through some tangible action. It was clear to some that chief probation officers needed to move more assertively into a leadership role as an antidote to centralism, and to assert probation's position in the criminal justice system. Although not apparent to all, a climate created by a series of measures, beginning with SNOP in 1984 and embellished by cash limits and national standards, was to be reinforced by a national programme of Quality and Effectiveness Inspections to be implemented by HMIP. The need for services to be led and to be seen to be led and rigorously managed was now palpable. It was the ACOP Management Training Sub-Group (MTSG), which had been promoting management training and development for some time, that came up with the idea of a conference for senior managers devoted to leadership. This proposal was not without controversy because it was an attempt to set an assertive proactive agenda that required all chiefs to be able to recognise that issues of performance would not go away and that leadership was now a requirement.

Cranfield Leadership Conferences 1997 to 2001

The fragmented nature of the services' structure and leadership, an undoubted strength in an innovative past, became an impediment in a political era in which centralisation, as opposed to small is beautiful, had become a compelling aspiration. Democracy and individualism were also central components in an area service's culture, where the concept of collective responsibility could be perceived as inimical. Those who grasped the management agenda were therefore viewed with suspicion and risked an authoritarian label. It was against this background that the first Leadership Conference was planned by ACOP's MTSG, held in February 1997. Whilst it was largely an ACOP initiative it had the support of the Home Office. The Cranfield

Conferences ran from 1997 to 2001, thus neatly spanning the years covered by this chapter, and we are going to review them sequentially because they provide an important barometer of change within the service. Cranfield University was chosen as the venue because of its management school of proven reputation and links with probation through its public sector leadership programme; it could also provide good resources in conference planning.

The first conference carried the title 'Leadership and Cultural Change' and was attended by 96 delegates. Most Chief Probation Officers attended in addition to representatives from the Home Office, including the Head of the Probation Division. The conference's timetable concentrated on strategy development in probation and was intended to provide a theoretical framework for individuals to take back to their areas. It also endeavoured to create greater cohesiveness in the chief officer group with inputs on leadership in times of change and an exploration of the concept of stakeholder value. Whilst the Home Office made a significant financial contribution, it was ACOP that provided the organisational umbrella, to some degree a reflection of the commitment to promoting awareness of leadership issues.

In fact this was to become a more explicit issue for the second event. Roger Statham the Chair of ACOP's MTSG, working with Peter Trusler, its Secretary, developed the agenda with Cranfield staff and with the support of the ACOP leadership. Planning for the second event began in the autumn of 1997 and the conference was held on 6th–7th May 1998, just one year after the election of New Labour. The Prisons–Probation Review, announced by the new government soon after its election in 1997, was seen as a critical environmental factor, in addition to the comprehensive spending review, local area autonomy, over-regulation, and the political climate. It was decided to hold the event for chiefs only, with a small and politically necessary representation from the Home Office and CCPC. Experience from the previous year and the growing threat to the service added an extra dimension to the leadership debate. Cranfield 1997 had produced an outcome which suggested that chiefs were prepared to work more cohesively, an issue of great significance. The major breakthrough at the 1998 conference was the empowerment of the ACOP Chair, Howard Lockwood, to speak on behalf of the service when dealing with the Home Office and other major players during his year of office. This was a significant event in service history and one of the groups at the conference suggested that a quorum of 36 CPOs might empower a decision. Another group suggested that a standing conference of CPOs should be established to decide a clear position on national issues.

The sense of change for the service was so palpable that planning for the third Cranfield conference began almost immediately and it was subsequently held on 5th–6th May 1999. The Prisons–Probation review was still ticking away in the background, holding the service in a kind of hypnotic trance, and going through a largely bogus process of consultation. However, the review and the changes that it heralded were already seeping into the consciousness of the service and there was a palpable sense of a fatalistic drift towards the inevitable. The other big issue was the government's determination to maintain its political credibility by strictly controlling public expenditure, and the impact that this was having on the service operationally was by then a major preoccupation. In a planning group held on 15th January 1999 it was reported by the Home Office representative that the financial situation was dire and that there were threats to the funding of management training in probation. The planning group was urged to devote some time to the concept of 'Best Value', the government's latest mechanism to ensure the delivery of value-for-money services. These were the issues that were to shape that event.

Therefore, the third Cranfield event, called 'The Modern Probation Service: Successfully Delivering Best Value Through Cultural Change', had a target audience of Chief Officers and another member of their senior management team. It was an attempt to explore some of the political pressures driving the service and, through the delegates, to ensure that the messages of the conference were relayed back to areas. The objectives of the conference were: (1) to enable Chief Officers to explore the political environment driving the Probation Service; (2) to understand the implications of Best Value and Business for local business planning; (3) to develop strategies for the promotion of a performance culture in local services. Speakers at the conference gave insights into the government's approach to public service, best value and business excellence, in addition to modernising government (which was the clichéd initiative of the time and to which we have already alluded within a specific probation context above). The keynote address given by the Director of Sentencing and Correctional Policy had as its title 'Modernising Probation Services: Exploring the Context' and one of the authors attended the briefing with the Director prior to the address. It was suggested that how probation 'positioned' itself would be important; the Home Secretary's expectations were critical; and that a leadership response was required from Chief Officers as they were the ones expected to promote the cultural changes perceived to be politically necessary. The address itself drew attention to Home Office Aim 4 that was the 'Effective execution of the sentences of the courts so as to reduce offending and protect the public' as a key determinant behind the Prisons–Probation review. A review of the slides used in this address and notes made at the time leads us to conclude that this was one of the most important political messages ever received throughout the history of the probation service. We were told that Chiefs were seen as barons, the service being more concerned with making the offender happy and of valuing the individual above the perceived political outcome. It was suggested that a respected liberal newspaper had described the service as universally unpopular. It was also stated that we needed to be a meaner and leaner service, reflecting the 'more for less' rhetoric of the time. Moreover, outcomes were what mattered and action urgently needed to achieve the central objective of reducing reconviction rates. The Home Secretary had attended ACOP's AGM on 13th April 1999 to make pronouncements about the Prisons–Probation review, followed by a letter to Chiefs on 15th April 1999 building on these after careful consideration of responses received concerning the consultative document 'Joining Forces to Protect the Public'. At Cranfield the messages from the Home Secretary, conveyed through our senior civil servant, had been articulated with a cogency that could not be ignored. It had taken New Labour less than two years to signal the end of the probation service.

The fourth event occurred on 3rd–4th May 2000 and once again focused on the prevailing political issues. The modernisation and nationalisation of the service was now going to happen, but there was little understanding of the detail of these unprecedented and momentous changes. The conference was used to identify the critical issues that required clarity and its purpose was described as defining the structure and dynamics of governance for the modernised service and to ensure the effectiveness of performance accountability within the new structure. Again it was attended by CPOs and another member of their senior management teams. The role and purpose of the proposed National Director of Probation, Area Chief Officers, Local Boards and the regional structure were all topics for discussion and both the Director of Sentencing and Correctional Policy and the Head of the Probation Unit were speakers at the event. The lack of detailed thinking was apparent and a transcript of a question and answer session on the first day of the conference reveals the width of concerns. The first question was about the accountability of chief officers and who would do their appraisals in the era beyond the *ancien régime*. It was suggested by the person who was to become the new national director and who was at the time working as the New Services Adviser in the Home Office modernisation team, that the local Chair would play a part in appraisal and that the National Director would also have a role to play in appraisal and performance related pay. The national versus local and governance issue dominated the session, with an admission being made that some secondary legislation may be needed. The conference planning team had anticipated some of the central concerns and an input from a health service perspective explored some of the dynamics between chief executives and Chairs which in that setting seemed to be producing a high turnover of chief executives. The corollary in probation was that chiefs might be expendable in any power struggle. Therefore this event provided a useful opportunity to explore critical yet also alarming issues. It also provided clear evidence that the script was being written on the hoof, almost made up as it went along. As the deadline of 31st August 2000 loomed for existing Chief Officers to indicate whether or not they wished to change their employment contracts and become civil servants, these two days had been significant in their decision making.

The fifth and last Cranfield conference was held on 27th–28th June 2001 and, as the national service had now been created (on 1st April 2001), the Statham-Trusler organising partnership was retained by special agreement even though they had both opted to retire. The decision provided continuity in the planning process which reflected the importance of these events. Inevitably, the dynamics of the event, 'Leadership in The New Probation Service – Delivering Change', reflected the changes that had taken place; and the conference was attended by the new National Director, other members of the National Probation Directorate, Chief Officers (no longer Chief Probation Officers, having been re-designated civil servants), Board Chairs and Regional Managers. It provided the opportunity for the National Director to give important messages to the conference. Her input to the conference on 27th June, which of course was after New Labour had been re-elected, was an evocation of the new Blunkett dispensation (David Blunkett replaced Jack Straw as Home Secretary, the latter going to the Foreign Office). The question of resources and staffing levels was considered but the need to reduce reconviction rates was unequivocal. The central priorities were identified as: enforcement (twice yearly audits were not enough); programme completions (getting

10,000 through the accredited 'What Works' innovation); Drug Treatment and Testing Orders (the political weight and potential for crime reduction); sickness and retention (the need to get sickness down to an average of nine days for each member of staff); to retain black and Asian staff (diversity targets for staff and offenders).

Comments were also made about the estates strategy for the newly nationalised service. The existing property estate, currently owned by probation areas, would go to the Crown; and, with management going to the centre, there were expectations of cost savings of £30 million over 10 years. Another contributor to the conference suggested that the service was losing 50% of offenders to the new 'What Works' programmes between the making of the order and when the additional requirement commenced, and that higher profile offenders were contributing to a high attrition rate. The National Probation Service had now been born and was less than three months old when the last Cranfield event was held. Would it proceed to live as long as its predecessor with its roots stretching back to 1876 and the legislative provision of 1907? Reviewing the Cranfield events has yielded an important insight into the political dynamics at a time of unprecedented change. The authors, now cast in the role of political diarists, will reserve analysis for our final chapter. Nevertheless, the events just described are worthy of some review, albeit briefly, at this point.

The Cranfield events were born in 1997 as an expression of the need to respond to the increasingly negative political climate in which the service was operating. The initiative was a reflection of the fact that crime was such a high-profile political issue that general election victories might depend on projecting New Labour as being a tougher animal than the Conservatives. Labour seemed to be walking in Tory footholds in its handling of probation, with civil servants providing the choreography as we lurched from one negative regime to another even more negative regime. The conferences in themselves, despite a brief moment of belated solidarity, failed to ignite any organised opposition to New Labour's aspiration to centralise power within the service and therefore neutralise opposition to the political will. In this respect ACOP was no more successful than the other probation representative bodies. Some of us could only look at the power of chief constables with envy, but then the police had never lost public support in the way that probation had. Again the point should be made that the announcement of the Prisons–Probation review in July 1997 was really the beginning of the end, which is why we need to address this next.

Prisons–Probation Review

In response to a parliamentary question in July 1997, Jack Straw announced the Prisons–Probation review, which was seen as a mechanism for joining the two services (Association of Chief Officers of Probation 2001 p27). The review was intended to be a wide-ranging exercise and therefore part of an inclusive process synonymous with a democratic exercise. All probation representative organisations were expected to play their part and after phase one, by the end of 1997, ACOP produced a draft response to the review that was circulated to probation areas for a further round of comment. ACOP appended a questionnaire to the document which was intended to provide a framework for collating responses. These questions provide a benchmark for the issues emerging from the first phase of consultation and the consequent evolving thinking. The questions were also intended to help in the exploration of important issues, with the restructuring of the service emerging as one of the most critical being raised at this point. ACOP was also asking whether probation should be a national or local service and whether it should be delivered in a regional and/or local way. It was also hoped that there might be an assessment of whether working at a regional level would add value. There was also an interesting suggestion that greater professionalism and authority at a national level could help to develop service delivery. The implications of this were simply that an individual at the centre would be more effective in influencing local practice than local area chiefs had been. From a strictly practical perspective the link was made between probation being delivered on the same geographical basis as the 42 police areas. The service was asked to look at the implications of such amalgamations, with the creation of a London area recognised as having a unique set of issues.

Towards a Unified Service

The second phase of the review began with the publication of *Joining Forces To Protect The Public: Prisons–Probation*, a Consultation Document, in August 1998. The 22-page document indicated that the government had in fact decided *not* to merge probation with the prison service, but instead to make probation a 'next steps' agency. The newly created unified national probation service would also have a new name, and all the members of staff would be civil servants directly responsible to the Home Secretary. Comments on these proposals were invited to be submitted to the Home Office no later than 27th November 1998. ACOP, as required, submitted its response in

November, suggesting that probation should be 'a public protection service; based on effectiveness; with a strong centre; authoritative local governance; and linked to whole service planning' (Association of Chief Officers of Probation 2001 p29). The tone of ACOP's contribution to the consultation process illustrated the extent to which many in the service had already acquiesced to the centralist-driven changes. However, as the amalgamation of prison and probation had been avoided (for now anyway), there was still the chance that government thinking could be influenced and the Correctional Policy Unit in the Home Office continued to handle consultation, which was to continue throughout the whole of 1998. The Home Secretary, at the ACOP AGM on 13th April 1999, finally made announcements.

Two days later, Chief Probation Officers received a letter from the Home Office Correctional Unit, and attached to it were the key points for Modernising the Probation Service, as the initiative was now known. These proposed changes, although falling short of the more fundamental aspiration to create a 'next steps' agency that still required legislation, were nevertheless profound:

- A unified national probation service for England and Wales comprising 42 local operational areas which will match police force area boundaries.

- The new service to be led by a national director with a full range of operational responsibilities.

- The day-to-day running and management of the service in each area will be, as now, in the hands of chief probation officers, but they will be employed and appointed by the Home Office and led by the national director.

- A local probation board will govern each area.

- The chairman of each board will be appointed and paid by the Home Office, and the appointment of individual members of the board will be approved by the Home Office.

- Chief probation officers will be members of these boards.

- · Boards will have a more strategic role and more diverse composition which will still include sentencer representation, but it will be more representative of key partners and the wider community.

- The boards will employ – as the committees do now – the remainder of staff.

- There will be a light regional touch, recognising the importance of matching regional boundaries with government offices of the regions, and which the prison service is planning to reflect in its future management structure.

- The service will be entirely funded by central government, thus ending the 80/20 arrangements.

- The Home Secretary will take full responsibility for the performance of the service and be accountable to Parliament for it and crucially will take greater powers to require necessary outcomes and standards for service delivery.

Consequently, the service received its 'black spot', not from Robert Louis Stevenson's blind Pew, but from the first New Labour Prime Minister. Given the emerging presidential style it would be foolish to believe that this continuing drive to reform the service was solely the work of the Home Secretary. This apparently innocuous little missive was to herald changes that would destabilise the service and allow bureaucracy to seep its stupefying poison deeper into the value base of a people oriented service.

The proposal for 42 services instead of 54 did not cause surprise, indeed Oxfordshire and Buckinghamshire had already joined together in a voluntary amalgamation that at one time had also intended to include Berkshire. The creation of the post of national director had also been expected, but what were we to make of 'a full range of operational responsibilities'? Equally intriguing was the indication that the Home Secretary was to take full responsibility for the performance of the service and to be accountable to Parliament. What seemed to be suggested was a process of delegation with the national director pivotal in ensuring that the service performed. In effect, one individual was becoming responsible where hitherto 54 chiefs had been culpable. In fact, under a nationalised service dominated by the centre, chief probation officers were re-designated chief officers, fitted with the gags of civil service contracts. However, the proposals had fallen short of the 'next steps' agency idea and all other staff would still be employed locally. Boards in each of the areas would employ staff whilst the chief officer would be responsible for the leadership of the service. These proposals suggested an unusual set of governance dynamics. Regions would also be part of a new governance structure, although again just how this was to work was not clear. The intriguing phrase 'light regional touch' prompted interpretations that would be a preoccupation for some time. The issues paper also reinforced the trend towards weakening the links between the probation service and local sentencers. Furthermore, the government was to take responsibility for the entire financing of the service, thus severing local authority funding links and further increasing the influence of the centre. The whole process was an exercise in political power and control; it gave further impetus to the abandonment of traditional probation values; it also indicated a total lack of understanding of the dynamics of organisations and of the creation of a working environment in which individuals felt motivated to perform. The letter was so lacking in detail and so open to interpretation that, not only did it invite endless speculation, it also created anxiety and inevitably anger. The letter was quite breathtaking in that it squandered a century of incremental and often thoughtful change, to an exercise in destabilisation triggered by a tendentious, politically inspired, interpretation of the nature of crime and its treatment. It is interesting that these key points, written in such an ad hoc way, could be viewed as a new vision. In its restless pursuit to modernise and make all things new, New Labour lacked the wisdom to appreciate that the probation service had deep roots with committed staff, and that it should therefore proceed with caution. However, it was acknowledged that a great deal of additional work would be needed in order to make the vision (some might say dystopian nightmare) a reality.

We have already reviewed the Cranfield events and the developing awareness of the need for probation leadership that emerged in 1998. But it was all too late, and the political drive for change and modernisation was not responded to by an alternative vision from within the service itself. There were some attempts to continue to involve members of Parliament in asking questions, but there was no organised or widespread groundswell of opposition to the latest manifestations of political control. The service's capitulation might be regarded as a lack of moral passion that would have been a huge disappointment to the probation pioneers of almost a century ago. We have also acknowledged that change in social attitudes meant that probation had little support to call upon from the media or wider public. Indeed, one attempted sortie into print with a well-known liberal broadsheet was greeted with the suggestion that the rehabilitation debate was over. It is surprising and disconcerting that there was meagre resistance to those changes that were going to challenge the very nature and existence of the idea of probation. As things unfolded it became clear that civil servants were also harbingers of the negative perceptions about the past leadership of the service with the result that probation required a new recipe for success. However, it was a recipe created by chefs who had never been into the kitchen, and who had no understanding of operations or of making organisations work.

New Labour wanted to create all things new and within the service the government embarked on a strategy (charm offensive or polite mugging?) aimed at getting chiefs and other key players to cooperate with the proposed changes. Lord Williams, a junior minister, who had memorably become visibly angry when resorting to class war rhetoric with a member of the audience at a CCPC AGM, set up a series of lunchtime meetings with CPOs at the Home Office. One of us was invited to the first of these events. Whilst the lunches purported to be a mechanism for dialogue, we were treated to familiar arguments about being tough on crime in order to assuage public concerns. It was typical of the discussions at the time that ministers seemed incapable of moving from their prepared positions on these issues. That the government was not prepared to depart from its tough stances on crime illustrated its own lack of political courage in attempting to influence public opinion. Consequently, when some of the wider issues were raised about the social circumstances of offenders so well encapsulated by Downes (1997), they were not seized upon. New Labour was too unsure of its political position to be seen as being soft on crime.

Such exchanges resulted in an uncomfortable recognition that we did not have a set of cogent arguments that would be convincing in the prevailing political climate. And the impact of this get-together contrasted sharply with a similar, though this time after-dinner, meeting with John Patten when he was a junior minister working with Douglas Hurd. On that occasion there was a much more open dialogue, CPOs had a more sympathetic hearing and, curiously, the ambience was far more compassionate despite Tory rhetoric in the press. We explored this period in Chapter 4 and (it will be remembered) at that time CPOs were being urged to pursue the doctrine of punishment in the community. By contrast, in 1999 there was little dialogue; the message from government was that probation had failed. Whilst the threat did not galvanise the service in any organised resistance, neither did it provide an impetus for the formulation of an alternative contemporary probation strategy that would have attracted public appeal. The ability of the service to supervise potentially dangerous offenders in the community, particularly in an atmosphere of escalating public concerns about criminals in general, and paedophiles in particular, was not grasped as an opportunity. Through the service's expertise in risk management, and the growing effectiveness of links with other agencies such as the police, there was an opportunity to promote probation as an agency of community safety. Instead, What Works and the effective practice agenda were allowed to become a panacea.

The modernising exercise was a huge undertaking. The translation of the key issues paper into a strategy that had a prospect of delivery was always going to be difficult. In order to succeed it required an organisational blueprint that staff in the service could understand, underpinned by a governance structure that was workable. It is important to remember that the old governance structure had evolved over time and had been subjected to substantial testing. A new structure separating the employment of the chief officer from other staff with an uncertain regional dimension, and without having clarified the role of a paid Board, was simply flawed. What was clear, however, was the political aspiration for the newly created post of national director to impose a new sense of order and control on an acquiescent subordinate structure. It was a simple case of who pays the piper will call the tune from now on. There were early indications of a sense of intimidation in the new management structure, reinforced by exchanges during the final consultation process in the lead up to the legislation that created a national service. The appointment of the national director brought with it clear signals that subordinates were expected to be on message. What followed was a plethora of aspirational statements with little practical detail. Whilst quite legitimately it could be expected that the changes would take some time to implement, it was clear that the sheer scale of change had not been matched by the quality of the planning process. Consequently, what began to unfold was a series of piecemeal initiatives. The emergence of the National Probation Service began to resemble the fiasco of the Child Support Agency. However, it should be acknowledged that in one important respect the exercise was an enormous success because it established central control from the Westminster village, which was the essential goal of the exercise.

Chief Probation Officer Learning Sets

Throughout the 1990s a system of learning sets had been established and overseen by ACOP's MTSG and the Home Office. It had been recognised that some CPOs had served for many years and had little opportunity to undertake formal learning about management and leadership. Some had availed themselves of the opportunity of attending programmes at business schools, but others chose not to. The concept of leadership was always problematic in an organisation that so valued individualism, but nevertheless was an essential ingredient. The learning sets comprised groups of 8–10 CPOs usually meeting for a 24-hour event with a facilitator external to the probation world.

These learning sets were given free rein in deciding their own development needs and it was customary to invite important people from within the government machine or amongst the thinking classes to explore pertinent issues. One of the authors was a long-standing member of such a learning set. Under the protection of Chatham House rules it had been possible to explore important issues of social and criminal justice as well as the organisational dynamics associated with leadership. In the lead up to 2001, using the very same structure, it was possible to listen to the views of those whose contributions were valued, at the centre, more than CPOs. This was the time when headline-grabbing initiatives, such as instant fines, and losing benefit for failing to keep appointments, were thought up by agile minds, and as such were more important than the thinking about their wider implications or practical implementation.

The probation service was an intelligent organisation. It is inevitable that, in a culture where individuals should be encouraged to think for themselves, scepticism or even agnosticism breaks out on occasions. Indeed, it might be argued that these are also the qualities of a mature and democratic society as well as organisation. However, in one learning set as the new millennium dawned, it became clear from the input of a civil servant close to the thinking of government that a new brand of unquestioning loyalty was an essential prerequisite of the nationalised service. It was also apparent that no aspect of leadership in the new service would be invested in the new chief officers. Having now dealt with a number of issues that culminated in the creation of a national service, we now turn to address a number of other concerns.

Mr Justice Collins' Judgment on Staffing the Modern Service

Throughout the period covered in this chapter, the lack of money remained a continuing problem for many probation areas and as a result led to another significant event, some would say cause célèbre, in one specific area in 1998. The Howard decision to abolish the social work qualification for probation officers left a significant vacuum that we explored in the last chapter. Operationally, some services were now in difficulty as the supply of suitably trained staff dried up. The problems were so acute that imaginative and radical thinking about potential solutions seemed to be forced upon the service. At this time the Teesside probation service was short of staff and struggling to meet workload demands. This service in the North-East of England had traditionally found recruitment difficult because it was perceived as a demanding area in which to work, having consistently high caseloads and acute social problems. Therefore a crisis was in prospect that challenged the leaders of the service and ultimately prompted some lateral thinking about the roles and functions of staff. It also led to some fundamental rethinking of the supervision process.

The Teesside argument was developed from the perspective that, whilst supervision had a legal context in probation, there was no single definition of this process. Supervision had evolved over time, as had the required qualification for probation officers. By the 1990s the supervision process was broadly based and, for an individual offender, it could include a number of individuals from volunteers to members of partner organisations, yet probation officers retained oversight of these devolved activities. The Demonstration Projects had provided evidence that the courts had confidence in a supervision process that had contributions from different individuals when it was delivered in a properly planned and managed way with appropriate managerial oversight. Consequently, the Teesside proposal was that risk assessment should be the critical factor in defining the parameters of the different phases of supervision. Cognitive or behavioural change work was differentiated from community reintegration work and it was suggested that different levels of skill and qualification could be applied to these phases. Probation officers would handle the higher risk work but other aspects could be handled by a new grade of staff called community offender supervisors, a title designed to describe the precise nature of the job (later truncated to offender supervisors).

It was also recognised that, even if it were possible to have all the work of the service handled by a large cohort of probation officers, the newly planned initiative to create a structure for probation officer training would not produce enough to meet workload projections; the range of tasks in the service simply did not fit with one grade of staff. It was also clear that not all duties carried out by probation officers required a high level of skill. Equally, the new range of NVQ qualifications opened up a potential route for local people to join probation and to embark on a process of career progression that could take them through the whole grade structure of the service. Discussions about these proposals with NAPO failed to produce any agreement and the union remained implacably opposed to the appointment of offender supervisors. National officers of NAPO took a similar stance and, as a consequence of an advertisement for community offender supervisors in a local paper, legal action was taken. A hearing took place in the High Court on 28th August 1998 and, in his judgment on 11th September 1998, Mr Justice Collins said: 'The applicant, whom I shall call NAPO, is the trade union and professional association which represents Probation Officers throughout the country. The respondent probation committee has, largely as a result of an initiative developed by The Chief Probation Officer on Teesside, Mr Roger Statham, determined to set a new grade of employee within the service known as offender supervisor. In May 1998 the respondent decided to invite applications for this new grade and inserted advertisements in the local newspaper accordingly. NAPO believes that the action is unlawful because the offender supervisors are to do work which must be reserved to probation officers. That has prompted these proceedings' (Collins 1998).

In Mr Justice Collins' carefully worded judgment the arguments of both sides were reviewed. NAPO's arguments were described as opaque and their application was dismissed. The judgment prompted questions about the way in which all probation areas defined their staffing needs and ultimately led to decisions about differently qualified staff being employed. These were issues that did not need a High Court ruling in order to make progress; they should have been resolved by a commitment to consultation, with recognition that simply resorting to restrictive practices was an unhelpful position to adopt, particularly within the circumstances that prevailed in one local area. Equally, pragmatic decisions taken about the employment of different grades of staff did not obviate the need for the surrounding issues to be fully debated. There had been a number of approaches to defining the qualities, skills and training of probation officers since 1907, and this was a development that deserved a comprehensive and open debate. Notwithstanding the cogency of different arguments prosecuted by management and union that were aired at this time, we speculate on whether the initial vision had been diluted and to what degree different grades of staff were appropriately trained and therefore equipped to undertake different roles within the service. In addition to the appointment of offender supervisors alongside probation officers, the autumn of 1998 witnessed the start of the new probation officer qualification to which we now turn.

Diploma in Probation Studies from Autumn 1998

We have already given the subject of probation training a fair hearing in the previous chapter and alluded to the creation of the Dip.PS that began in the autumn of 1998 as the recognised form of training for probation officers (Whitehead and Thompson 2004; Elliot 1997). It had been questioned for some years whether the Diploma in Social Work met the needs of qualifying probation officers now that they were more criminal justice workers than social workers, particularly against the background of all those political changes since 1979. Consequently, the Dip.PS was organised around the concept of occupational standards and the achievement of core competencies. As such the new qualification has three main components.

First, the National Vocational Qualification (NVQ) element in community justice is normally commenced at the end of stage 1 after the successful completion of the Foundation Practice Portfolio (FFP),[3] which is a rite of passage from stage 1 to stage 2 of the two-year programme. Both the FPP and NVQ require the trainee probation officer to collect evidence, both practice-based and underpinning knowledge and understanding, in relation to the required standards of performance. Where the NVQ is concerned, 12 separate yet overlapping units must be completed in approximately 16 months.[4] Secondly, an approved degree that covers a range of relevant subjects must be completed in two years.[5] Finally, practice-based work involves the trainee being located in a probation team that provides opportunities to begin to learn the job, on-the-job, and also to collect evidence for the NVQ that should naturally evolve from practice. Therefore, the Dip.PS provides a variety of complementary theory and practice components, with the result that the trainee will be awarded a licence to practice at the end of the two-year period if all aspects have been successfully completed. Additionally, it is the role of the Practice Development Assessor (PDA), a critical function in the new award, to relate theory to practice, assess the NVQ evidence against the standards, and to develop the reflective, assessment and intervention skills of the trainee (Whitehead and Thompson 2004). The PDA must model the required knowledge and skill to those whose task is to learn, listen and understand.

It should be acknowledged that New Labour has invested significantly in the probation service, particularly since 2001, reflected in the number of trainee probation officers recruited. We can illustrate this by turning to the North-East consortium (comprising the Northumbria,

Durham and Teesside services) in which 17 trainees were recruited to start the new programme in October 1998. This was followed by 20 in 1999 and 15 in 2000. However the figures from 2001 to 2004 (cohorts 4–7) are quite astonishing: 66, 56, 69 and 50 respectively commenced training. At the time of completing this book, recruitment had dropped to 22 trainees for the North-East consortium in 2005. It should be noted that the previous dramatic increase in trainees in the North-East has been replicated in the other eight consortia in England and Wales. After reflecting upon staffing and recruitment issues, let us now turn to more practice oriented matters in the next section.

Accredited Programmes: Introducing What Works

It can be claimed with some justification that since the election of New Labour in May 1997, What Works, or Accredited Cognitive Behavioural programmes, have been an important feature of probation practice and probably 'saved' the service from dissolution (Mair 2004). It should be stated again that the Major–Howard period was a difficult time for probation; its future was in doubt; and the focus had been on prison rather than probation works. Consequently, George Mair suggests, it was a combination of Chris Nuttall as Head of Research and Statistics at the Home Office, Graham Smith as Chief Inspector of HMIP who championed What Works in 1997, in addition to the development of accredited programmes, that managed to breathe new life into probation. In fact, Mair goes on to suggest that the What Works initiative became 'the foundation stone for the National Probation Service (NPS), the rock upon which the new church has been constructed' (Mair 2004 p13).

Over recent years the service had recourse to a range of methods of working with offenders (Whitehead 1990). Increasingly, since the 1970s, serious questions were being posed about what exactly the service gets up to, effectiveness and performance that left the service vulnerable to criticism. Robert Martinson (1974) had indicated that nothing works, in addition to other empirical research that we have alluded to in Chapter 2. Eventually, the work of Don Andrews, James Bonta, Paul Gendreau and Frank Porporino in Canada developed cognitive-behavioural programmes for offenders to counter the nothing works doctrine; James Maguire and Philip Priestly in England complemented the Canadian contribution. Subsequently, meta-analysis, a statistical technique for analysing a large number of research studies, was yet another road that led to the What Works phenomenon from 1997 and the renaissance rehabilitative thinking. This, to some degree, was an encouraging beginning to the regime of New Labour compared to the penchant for prison under the Conservatives (see Mair 2004 for the history of What Works).

The cognitive-behavioural approach to offending behaviour is that offending behaviour is a consequence of faulty thinking. A basic premise is that thinking or cognition affects the way people feel (emotional state) and, in turn, behaviour. Therefore, if we can change the way people think and feel, we can change behaviour via a repertoire of thinking skills, social skills and problem-solving skills administered by probation staff. What has in fact been learned by faulty socialisation, a failure to internalise certain norms, can be unlearned by a cognitive-behavioural programme. However, Kendall (2004), in an interesting paper, suggests that this approach within probation is commensurate with a neo-liberal society, as opposed to a welfare state society. Within the post-war period of welfare and rehabilitation, the state and its experts did things to people to encourage but also coerce them to reform and comply with certain behavioural expectations. By contrast, in a neo-liberal society and more neo-classical oriented penal system that has adopted a cognitive-behavioural approach, it is the individual who becomes responsible for his own cognitive transformation rather than an overt form of the welfare state. As we said in Chapter 2, one of the main criticisms of the political, penal and probation system is that it puts the focus on the faulty individual, cognitive deficits, the individual as the focus of the problem. From saving souls, to curing by casework, to cognitive-behavioural 'What Works' programmes, the focus of attention largely remains the individual malefactor and his transformation. Whilst it can be argued that there is something to be gained by teaching thinking, social and problem-solving skills to offenders, equally we say again that this must be complemented by addressing those wider social factors that are associated with certain forms of behaviour. This is both a political and probation responsibility that takes one beyond a crude 'blaming the individual offender' approach.

Summary of Legislation 1997 to 2001

Probation has always functioned within a legislative context and we have had cause to mention many pieces of legislation during the course of this book. Where the period travelled within this chapter is concerned, it should be acknowledged that we have already alluded to the Crime (Sentences) Act 1997 in Chapter 5. We should also refer briefly to the Protection from Harassment Act 1997 and the Sex Offender Act 1997 which established the sex offender register.

The Crime and Disorder Act 1998 draws attention to extended sentences/prison licence periods at sections 58–60, which became section 85 of the Powers of Criminal Courts (Sentencing) Act 2000. Section 2 of the Crime and Disorder Act is the legislative basis for the sex offender order; and this legislation introduced the Drug Treatment and Testing Order that has been operated by probation areas. It also facilitated a more collaborative approach between agencies in relation to multi-agency public protection (at section 115). Importantly, it introduced new offences to deal with racist incidents: racially aggravated assaults, criminal damage, public order offences and racially aggravated harassment. Finally, Youth Offending Teams were established, following the Crime and Disorder Act, in 1999–2000 which resulted in 14–17-year-old juvenile offenders being transferred from probation caseloads to the new youth teams. We should also add that from January 1999 Home Detention Curfew (HDC) was introduced, which is a mechanism for ensuring the possibility of early release of those offenders sentenced to three months' imprisonment and over but less than four years. Probation is involved in assessing the suitability of offenders for early release under HDC provisions.

The Human Rights Act 1998 came into force on 2nd October 2000 and it is anticipated that, over time, it will call into question certain aspects of current sentencing law and practice. In fact it requires all public authorities, including the courts and probation service, to act in conformity with the European Convention on Human Rights (Ashworth 2000 p79). Some of the articles are as follows:

Article 2: the right to life protected by law;

Article 3: no one should be subject to torture;

Article 4: no one should be held in slavery;

Article 5: the right to liberty and security of the person;

Article 6: everyone is entitled to a fair and public hearing under law;

Article 7: 'No one shall be held guilty of any criminal offence on account of any act or omission which did not constitute a criminal offence under national or international law at the time when it was committed [etc]…';

Article 8: the right to respect for private and family life;

Article 9: 'Everyone has the right to freedom of thought, conscience and religion';

Article 10: 'Everyone has the right to freedom of expression'.

Next the Powers of Criminal Courts (Sentencing) Act 2000 was an important statute because it brought together relevant sentencing law in relation to probation located in other statutes: for example, Criminal Justice Act 1991; Crime (Sentences) Act 1997; Crime and Disorder Act 1998. However, this attempt to tidy up and consolidate was quickly overtaken and rendered incomplete by the second important piece of legislation in 2000, which we will now consider.

The Criminal Justice and Court Services Act 2000 created two new sentences: the Exclusion Order and Drug Abstinence Order. It is a significant statute because it cosmetically changed the name of certain well-known orders: Probation Order to Community Rehabilitation Order; Community Service Order to Community Punishment Order; and the Combination Order became the Community Punishment and Rehabilitation Order. This was also the legislation that created the National Probation Service in April 2001. It was considered that in the new political climate a community rehabilitation order, rather than probation order, had far greater cachet. There was also the possibility, prior to April 2001, that the word *probation* in the title of the organisation would be dropped, but a change of heart by Jack Straw saved the day.

Finally, we must refer to the Child Support, Pensions and Social Security Act 2000 because sections 62 to 66 are significant for enforcement proceedings in that this legislation introduced the inimical benefit sanction, which requires more detailed consideration.

Inimical Benefit Sanction

The withdrawal of benefit from offenders under sections 62–66 of the Child Support, Pensions and Social Security Act 2000 has been piloted in four area services since 2001, Teesside being one of them. The rationale appears to be encouraging offender responsibility when subject to a community sentence. Consequently, state benefit is not perceived as an absolute right or entitlement because if you are an offender it is conditional on keeping all probation and/or community service appointments. It can be argued that it signals a shift in political discourse from rights to responsibilities and it promotes normalisation and citizenship by the punitive threat of benefit withdrawal. To be precise, if appointments are not kept with the probation service then all or part of benefit can be withdrawn for up to four weeks if the offender is aged between 18 and 59 and subject to a community rehabilitation, community punishment, or community punishment and rehabilitation order. Moreover, the offender must be claiming jobseeker's allowance, income support, or claiming certain training allowances.

An evaluation of the policy began in 2001 but it should be acknowledged, we suggest, that it must be understood in relation to the social policy context we explored in the previous chapter. Furthermore, it needs to be said that it is difficult for probation officers, researchers of government policies, politicians who formulate legislation and magistrates who enforce it, to appreciate the impact of the loss of benefit on the lives of individual offenders and their families. Having said that, some magistrates deserve credit for not imposing a financial penalty in certain breach cases where the benefit sanction applies because they recognise it will create severe financial hardship. This sensible course of action will no longer be possible under the Criminal Justice Act 2003 because of its emphasis on 'onerousness' if someone is in breach (see Appendix 2). It has been estimated that the legislation under review has been responsible for 'a small but positive impact on compliance' (Benefit Sanction Report 2003/04). However, in a political climate that pursues examples of discrimination with alacrity, the benefit sanction makes it clear this does not apply to offenders. In other words, why were Teesside and three other areas selected to implement the benefit sanction with the result that some offenders would experience greater difficulties than offenders in areas not selected? Why do we have to penalise and discriminate against the unemployed, who are the least able to withstand such a harsh policy? Why make impoverished lives even more poor and difficult and in the process militate against rehabilitation? It seems to us that personal responsibility and citizenship can be better facilitated by helping offenders develop a stake in society rather than punitively removing benefits. We are surprised that this discriminatory policy has not been pursued by the legal profession under the human rights legislation and made into a cause célèbre.

The fact that we feel exercised by the benefit sanction can be illustrated by the following anecdote. One of us was present at a busy magistrates' court when a young female offender was appearing in breach proceedings and the benefit sanction was applied. She had already lost a proportion of her benefit because she was repaying a loan from the benefit agency. Therefore, when the sanction was applied she lost a further amount which meant she had not enough money to live on.

Helena Kennedy has referred to a publication called *National Association of Probation Officers News, 2003* that evaluated the cost of processing each benefit sanction case as £730; but the amount of benefit saved in each case was £132. Baroness Kennedy castigates her own party by saying that 'Inventing new ways to punish the poor is a disgraceful activity for a Labour government' (2005 p245).

National Standards 2000 (revised 2002)

During the course of this book we have periodically referred to national standards that were introduced in 1988/89 for community service, and which were expanded and metamorphosed during the 1990s. At this point it is necessary to contrast the 1995 standards with the 2000 standards in relation to enforcement practice (having just referred to the benefit sanction) (Home Office 1995a; 2000 (revised 2002)). By the mid-1990s offenders subject to community sentences could receive two final warnings prior to an intention to breach letter at the third unacceptable absence. This was reduced to one final warning before intention to breach in 2000, confirmed in 2002. This is a form of 'two strikes and you're out' because breach proceedings from 2000 carried the threat of prison and benefit sanction (Whitehead and Thompson 2004; Hedderman and Hough 2004).

Prior to drawing together some of the salient threads of this chapter we need to consider two important reviews, one of which we will return to in the next chapter.

Auld and Halliday Reviews

In December 1999 the government established a review of the criminal courts that was undertaken by Lord Justice Auld. It remains to be seen what the full implications of this could be for the probation service during the next few years. By contrast, and of more immediate impact, is the review by John Halliday, formerly Director of Criminal Justice Policy at the Home Office. The full implications of this review will be considered in the next chapter when we turn to consider the Criminal Justice Act 2003. Nevertheless, it should be elucidated here that the Halliday review of sentencing began on 16th May 2000 and its terms of reference were as follows:

'In the light of the Government's objectives to protect the public by reducing crime and re-offending, and to dispense justice fairly and consistently, to consider:

(i)   what principles should guide sentencing decisions;

(ii) what types of disposal should be made available to the courts in order to meet the overarching objectives;

(iii) the costs of different disposals and their relative effectiveness in reducing re-offending;

(iv) what changes therefore need to be made to the current sentencing framework, as established by the Criminal Justice Act 1991, so as more effectively to reduce re-offending, including any transitional and consequential arrangements; and

(v) the likely impact of any recommendations in terms of costs and the effects on the prison population.

In particular, the review should bear in mind the desirability of promoting flexibility in the use of custodial and community based approaches.'

The review focused on sentences that should be available to courts; greater sentencing flexibility; enforcement issues; prison sentences and licences; court decisions whilst sentences are in force; judicial discretion and costs-benefits. Halliday did not propose the abolition of the philosophy underpinning the Criminal Justice Act 1991, but certain refinements were required in relation to: persistent offenders; custodial sentences of less than 12 months being of questionable value; and closer links between prison and probation being reinforced. Importantly, Halliday stated that the severity of the sentence should incrementally increase, based upon the current offence and previous convictions. This changes the approach envisaged by the 1991 Act that put the emphasis on the seriousness of the current offence and diluted the weight that should be given to previous convictions. Therefore, it may be said that the relationship between seriousness and proportionality remains but previous convictions will have more weight attached to them. John Halliday proposed a range of new sentences that will be discussed in the next chapter when we turn to the Criminal Justice Act 2003. Suffice to say here that the underlying principles were:

(a) the severity of the sentence should reflect the seriousness of the offence and previous convictions;

(b) the seriousness of the offence should reflect the harm caused and the offender's level of culpability;

(c) sentence severity should increase as a consequence of previous convictions;

(d) prison sentences should only be imposed when no other sentence is adequate to reflect the need for punishment;

(e) non-custodial sentences should be used when they are punitive enough and can reduce re-offending and protect the public.

The review began in May 2000; 12 months later, on 1st May 2001, it was presented to ministers; it was published by the Home Office in July 2001 and a period of consultation ensued until 31st October 2001 (Home Office 2001b). All we need to add here is that the Halliday review of sentencing culminated with the suggestion that the probation service would be working at any one time with up to 80,000 more offenders, with obvious implications for staffing resources. In fact, this helps to explain why the Home Office has been investing heavily in additional staff through the expanding trainee probation officer programme since the autumn of 2001, as we mentioned earlier in this chapter. (We will develop this section when we turn to the Criminal Justice Act 2003 in Chapter 7.)

Summary and Conclusion

We have covered much ground in this chapter, which began in May 1997 with what became a misplaced optimism about what New Labour would do for probation after 18 years of Conservative administrations. We conclude with the creation of the National Probation Service in April 2001, a nationalised, centralised and Byzantine megalith. In August 2001, the National Probation Service for England and Wales, in addition to the Home Office Communications Directorate, published *A New Choreography* (Home Office 2001c). Presumably the document is a metaphor to capture the notion that the national service must learn new steps; dance to a new tune; teach an old dog new tricks. But no one explained to members of staff, in a coherent manner, why this should be the case. The new choreography resorted to the language of 'stretch objectives' to illustrate those areas of greatest challenge, which are: assessment and management of risk and dangerousness; victim work; accredited programmes; young people and crime; enforcement; court reports; valuing diversity; building an excellent organisation and an effective performance management framework.

It can be argued that even more emphasis was placed upon bureaucratic systems and procedures (for example, the electronic Offender Assessment System), rather than enhancing practice skills, reflecting on the needs of probation clients, care, compassion, values, understanding people who offend, decency and humanity, in what is fundamentally a people-based organisation. In our naivety we imagined that New Labour would restore these latter priorities in 1997; in fact it did the opposite by exacerbating the bureaucratic and punitive climate that had been pursued during the previous five years under Mr Major and Mr Howard.

In summarising this chapter we need to provide the reader with a few examples of New Labour's punitiveness to illustrate that the probation ideal hardly stood a chance. First, there is evidence from a number of sources to support the view that New Labour is associated with a set of attitudes that are of deep concern in general terms, but particularly for probation officers: disciplinarian instincts, moralistic and authoritarian tendencies (Windlesham 2001 p73; Seldon 2004 pp180, 244 and 600; Baroness Kennedy 2005 p283). Secondly, there was no attempt after 1997 to reverse the rising prison population promoted by the previous Conservative administration. New Labour is the heir of Thatcherism in the way it has pursued choice, opportunity and competition, but also in its approach to law and order (Sargeant 2005 pp369–370). Consequently, the comment made by Baroness Kennedy, in her powerful book on the need for justice, is telling: 'That Labour took the decision to continue Michael Howard's incarceration binge is one of the blackest marks against this government's record on social justice' (2005 p283). Thirdly, community sentences must be even tougher; there has been a tougher enforcement regime since National Standards 2000/02, reinforced by a punitive benefit sanction that adds another layer of discomfort for the unemployed and disadvantaged offender. Even area services can be punished, if they do not meet certain central government cash-linked targets, by having a proportion of their budgets removed. All this amounts to a difficult political and penal world for probation, where criminal policies have been reduced to sound bites such as 'Find me an eye-catching initiative on crime'.[6] How is it possible to develop and implement carefully considered policies on crime that involve probation in a climate where crime has become a political tool to inveigle votes out of the electorate and defeat your opponents?

We accept that an organisation that has been in existence since 1907 would require some modernisation by the 21st century; yet there is a difference between modernisation and destruction. The danger in making all things new is that you tear up much that is good, decent and mature within an organisation, qualities that have evolved over many decades. Part of probation's appeal is its moral commitment to a set of attitudes that include humanitarianism, decency, and an understanding of people. Yet these are being replaced by a set of oppressive systems, procedures and targets linked to punishment, which is a deep concern for some of us within the service who are concerned about how we treat and work with people.

Finally, as part of the process of creating the new probation service, existing chief officers were given a deadline of 31st August 2000 to decide whether they wished to be made redundant or have a civil service contract within the new national structure. The deadline was fair within the context of the enormous planning process that was underway, and exit terms had been carefully negotiated. Decisions had to be taken by individual chiefs but, in the sharing of concerns that is sometimes possible in such circumstances, it was clear that people were much exercised. Probation had been a way of life, and being a Chief Probation Officer a privilege. The prospect of being accountable to whimsical ministers and losing the freedom to exercise any local leadership dulled the enthusiasm for the proposed changes. It was clear that much of what was being proposed would not work and there would be a lengthy process of destabilisation. Of the 54 Chiefs, 26 left the service on 31st March 2001: 23 took various forms of retirement and 3 moved into other jobs; an astonishing cull. But the upheaval created by establishing the National Probation Service was not the end of major disruption and change. In little over two years, yet another round of change would occur (considered in our penultimate chapter).

NOTES – Chapter 6

[1] For many years after 1945 the 'principled pragmatism' that was penal policy was largely in the hands of civil servants (Rutherford 1996). However, due to the increasing politicisation of crime and probation since 1979, taken to a new level since 1997, we question the degree to which the moderating role of civil servants has been diluted under the weight of political interference. Therefore, what are the implications of this development for the democratic processes of government?

[2] Niccolo Machiavelli (1469–1527) was an Italian statesman and writer and one of his publications was *The Prince*, published in 1532. This book describes both the achievement and maintenance of power by a determined ruler who is indifferent to moral considerations.

[3] The Foundation Practice Portfolio is structured around seven areas of probation practice:

1. Demonstrate through practice an understanding of the nature of risk.
2. Assist in the assessment of individuals.
3. Support individuals experiencing difficulties.
4. Help individuals address problem behaviour including abusive and aggressive behaviour.
5. Develop working relationships with staff in other agencies.
6. To assist in the delivery of either group or individual interventions.
7. To be able to record accurately and appropriately.

[4] The 12 NVQ units at Level 4 are:

B103: Contribute to developing awareness and community action in relation to crime.

D102: Process information relating to individuals' offending behaviour.

D103: Assess individuals' offending behaviour and prepare sentencing proposals.

D202: Plan, supervise, enforce and review sentences in the community.

D302: Enable individuals to change their offending behaviour.

D308: Deliver externally-validated evidence-based programmes designed to reduce the likelihood of re-offending by offenders who pose a medium to low risk of harm.

E203: Contribute to the prevention and management of abusive and aggressive behaviour.

E205: Evaluate risk of abuse, failure to protect and harm to self and others.

E409: Enable individuals to understand and address their difficulties.

F307: Develop one's own knowledge and practice.

F403: Develop and sustain effective working relationships with staff in other agencies.

F407: Represent the agency in courts and formal hearings.

[5] Some of the subjects covered at the University of Portsmouth are:

Introduction to criminology   Issues in criminal justice
Introduction to criminal justice studies   Research and effective practice
Understanding society   Issues in criminology
Understanding social problems   Penology.

6   Baroness Kennedy refers to a leaked document between Mr Blair and pollster Phillip Gould in July 2000 that yields a disturbing insight into the formulation of criminal justice policy when the Prime Minister is reported to have said: 'Find me an eye-catching initiative on crime.' *(Kennedy 2005 pp21–22)*

Part 3

DECLINE AND FUTURE OF PROBATION

Chapter 7

FROM THE NATIONAL PROBATION SERVICE TO THE NATIONAL OFFENDER MANAGEMENT SERVICE: 2001 TO 2004

'The current Labour government has knowingly adopted policies known to be ineffective or unlikely to work because of an arguable belief that its own continuation in office justifies the unnecessary human suffering and waste of public resources that its policies produce.' *(Tonry 2004 pix)*

'Two questions remain. Why did these politicians, and this government, in this time, and this place, play the crime card, and why in a time of falling crime rates do they keep doing it? Those answers are known, if by anyone, only by senior figures in the Labour Party.' *(Tonry 2004 p70)*

Introduction

The first substantive section of our penultimate chapter sequentially addresses numerous events in probation from the government's ten-year plan in February 2001 to the appearance of proposals for a National Offender Management Service on 6th January 2004. We also consider a number of probation practice issues that we feel have been neglected by recent organisational developments. This is because, it could be argued, the agenda for change has been preoccupied with new governance arrangements; the changing role of chief officers; the driving through from Whitehall of a centrally determined agenda that has attempted to create a new culture manifested in the NOMS structure.

Criminal Justice: The Way Ahead *(Home Office 2001a)*

In February 2001 the Labour government published its ten-year plan for the criminal justice system. This was a pre-election document (the general election was held on 7th June 2001) that drew attention to a number of reforms which included: improving the police service; more effective criminal prosecutions with more investment in the Crown Prosecution Service; more flexible punishments that linked with the work being undertaken by John Halliday; putting the needs of victims and witnesses at the centre of the criminal justice system; and better care and rehabilitation inside and then following a custodial sentence.

213

Next, as has been mentioned several times, on 1st April 2001 the National Probation Service was created and the *Choreography* document, published in August, enumerated the new organisation's objectives (Home Office 2001c). In July 2001 the Halliday Review on sentencing was published: *Making Punishments Work* (Home Office 2001b). We saw in Chapter 6 that Jack Straw announced a review of the sentencing framework on 16th May 2000, which was presented to ministers on 1st May 2001. Following publication in July 2001, after the election that returned New Labour to office, the new Home Secretary, David Blunkett, responded to the Halliday Review at the first National Probation Service conference, held in London on 5th July 2001. Subsequently, there was a period of consultation until 31st October 2001. Therefore, we can summarise by saying that a lengthy process that began with Lord Justice Auld (2000), continued with the Halliday Review and the Home Office ten-year plan, culminated in July 2002 with the publication of the White Paper, *Justice For All* (Home Office 2002). At this point we need to turn to the White Paper prior to considering the Criminal Justice Act 2003 and other associated matters.

Justice for All

This White Paper prepared the ground for the Criminal Justice Act 2003 and drew attention to one of the central concerns of New Labour, namely anti-social behaviour. There are references to drugs and the fact that custody will be used for sex, violent and dangerous offenders in order to protect the public. Another New Labour theme given emphasis is that too few people are brought to justice, in addition to the need to re-balance the criminal justice system in favour of victims (see discussion in Tonry 2004 on this issue). When reflecting on bringing people to justice, perhaps the government had in mind the analysis of Andrew Ashworth when confirming British Crime Survey findings that only about 2% of offences committed annually result in court convictions and sentences (2002 p1084).[1] The document proceeds to confirm that a small group of people commit the majority of offences, which means that government has a duty to focus on persistent offenders. It also touches on breaches of community sentences: community sentences must be tougher and more demanding on offenders; new sentences should be introduced; and greater consistency is required across the country when courts sentence offenders, hence the creation of a Sentencing Guidelines Council. To achieve its objectives in relation to what we have just alluded to, including protecting the public and expediting justice, the government by this stage had already begun to modernise the police service, prisons, the Crown Prosecution Service, the National Probation Service, and the courts, that comprise approximately 300,000 people working for the criminal justice system. Subsequently, the Criminal Justice Bill was published in November 2002, culminating in new legislation with implications for the probation service, which we shall now consider.

Criminal Justice Act 2003 and Probation

It is not possible or necessary to summarise all the different parts of the CJA 2003. This is a comprehensive and complex piece of legislation that covers a wide range of issues: police powers, bail, juries, double jeopardy, hearsay, and of course introduces a new sentencing framework (Taylor, Wasik and Leng 2004; Gibson 2004). It replaces, but at times it is more accurate to say refines, the Criminal Justice Act 1991 and Powers of Criminal Courts (Sentencing) Act 2000 as the primary legislation for probation practice. The first point to establish is that some of the language of the 2003 Act resonates with the 1991 Act (considered towards the end of Chapter 4): seriousness of the offence; the punishment should fit the crime; aggravating and mitigating factors; restriction of liberty; reparation to victims; prevention of re-offending; and the balance of risk and need. By contrast, the new legislation establishes significant changes in relation to:

- The weight that will now be given to previous convictions.

- The 'seriousness' test, which can be bypassed for persistent offenders.

- The creation of a new sentencing framework that draws attention to dangerous offenders.

- The creation of a Sentencing Guidelines Council to promote greater consistency in sentencing throughout England and Wales.

CJA 2003: Some Key Issues

When dealing with adult offenders the court, when arriving at its sentencing decision, must have regard to the *purpose of sentence* (s 142), of which there are five (intellectually incompatible) possibilities in the legislation:

- Punishment

- Reducing crime through deterrence

- Reform and rehabilitation
- Public protection
- Reparation.

Seriousness is a key feature of the Act and the sentence imposed must be proportionate to and commensurate with the level of seriousness. The 1991 Act's language of 'serious enough' and 'so serious' (s 152) is retained with certain modifications. These are the two categories of seriousness that define the community sentence and custody thresholds respectively. It should be acknowledged that the 2003 Act contributes to our understanding of seriousness by saying, 'In considering the seriousness of any offence, the court must consider the offender's culpability in committing the offence and any harm which the offender caused, was intended to cause or might foreseeably have caused' (s 143(1)). Of course, the level of seriousness that the court must formulate a judgment upon will be influenced by, amongst other things, aggravating and mitigating factors. Some examples of *aggravating* factors are: previous convictions (s 143); offences committed on bail (s 143); racial and religious aggravation (s 145 and Crime and Disorder Act 1998); hostility based upon sexual orientation or disability (s 146). By contrast, a timely guilty plea is a *mitigating* factor (s 144). Furthermore, it is important to unpack the notion of culpability into the following gradations of *harm*: intention to cause harm; recklessness; knowledge of risk of unintended harm; negligence.

Consequently, the point we make after perusing, albeit briefly, some of the important features of the new legislation is that they have profound implications for probation staff, particularly when preparing reports for courts. For example, the Act has clear implications for interviewing offenders, assessing risk and need, considering appropriate interventions, resulting in proposals for sentence to the Magistrates' and Crown Courts. If the legislation is implemented effectively then it may be envisaged that offenders will be sentenced appropriately to fines, discharges, community orders or custody, according to the criteria alluded to above, facilitated by the guidance provided by the Sentencing Guidelines Council. Alternatively, a more pessimistic scenario comes to mind if the courts, for example, place onerous burdens on offenders by imposing too many requirements from the menu of 12 that comprise the new community sentences, which could result in more breach proceedings that will commit more offenders to prison by the back door. Additionally, more offenders could breach licence requirements and therefore continue to swell the prison population. Inadvertently and unwittingly, probation officers could contribute to this outcome by inappropriate recommendations in their reports. The politics of the new Act are intended, we think, to peg the average prison population to no more than 80,000. Having said that it is a salient reminder that legislation, beginning with the Criminal Justice Act 1961, intended to reduce the prison population, has hardly achieved this objective.[2]

CJA 2003: Sentencing Framework

The new sentencing framework can be divided up into five substantive sections that comprise the following sentences: first, there are four custodial sentences of over 12 months that are the province of the Crown Court; secondly, there are three custodial sentences of 12 months or less that comprise custody 'plus', intermittent or part-time custody, and the new suspended sentence or custody 'minus'; thirdly, the new generic community sentence, which can be assembled from 12 requirements; fourthly, fines and discharges; finally, we should include deferment of sentence, individual support orders, parenting and referral orders. (Appendix 2 provides the reader with a more comprehensive overview of the new sentencing framework provided by the Criminal Justice Act 2003.) Before moving on it is important to clarify that from 4th April 2005 the provisions under the new Act introduced were: public protection sentences for dangerous offenders; the new generic community order; custody minus; and the new release and recall arrangements for all custodial sentences of 12 months and over.

Patrick Carter's Correctional Services Review

In March 2002, Patrick Carter, 'a businessman with impeccable credentials' (Ramsbotham 2003 p254) who had previously been a non-executive member of the Prisons and also Corrections Board, was asked to review correctional services in England and Wales. Notwithstanding improvements in prisons and probation since 1997, the work of Halliday that culminated in the 2003 Act suggested the necessity for even further reforms. Therefore, to ensure the effective implementation of the new legislation, to impose custody for the most serious offenders, and to make community sentences even more demanding, the most effective and efficient use of both prison and probation resources had to be achieved. Intriguingly, the decision not to proceed with closer cooperation between prisons and probation following the review of 1997–98 (discussed in the previous chapter) was now resurrected by Carter, because to ensure maximum cooperation between the two organisations he advocated their merger through the creation of a new National Offender Management Service. So what did not occur in 1998 was about to emerge in 2003–04. The Carter Report on *Managing Offenders, Reducing Crime: A New Approach* (Carter 2003) was published and circulated to probation areas in January 2004, causing quite a stir. Fundamentally, Carter advocated a more integrated criminal justice system, the end-to-end management of offenders, which of course had profound implications for probation. Therefore, we begin with a summary of the context within which Patrick Carter produced his report that includes some interesting but disturbing statistics.

Context of Carter Review and Some Statistics

The Carter Review states that the use of probation and prison had increased by 25% since 1996, with a corresponding decline in the use of the fine. Moreover, sentencing had become more severe and instead of using community sentences for more serious offenders, they were being used for a relatively high proportion of first offenders when fines and discharges would have been more appropriate. We would want to add, and the book has made this clear at certain points, that both Conservative and Labour politicians must accept some responsibility for this. If you continue to talk-up punishment, demand tougher sentences and proclaim that prison works, then over time public attitudes will be affected, including those of sentencers and the media, resulting in a harsher criminal justice culture. This is what has happened. Carter's statistics illustrate our point because, in 1996, there were 85,000 custodial sentences and 133,000 community sentences. By 2001, the figures were 107,000 and 166,000 respectively – a 25% increase for both. Prison statistics can also be looked at another way by saying that, in 1996, the average prison population was 55,000; in 2001 it was 66,000; and by late 2003 it was 74,000. In fact England and Wales, in 2004, had the highest prison population in the European Union at 139 offenders per 100,000 populations. If we turn to community sentences, in 1996 there were 127,000 under supervision and by 2001 this had risen to 141,000. Carter illustrates the fact that sentences have become more severe by stating that 15% of offenders found guilty of an indictable offence received a custodial sentence in 1991; 22% in 1996; and by 2001 it was 25%. On the basis of his analysis of available data, Carter forecast that by 2009 the average prison population could be as high as 93,000 in addition to 300,000 under probation supervision. However, Blunkett revised these figures downwards in his reply to Carter (Home Office 2004c) by predicting an average prison population of 80,000 by the end of the decade. It may be said that we have come a long way since the Hurd, Patten and Faulkner era (1985–91) in our thinking about what is an acceptable prison population.

The Review reminds us that spending on both prisons and probation had increased by over £1 billion during the last ten years to £3.5 billion per year. Yet, despite the achievements in probation since 2001 that saw the creation of the National Probation Service, the introduction of new multi-agency public protection arrangements, a new focus on performance management and the fact that area services are penalised if certain targets are not met, Carter laments the 'silo-like' structure of these two organisations. In other words, according to his analysis there is a lack of strategic end-to-end offender management. Therefore, after perusing the context within which the review was conducted, statistical data, the allocation of resources over recent years, achievements but also deficiencies, what is Carter's vision for the future?

Carter's Vision for a National Offender Management Service

Patrick Carter argues that the criminal justice system must have a clear set of objectives that include the proper punishment of offenders; public protection; persistent offenders should be punished incrementally more seriously; but offenders should also get help to stop offending. Therefore, he builds upon the Criminal Justice Act 2003, in addition to which prisons and probation must focus on the management of offenders throughout the entirety of the sentence, which means much closer cooperation, hence the creation of a National Offender Management Service (NOMS) that will have a Chief Executive, National Offender Manager, Regional Offender Manager, and offender manager to coordinate the work being undertaken with offenders.

David Blunkett's Response to Carter

Concurrently to the appearance of the Carter Report in December 2003/January 2004, the Home Secretary published his response, *Reducing Crime – Changing Lives*, that basically approved the creation of NOMS (Home Office 2004c). Comments were requested in response to the Home Secretary's document by 18th February 2004. It is interesting to recount statistics included in the Blunkett response. For example, since New Labour came to power in May 1997 seven new prisons have been opened creating 14,700 extra places and, by 2006, government is planning to expand prison capacity to 78,700 places. Moreover, probation funding has increased by 46% in 'real terms' between 1997/98 and 2003/04 and probation staff are expected to increase from 14,700 in 1997/98 to 19,000 by 2003/04. As we have already seen, the service has recruited unprecedented numbers of trainee probation officers to the Diploma in Probation studies programme since 2001 and the CJA 2003, with its new sentences and therefore additional responsibilities for probation, has generated additional demands for more staff. It must be acknowledged that the Carter Review and David Blunkett's response generated a good deal of activity that was reflected in yet another publication, *National Offender Management Service – Next Steps: Summary of responses to the two Government consultation exercises* (Home Office 2004b). This document contains (a) the results of a consultation exercise precipitated by Blunkett's response to Carter, and (b) the results of a second consultation exercise on proposed organisational change that interestingly culminated in a decision to defer the decision to proceed with structural change that would see the creation of NOMS. We address some of these issues below.

David Ramsbotham (2003), formerly Her Majesty's Chief Inspector of Prisons, lamented that the Carter proposals were not given more careful and detailed consideration by the Home Office. This is because, as he correctly points out, both the Carter proposals and the response of David Blunkett occurred almost simultaneously. There was a feeling at the time that proposed developments were being rushed; there was going to be yet more major change for probation to cope with; the government expected that NOMS would be introduced by June 2004, yet had to pull back from this overly ambitious plan. For something as far reaching as NOMS, on top of everything that had changed since 1997, it can be argued that it was unwise to proceed with such unseemly haste. We make this point because it is interesting to compare the process and timescale that culminated in the NOMS proposals with those Departmental Committees summarised in Chapter 2.[3]

At this point, and for the sake of completeness, we want to allude briefly to other documents prior to reflecting on some of the implications for probation practice during the period under review, before returning to NOMS towards the end of the chapter.

Heart of the Dance Diversity Strategy

One of the stretch objectives of the *Choreography* document was to value and achieve diversity in the new National Probation Service and the services it provides. Consequently, during 2003 the National Probation Directorate published its diversity strategy called *Heart of the Dance* (Home Office 2003). The document endorses a commitment to quality, excellence, justice, fairness and equality as the building blocks of the new organisation in relation to members of staff and offenders.

Setting the Pace: Achieving *Choreography* Objectives

Another document with athletic undertones, *Setting the Pace*, was published in January 2004 (Home Office 2004d) and once again emerged out of the *Choreography* document because it considers some of the achievements of the National Probation Service during its first 1,000 days in relation to a number of issues, including:

Multi-agency Public Protection Arrangements	Curfew Orders
Intensive Control and Change Programmes	Enforcement
Enhanced Community Punishment	Basic Skills
Drug Treatment and Testing Orders	Victim issues
What Works and reducing crime	Court reports
Home Detention Curfew	Tagging
Offender Assessment System (OASys)	Community Sentences

It makes the point that the NPS has been involved in much good work since April 2001, so much so that the Director General, Eithne Wallis, stated: 'We have achieved a great deal in the past 1000 days. We have a continuing job to do under *Bold Steps*, giving service to victims and supervising offenders to reduce re-offending' (Home Office 2004 p21). In fact Eithne Wallis left her job as the first Director General of NPS in April 2004 to become Director of Change as the service began to feel its way towards the new structure created by the National Offender Management Service. But before doing so she referred to *Bold Steps* and so must we.

Bold Steps

In July 2004 a new business plan for the period 2004–05 was published for the National Probation Service called *Bold Steps* (Home Office

2004a). It contains a summary of priorities, objectives and targets that we can enumerate as:

1. Effective implementation of the CJA 2003.

2. Effective offender management to reduce crime.

3. Providing a more efficient and effective reporting service to courts.

4. The delivery of offender programmes and interventions to reduce re-offending.

5. Managing and reducing dangerousness.

6. Providing a quality service to the victims of serious sexual and other violent crime.

7. Valuing and achieving diversity in the NPS and in the services it provides.

8. Building capacity in Wales and in the English regions.

9. Building effective support.

The above provide us with an insight into national probation priorities. Furthermore, and perhaps more importantly, we want to focus on the national targets contained in the document, which are instructive.

Probation Targets 2004 to 2005

The national targets for the period 2004–05 are as follows:

Enforcement and Compliance: initiate breach proceedings within 10 days in 90% of cases and increase to 70% the proportion of orders and licences in which the offender complies.

Offending Behaviour Programmes: 15,000 completions.

Enhanced Community Punishment: 30,000 completions.

Drug Treatment and Testing Orders: 13,000 orders including 1,000 lower intensity orders; there are other targets associated with DTTOs.

Learning and Skills (basic skills): 32,000 starts and 8,000 awards.

Intensive Control and Change Programme: 17 schemes; 1,788 orders made and 1,101 completions.

Reports to Courts: there must be a clear proposal in 95% of reports on minority ethnic offenders.

Victim contact: 85% of victims to be contacted within 8 weeks of offenders receiving 12 months' or more imprisonment for serious sexual and violent offences.

Youth Justice: probation and youth justice board to achieve 5% reduction in reconviction target.

In addition to national targets each of the 42 area services has its own local targets to achieve.[4] Finally, we need to acknowledge that on 20th January 2005 the latest Draft National Standards were issued to areas in Probation Circular 07/2005. The latest standards are expressed in measurable terms as General Standards and Specific Standards, which are in the control of probation area managers and staff and for which they must be held to account (National Probation Directorate 2005). Consequently, as we summarise the above we suggest that events from 2001 into 2005 indicate yet another busy period for probation and a great deal of change to assimilate. Notwithstanding two major periods of change within probation, from the creation of the NPS in 2001 and then the merger of prisons and probation to create the NOMS structure beginning in 2004, we suggest little attention was given to probation practice. Therefore, in what follows we want to reflect upon what we consider to be a neglected feature of recent probation developments, namely the face-to-face contact between probation staff and people called offenders and accompanying practice oriented skills. We progress from a few general to more specific points.

Probation Practice: A Discussion

First, the 2003 Act was partially implemented on 4th April 2005 and it is anticipated that more people will be subject to community sentences over the next few years. In fact, as we have already seen, the Carter Report (2003 p39) predicted that 300,000 offenders could be under probation supervision by 2009. This projected figure can be compared with 127,000 in 1996 and 141,000 in 2001. Therefore, it will be interesting to observe how magistrates and judges use the new community sentence with its 12 requirements and whether probation within the NOMS structure has the resources to work with a substantial increase in workload across the 42 areas (see Appendix 2 for details of the 2003 Act).

The second issue concerns the number of offenders who will be on licence following a prison sentence. We know that once custody 'plus' is introduced all offenders sentenced to 12 months' imprisonment or less will receive a minimum period of licence of 26 weeks. Furthermore, offenders who receive a custodial sentence of more than 12 months at the Crown Court will normally be released on licence at the halfway point and it will remain in force until the termination of sentence. Therefore, more offenders will be on licence for longer. Again we can remind ourselves that Carter predicted a prison population of 93,000 by 2009, which was revised to 80,000 by David Blunkett. If the prison population does rise to 93,000 by 2010, then more prisons will need to be built because the expected capacity by 2006 is 78,700 places. Additionally, the prison population could be given a boost, albeit inadvertently, by the new onerous breach procedures under the 2003 Act (custody by the back door). Again we ponder the implications of these potential developments for probation practice and resources.

Thirdly, additional demands will be made upon report writers within the new sentencing framework established by the CJA 2003. Probation officers who write reports will have to think extremely carefully about a number of issues, including offence seriousness, risk of re-offending and gradations of harm, aggravating and mitigating factors, relevance of previous convictions, and the needs of the individual, to make a judgement about the most appropriate disposal to propose to the sentencing court. Consequently, there are clear implications here for ensuring probation staff have the required practice skills to work with offenders that have always fundamentally consisted of: the ability to build and sustain professional working relationships; interviewing, assessment and intervention skills; insight and awareness; listening and negotiation; and, critically, an understanding and appreciation of an offender's behaviour influenced by their social circumstances. Nevertheless, it is our contention that since 1997 the development of practice skills has been neglected because of a preoccupation with modernisation, governance, bureaucratic systems and cultural change. In other words, the focus has been on macro organisational issues rather than refining the skills of individual members of staff to work with offenders. (This point requires expansion and justification.)

Fourthly, even though a combination of the *New Choreography, Bold Steps*, National Standards and E-OASys have drawn attention to the importance of assessment of re-offending and harm, we would argue that the National Probation Service should be reminded that to produce an insightful risk assessment the practitioner must be in possession of a range of sophisticated skills (as just enumerated). The foundation

Hayles point

too techno — abandons personal

for these skills is an interest in and understanding of the person the officer is working with. Yet the point should be entertained that people oriented skills are acquired over a considerable period of time through doing the job and gaining knowledge based upon experience; making mistakes and learning from them; training, coaching and feedback from those who, over many years, have themselves acquired these skills; and the ability of practitioners to reflect on their own practice. Over recent years it may be suggested that some staff have not given themselves sufficient time to learn these skills before applying for managerial posts that inevitably reduce opportunities to work with offenders. One major problem with this is that, if the practitioner has not acquired these skills prior to promotion, they cannot subsequently hand them on to other staff. Furthermore, and this is a critical problem with the way in which probation has evolved since the 1970s, even though it is fundamentally a people oriented organisation, upon promotion managers increasingly lose touch with offenders. Bill McWilliams encapsulates this problem by making a pertinent observation: 'In a profession the most senior members, no matter how eminent, practice their professional skills; the consultant surgeon operates on patients, the university professor teaches students, the greatest lawyer appears in court' (1992 pp9–10). So why does this not apply in probation? Until the 1970s *all* probation staff held a caseload including senior and principal probation officers, albeit restricted. This fact alone is indicative of profound organisational change within probation. Other factors have contributed to weaken practice knowledge and skill, which we shall now explore.

1. We repeat that a climate of punishment rather than welfare since 1979 has hardly been conducive to cultivating a deep understanding and appreciation of probation service clients.

2. There has been more emphasis on *presenting* rather than *underlying* problems. This means that to a greater degree practitioners sometimes appear more concerned with surface issues, such as drink and drugs, that are of course importantly related to offending behaviour. So the question being posed is: *What* problems are associated with offending? However, insightful probation officers are interested in getting behind presenting problems by reflecting on *why* offenders are dependent on drink and drugs, which could be associated with, for example, traumatic childhood experiences. To understand why someone has problems enriches both assessment and intervention. In fact, how can we intervene unless we have a good understanding of why someone behaves in a

particular way? Therefore we pose two questions to practitioners: When was the last time you were given opportunities to develop your practice skills such as interviewing, listening, risk assessment, understanding clients, insight and awareness? When did you last receive feedback from a senior officer on your practice *that had been observed*, as opposed to a file check for audit purposes?

3. There is now a politically inspired sense in which offenders are not a deserving category. The fact that we have such a high prison population helps to illustrate this point. It is no longer *de rigueur* for probation to be associated with a modus operandi exemplified by sympathy, empathy, tolerance, and therefore understanding. Political and in turn social and probation sensibilities have changed and delicate balances have been affected.

4. There is more focus on victims than offenders. We do not have a problem with this proposition but it must be balanced by saying that probation staff have a professional responsibility to consider both groups.

5. The prevailing political culture also demands more from offenders in terms of personal responsibility. If they do not shape up and act responsibly as citizens within their local communities and accept opportunities probation provides, then breach action threatens which could culminate in removal from their communities if they do not play by the rules of citizenship. Yet some struggle to play by the rules because of experiences they have had that have burdened them with certain problems. Therefore, tolerance, care and compassion must have a part to play in probation work. However, in the world of New Labour and its modernised probation service, with its roots in the Thatcherism of the 1980s, this constitutes a challenging predicament.

6. A significant point to mention is that over recent years more emphasis has been placed on training in policies, procedures, systems and computers than on people skills. This has facilitated the ongoing bureaucratisation of probation. We caricature this point as we suggest a growing division within the organisation. There are those who do the job by the strict application of rules and procedures, promoting a working environment in which decisions about people are made within a moral vacuum: the role of bureaucratic technician (Nellis 2004). Alternatively, there are those who operate with a therapeutic imagination (Millard 1977),

characterised by an acute awareness that they work with people; they belong to a moral universe so that judgements and decisions affect people for good or ill. Additionally, they have a *feel* for the individuals they work with, often agonise over decisions, and try to live with the many conflicts generated by the job in pursuit of criminal and social justice and doing what is right for individual offenders and victims. The tragedy of what has been happening within the organisation since the 1970s is that this division has been accentuated. The service has become more bureaucratic and routinised, with a plethora of top-down procedures, systems and targets. But we still need those with a therapeutic imagination to promote decency, humanity and understanding in probation practice.

7. Under NOMS, probation officers are being re-labelled offender managers/directors and the new designation is highly suggestive, indicating a further cultural shift from supervising people to managing various categories and degrees of risk. Perhaps another way of expressing this point is to draw attention to an organisation that is top heavy with the quantitative features of national standards, key performance indicators, targets and efficiency; rather than the quality of relationships, the qualitative and ineffable dimensions of the job, and those practice skills alluded to above.

Having considered a series of events between 2001 and 2004, in addition to reflections on practice issues, within this framework we turn to address a number of associated developments.

Governance in Probation

The new governance arrangements created for the national service from April 2001 were dramatically different to those that had evolved over the previous 75 years (Statham 2000). Since the Criminal Justice Act 1925 made the appointment of paid probation officers a legal requirement for each petty sessional area, oversight or, in modern parlance, governance had been the responsibility of probation committees. The handbook for probation committee members produced by the Central Probation Council (1987) outlined governance arrangements for local probation services. It stated that probation committees were bodies corporate (p3.2) and the duties and powers of probation committees were contained in two pieces of legislation: Probation Rules 1984 (as amended) and the Probation Service Act 1993 which in effect consolidated earlier legislation. The duties and powers of probation committees are contained in sections 3 to 9 of the Probation Service Act and summarised in the CPC document as follows:

(a) To appoint and remunerate Probation Officers

(b) To provide for the efficient work of Probation Officers

(c) To make arrangements for Probation Officers to supervise cases as required, both adults and children

(d) To make any payments to those under supervision that are considered necessary

(e) To decide how many Probation Officers are sufficient for the area provided that this does not conflict with funding arrangements

(f) To provide, with approval of the Secretary of State, hostels and other facilities for use in connection with the rehabilitation of offenders

(g) To make payments to those required to use hostels

(h) To make grants to other bodies and to forge joint arrangements for service delivery.

The legislation also gave the Home Secretary the power to take default action against any committee that failed to fulfil its statutory duties. The Central Probation Council document suggested it was probably fair to say that committees derived their power through being held accountable by the Home Secretary and in turn holding managers and staff to account (p3.3). More accurately, what was being described was a system of delegated power, with considerable discretion being held locally. From 1925 to the 1980s perceptions and awareness about the governance of probation services had been somewhat low-key. However, the Central Probation Council, through its work in producing the handbook for committee members, attempted to promote greater accountability. This was an initiative which reflected wider concerns about boardroom governance promoted by Cadbury (1992) and later reinforced by Nolan (1997).

Two other developments also prompted discussion of these issues within probation: the Green Paper, *Supervision and Punishment in the Community* (Home Office 1990b); and Blue Paper, *Organising Supervision and Punishment in the Community* (Home Office 1991). The Blue Paper outlined thinking about the organisational structure of the probation service and, after consultation, in July 1992 the Home Office announced that ministers had agreed that probation committees should be replaced by Boards. The announcement indicated an intention by government to produce legislation that would change the old committee structure in favour of a Board membership of sixteen, comprising seven magistrates, one judge, two local authority appointees and five members of the local community; there would be fifteen non-executive Board members with the Chief Probation Officer being the one executive member of the Board.

Parliamentary time was never found for these changes to be enshrined in legislation and individual probation services in England and Wales were left in limbo contemplating a structural change that never happened. Whilst that may have been unhelpful, the debate and need for better governance arrangements proved to be a fertile one and consequently there was growing clarity, not only about the importance of the role of probation committees, but also about their duties and responsibilities. A number of probation services undertook reviews of their own arrangements and established 'Shadow Board' structures which attempted to emulate the model propounded by government. Shadow Boards in effect became sub-committees of probation committees allowable within the legal framework and there were examples of these new arrangements working well. The responsibilities of Chief Probation Officers were also defined in the 1984 Rules, including the direction of the area service, its effective operation and efficient use of resources.

By the 1990s, however, the climate was changing and Flynn (2000) provided a review of the government's approach to public sector governance. He takes the view that performance management is central, which in his view reflects some of the thinking of the Conservative administration about competition and the need for a business-like approach within the public sector. Flynn proceeds to explore the mechanics of systems which have been used increasingly to monitor performance in the public sector and in doing so reveals a burgeoning set of mechanistic controls driven by the centre. Here was a suggestion that bureaucracy beckoned. Furthermore, 'The Prisons–Probation Review' consultation paper set out possible models for new governance arrangements for probation, at the same time redefining its relationship with the prison service. Challenging deadlines were set for responses to these proposals and the government included its modified thinking in the Criminal Justice and Court Services Bill introduced into the House of Commons on 15th March 2000. Part One of the Bill set out proposals to create two new services from the existing probation structure, the National Probation Service for England and Wales but also the Children and Family Courts Advisory and Support Service. During the ongoing period of consultation a somewhat reluctant government, taking account of the feedback that it had received, changed its perception on a number of issues. It had changed its mind about the name of the service, adopting the title National Probation Service for England and Wales after an attempt to promote the Community Punishment and Rehabilitation Service. More importantly, the Next Steps Agency concept was dropped after a successful argument promoted by the Central Probation Council on the grounds that there remained the need for a local dimension to governance arrangements. However, seriously contentious issues remained: the most important was that Boards would not own the property in which their staff worked; another was the potential conflict of having the Chief Officer as a member of the Board whilst being appointed and employed by the Home Secretary. Wargent (2002) voiced misgivings about the new governance arrangements, which were to prove well founded. On 1st April 2001 the 42 newly created Probation Boards had a paid Chairman to work two days per week and paid board members. The 15 member boards were to include a judge appointed by the Lord Chancellor, who would not be paid by the Home Secretary.

Home Office Memorandum on Governance

In May 2001 the Home Office published its *Management Statement and Financial Memorandum for Local Probation Boards*, which spelled out the new governance arrangements. This was a 40-page document which not only replaced the 'old style' probation Rules, but also provided a governance framework that had greater detail and prescription than had been the case previously. The statement set out the rules and guidelines relevant to local Boards' functions, duties and powers, and how they were to be held accountable. The financial statement set out the financial framework in which the Board was to operate. In section 3 of the document the lines of accountability were delineated from the Home Secretary's accountability to Parliament through to the roles of the local Chief Officer, Treasurer and Secretary. Within this document there were important structural pronouncements as well as expectations of performance. The overall aims and objectives of the national service and local boards were: the protection of the public; the reduction of offending; the proper punishment of offenders;

ensuring offenders' awareness of the effects of crime on the victims of crime and the public; and the rehabilitation of offenders. The definitive message in paragraph 2.2 was that key performance indicators relating to these objectives would be set by the Home Secretary and contained in the Boards' business plan. The implications were clear in that the 42 local services were now working to a national strategy and there was no longer a place for local contextualisation.

The sections on responsibilities and accountability reinforced the hierarchical control from the centre. The role of the Home Secretary was defined in terms of ultimate responsibility to Parliament and in setting the policy and performance framework, determining the level of grants to Boards, and appointing Chiefs, Chairs and board members. The Permanent Secretary at the Home Office was also designated by the Treasury as the department's principal Accounting Officer. The National Director was designated as the National Probation Service Accountable Officer. The Chief Officer became the local Board's Accountable Officer (AO). As AO the Chief Officer was personally responsible for the propriety and regularity of public funds and for the day-to-day operations and management of the local service. The roles of the local Board Chair, Treasurer and Secretary were also defined, with the Treasurer having a particular responsibility in ensuring financial fidelity, with a right of independent access to the local Chair and Board. Paragraph 7 was devoted to staff management. The National Director was defined as having responsibility for paying the remuneration, allowances and expenses of the Chair and Chief Officer. The local Board had payroll responsibilities for local staff and also for their recruitment, retention and motivation. The Financial Memorandum spelled out that the local Board did not have any landowning powers. Consequently, all property rights to previously owned local property were ceded to the Home Office, which also took central responsibility for all local leases too. The repercussions of the loss of local control and subsequent property strategy were serious.

Overall it may be said this structure paid lip-service to the local dimension and the notion that small is beautiful, thus taking little account of the arguments that had been developed prior to nationalisation. The position of local Chiefs as Accountable Officer was interesting vis-à-vis Chairs who were to have limited influence. In the National Probation Service the direction would be set from the centre, monies would be provided from the centre, and the Chief, now virtually the puppet of the centre, could override the local Board. The reservations voiced by the Probation Boards Association (PBA) and others prior to the new legislation had little impact and very quickly into the new structure PBA were expressing considerable misgivings. The anticipated drive from the centre had been a feature of the way in which the National Probation Directorate had begun to conduct its business. In the PBA Newsletter published in February 2002 (Professional Boards Association 2002; see also Wargent 2002), extracts were printed from a letter expressing concerns which had been sent to the NPD Director:

> '... there is feeling that the principles of local governance are being undermined by patterns of behaviour within the directorate.
>
> ... the legislation that brought local boards into being is not understood by Directorate staff, who at times, circumvent the proper process of discussion with employers and does not listen to the voices of concern that are being raised.
>
> The cash limit: boards have expressed concerns over top slicing developments which have created a serious position. Services previously provided locally at an affordable level have now switched to more expensive and not demonstrably better central arrangements.
>
> IT contract: The contract with Integris and its substantial cost have caused local boards to question whether they will be able to deliver the full agenda of what is expected of them.
>
> Facilities management: members have commented on the inadvisability of contract services in Hostels where issues of security, vulnerability and liability occur more starkly.'

These brief extracts, so openly critical, provide not only a barometer of the relations between PBA and NPD but also provide an insight into how NPD had set about developing the new probation culture. PBA gained its intelligence from Chairs of local Boards who had expected to be able to promote a local dimension to the work of probation areas. The concerns being raised reinforced the fact that their roles had been marginalised from the outset. Additionally, the concerns voiced by PBA were exemplified by the behaviour of those at the centre in the new National Probation Directorate. Such behaviour was indicative of the way in which business was conducted by NPD in its dealings with its external world. Furthermore, the way in which NPD conducted business within the National Probation Service would be illustrative of the new culture.

Creating a New Culture

At the launch of new regimes it might be expected that those with the opportunity of building a new organisation would plan carefully in order to create a sense of identity but also to ensure a sense of mutual ownership vital to the creation of motivation within organisations. The same careful approach might also be expected as an organisation builds its links with key players in its environment. In the second of these dimensions, as we have illustrated by the reaction of PBA, the portents were not positive. Within the internal world of probation there were also worrying signs that the new regime was driven by a centralist political process reflecting a one-dimensional expediency of power and control. So 1st April 2001 began the new era for probation; it was the first day of the new nationalised structure. An assessment centre had been used in the appointment of the newly styled Chief Officers but there were still some gaps amongst the 42 areas that were filled on an 'acting up' basis until a further assessment centre was held. All the Chief Officers were now employed by the Home Office with, as we have illustrated, line management responsibility to the National Director. Whilst the governance structure would have a major dynamic change, it would take some time for the impact of the almost totalitarian style structure to be felt.

The first National Director, Eithne Wallis, began the task of building the national directorate, creating a structure that was primarily intended to influence performance in the 42 areas. To what extent this exercise required prior knowledge of probation culture is a matter for conjecture, but we can assume that in writing *A New Choreography* (Home Office 2001c) the Director had attempted to create a common perception, a shared agenda, a sense of ownership, even a rallying call for the new service. The draft document had been trailed, prior to April 2001, with a roadshow designed to enable the Director to speak to as many staff as possible. The success of this initiative would depend on its effectiveness in securing the commitment of staff. But the heavy political influence that had dictated change in probation prior to 2001 had increased scepticism in a service that had a long tradition of agnosticism. Consequently, the publication of *A New Choreography* in August 2001, accompanied by even tighter national standards, was perceived as the manifestation of political centralism. The measures acutely reinforced a sense of negativism at all levels in the organisation.

This was now a more authoritarian era and one factor that is beyond dispute was that all Chief Officers were expected to know the dance steps; the future of the new service was predicated on expectations of a new level of loyalty to the centre that would be rewarded, but dissonance would not be tolerated. Perhaps, as a result of this newly found authoritarianism, there was a sublime expectation that everyone would automatically fall into line and the need for a coherent change strategy was overlooked. It is not unrealistic to expect that the creation of this new organisational structure for probation might have been influenced by some accompanying theoretical model. Despite some misgivings in the world of probation, management theory does have an established academic credibility and might have been used in informing the various aspects associated with planned organisational and cultural change.

We revisited Stonor and Wankel (1986), Pugh (1984) and Handy (1985) to remind ourselves of the theory of organisations and management. These writers are but representative of many possible theoretical sources. But the chapters in Stonor and Wankel on 'Managing Organisational Change and Development' (Chapter 13) and 'Leading' (Chapters 15–19) would have provided some helpful reminders of the important issues that need attention in successfully handling change. However, careful attention and planning were not readily apparent, either in the process associated with change or the behaviours exhibited within NPD. In fairness, the need to create an effective team in the new national directorate must have been the major priority and, as there were so many new people in post and so much of the change was unscripted, it was always going to be a difficult challenge. However, there has been little evidence to suggest that change in probation was promoted through anything other than a series of coercive measures and with an expectation of uncritical conformity.

Prior to 2001 it could be argued that probation had developed a distinctive culture, created over many decades through a shared set of beliefs, norms, values and attitudes (Stonor and Wankel 1986 p374). Whilst probation culture could not be defined in an unqualified homogenous manner, there was enough of a shared perspective for people working within the organisation to be linked by some sense of common purpose. This sense of shared culture was probably at its strongest in the rehabilitative 1960s and 1970s and as probation made its collective decision that it was different to mainstream social work post-1968 Seebohm. However, it is important to recognise that culture is not static; it is subject to change through both internal and external influences. It also has both formal and informal dimensions and organisational culture is often described through myths and legends

(Whitehead and Thompson 2004 p136f). Despite these rather diffuse elements, organisational culture is recognisable as a binding agent to those who are part of an organisation. Therefore, events that threaten or challenge culture are seen as a threat to the perceived order and, if change is to be handled successfully, fear has to be diffused and resistance overcome. Quite simply, the process of cultural change, if there are good arguments for pursuing such a course of action, must be handled with great sensitivity. It should also be recognised that ultimately it will be individuals comprising an organisation who themselves define their loyalty and allegiance. It is axiomatic to most people that being part of an organisation requires more than an ability to take instruction. Being constantly directed is unlikely to promote a sense of self-worth or job satisfaction. It is much more likely that this is gained from some personal expression of values and commitment to a cause or a common sense of purpose, including emotional investment in a set of beliefs. At its very basic it is perhaps the kindling of a creative spark that is sustaining. We might ask: What makes us feel we are part of an organisation? What generates loyalty? In addition to believing in the rationale of an organisation, having confidence in its leadership seems essential. This is achieved through good communication that enables individuals within the organisation to understand decision-making processes, and also providing opportunities to influence them.

Against the background of these issues, which we would argue should play a part in the thinking of those driving change, how were events handled as the National Probation Service was launched? Given that the National Probation Directorate was committed to getting the best out of its staff, how successful have they been in achieving that objective? As we have intimated above, behaviour provides the best cultural benchmark in measuring the performance of individuals. So the way in which the National Probation Directorate behaved, the things they did and not just said, provides the best evidence of their intentions, direction and priorities, and ultimately the flaws in thinking and processes pursued.

New governance arrangements were a crucial factor as they defined the structure and ultimately the power in the modernised service. In 2001, within the new structure of the National Probation Service, there were two significant cohorts of staff: the senior post-holders in NPD and the newly-titled Chief Officers so clearly responsible for performance in area services. In order for the new organisation to be successful, both groups needed to understand what was expected of them and be motivated to deliver. There also needed to be a shared understanding of what was expected of each group and sympathy for the shared agenda. Inevitably, the National Director who had responsibility for both groups was drawn to the centre, as the creation of the new NPD senior management team was a major exercise. Whilst there had been some lead-in time in creating the new team, there was no existing culture that would ease them into their new roles supportively. Consequently, the effectiveness of the leadership role itself became a starker barometer of success in what was essentially a process of change management. A number of Strategic Heads were appointed to oversee key developments and these post-holders in effect became the senior management team in NPD. This senior management team, with the National Director at its head, was responsible for gaining the support of the Chiefs in the 42 areas and delivering the aspirations of the National Probation Service spelled out in the planning documents.

The significance of this exercise in organisational cohesiveness was neither understood nor delivered. The Chiefs operating in their local areas began to feel a growing sense of isolation followed by detachment from the centre. As a result of the preoccupations at the centre, the Director was unable to provide appropriate inputs into the supervision and appraisal process even for the newest Chief Officers, who were expected to conform. When performance after the first year of operation was reviewed and the performance related pay process handled in a dilatory and bureaucratic way, then the sense of alienation within the Chief Officer group was palpable.

It should also be made clear that the National Director was embroiled in a further and even more important set of dynamics as a member of the Home Office Board, chaired by the permanent secretary and the seat of power in the government machine. This Board is the policy-setting body and has oversight of the budget-setting process across all the areas of Home Office activity. At a personal level it must have been alarming for the National Director, an individual with such a massive change agenda within her own organisation, to devote so much energy to the internal political machinations of those seeking to determine political outcomes. By the beginning of 2004 the National Director found herself outflanked in a political process that saw the erstwhile prisons director, in the guise of Commissioner for Correctional Services at that time, Martin Narey, invited by the Home Secretary to be the first Chief Executive of a new National Offender Management Service. The vehicle for change was the Carter Report (which has already been discussed).

The Role of Chief Officer

Whilst Chairs of Boards retained an association, Central Council of Probation Committees essentially became the Professional Boards Association, which in principle enabled them to contribute to a dialogue with the centre, notwithstanding Chief Officers being denied an independent voice after the demise of ACOP. Chief Constables and Prison Governors have maintained their professional associations and, whilst Chief Officers in probation have an effective trade union, there has been no professional network that would provide them with a safe and effective way of presenting their views. The climate in which Chief Officers were operating from 2001 changed dramatically; they did not feel safe to speak out and were given little opportunity to influence the new system. ACOP may have had its frailties but its inclusive and comprehensive structure, which facilitated wide debate, was now both missing and missed. This made the whimsical little scenario of auctioning the ACOP emblem at the final ACOP event, bid for and successfully purchased by the new National Director, a curious phenomenon.

Chief Officers, denuded of experience and now part of a centralised and coercive structure after 2001, had been demoralised and neutralised. Efforts made in 2002 to create a more inclusive structure between areas and the centre through management development initiatives from within NPD were not sustained; and Chief Officer isolation continued. There was also a brief attempt made in 2003 to promote a Chief Officer association, fuelled by the recognition that the group had an important voice in a democratic society. Eventually the PBA recognised the implications of leaving the group voiceless and, in March 2005, began an initiative to create a mechanism for allowing them an independent voice again. However, it should be recorded that as a group they had little opportunity objectively and dispassionately to influence events as they unfolded after 2001. Consequently, an essential element of applied operational wisdom was missing from the outpourings of the centre, which continued with little understanding of their impact on local services.

NOMS and Parliamentary Scrutiny

Following the announcement of the Carter Review on 6th January 2004 and the publication of *Reducing Crime – Changing Lives*, an adjournment debate on the National Offender Management Service was secured in the House of Commons on 17th March 2004. Both

PBA and NAPO had been effective in lobbying activity and the impact of this kept alive important issues about the NOMS proposals from January 2004 through to the calling of the general election in April 2005. In fact, a series of adjournment debates were called during this period which provided an opportunity for a number of troubled voices to be heard. Issues were raised using parliamentary privilege and custom which illuminated some of the government's rather opaque practices. By trawling Hansard debates, we have been able to identify a number of concerns and report them below, preserving as much of the flavour of the parliamentary rhetoric as was feasible, in order to highlight some of the most glaring aspects. We have not identified the speakers, apart from those opening the debates, and sometimes we have joined contributions from different individuals if they were contributing to the same point. The extracts are in reported speech but on occasions the direct speech comes through as it provides important emphasis. We believe this approach is a more powerful way of recording the manifest and sustained disquiet amongst the elected representatives of all political parties.

Neil Gerrard, the Labour MP for Walthamstow, opened the first of the debates on 17th March 2004 by asking why the reorganisation was so important that it had to be done by June 2004; equally, why require feedback by 3rd March for a paper published on the 6th January? The issue of contestability was raised as the debate progressed and other MPs contributed. It was suggested that prison officers in the private sector received pay which was 24% to 32% less than those in the public sector, and that pensions were 10% to 13% more valuable in the public sector than the private sector. *Reducing Crime – Changing Lives* did not refer to the fact that probation had been substantially reorganised under the Criminal Justice and Court Services Act 2000 and these changes had not yet bedded down. NPD increased its staff from about 90 in 2001 to 460 in November 2003, and during that period there was no commensurate increase in the number of field staff. Prison numbers are a response to the panic climate of a 'bang 'em up' culture produced largely by the clamour of the *Daily Mail*. We face a retributionist mood that magistrates have been panicked into and the merger of the services will have no bearing on it. Carving out chunks of the service by privatisation will not produce a seamless service but rather fragmentation, which will make it difficult if not impossible to follow things through. Now we have contestability we might as well be straightforward and call it privatisation. It is extremely worrying that the concept will not be subject to legislation.

There is a general lack of transparency. In 2002 NPD privatised hostel facilities including cooks, cleaners and maintenance staff. The costs subsequently rose by 62%. In 2003 NPD decided to privatise the management and maintenance of probation premises and costs rose by 35% – outrageous. The situation is becoming a comedy of errors, a combination of *Fawlty Towers* and *Porridge*. Moreover, the probation service is becoming even more a correctional service than a social work service – a move in the wrong direction. We cannot overemphasise the good that can be done with the traditional method of advising, assisting and befriending. The document entitled *Reducing Crime – Changing Lives* states: 'Believing that offenders in the community will reduce their re-offending through occasional interviews with probation officers is also naïve'. This comment belittles what probation officers have achieved over the years because offenders have been able to trust them. Problems have been created by the National Probation Directorate's £20-million overspend which means cuts in funding of 2% this year and 8% next. The structures implemented in April 2001 should have been monitored and independently evaluated before further changes were introduced. Melding two organisations in possession of a different ethos and ways of doing things needs careful thought; I have no confidence that this has been done. I want to congratulate the Government on its speed. Patrick Carter presented his report to the Prime Minister on 11th December 2003 and the Government were able to produce *Reducing Crime – Changing Lives* on 6th January. This breaks all records for a Government's response. It is a miracle what can be achieved over the Christmas period when one sets one's mind to it. These comments are from the 17th March 2004 debate, which included contributions from both sides of the house and ended with a response from the Minister.

Ian Griffiths, Labour MP for Reading East, secured a further debate on 19th May 2004, which he applied for after a lobby from probation staff in his constituency. Inevitably, some of the ground covered in the earlier debate resurfaced, but again the emerging perspectives reflected parliamentary disquiet. Staff are concerned that the changes have not received any parliamentary scrutiny. A member of staff asked me that if there was value in a single coherent sentence to deal with prisoners why was not the same logic applied to offenders in the community, instead of breaking up the probation service into purchasers and providers. Local authorities who were forced down this route in the 1980s and 1990s have now put them back together again. Last week I was involved with 1,200 probation officers engaged in a lobby of

Parliament. It was clear that there was a degree of demoralisation, people feel extremely insecure and there is a danger that experienced staff will be lost. I shall concentrate my remarks on the latest Home Office paper, issued by Martin Narey on the 10th May, which asks for responses by the 11th June. The paper talks about being driven by the legislative timetable but – I am sure that the Minister will correct me if I am wrong – my understanding is that there is no need for legislation on reorganising service delivery. If the Home Office wanted to change the structures of the probation service and the prison service, or put them together, it would not need legislation to do so. The paper asks for responses to quite a number of questions and some of these raise even more questions. The structure shows a purchaser–provider split. The whole of the prison service is in the provider part, but a 70–30 split is proposed for current probation officers. Roughly 70% would go into the purchaser side and about 30% would be on the provider side, although the purchaser side as it stands would include such things as human resources, finance and back office support. I have seen comments suggesting that people in those parts of the service have no guarantee they will remain on the purchaser side for ever. Private sector involvement in the probation service has not been very successful hitherto. The privatisation of hostels saw costs rising by an average of 62%. A Brighton hostel was forced to call in environmental health officers because of the state of the kitchen. A hostel in Sheffield had no cleaner for 12 weeks. A hostel in London needed a boiler switching on and a carpenter was sent from Portsmouth. A call-out from Newcastle resulted in a contractor being sent from Chester.

Cheryl Gillan, Conservative Member for Chesham and Amersham, claimed to be the first Conservative MP since Willie Whitelaw to address such a parliamentary lobby. On the question of NOMS she urged the need to stop, think and slow down. She pointed out that the budget for the organisation would be enormous, £3 billion, and one man, Martin Narey, will handle it. He has been put in place and appointed, although I do not believe that there was any contestability for that post. I will let the Minister intervene to correct me if it was advertised but I do not believe it was. At the end of the 19th May 2004 debate the Minister, when summing up, replied that Martin Narey had been appointed to the job of Chief Executive of NOMS by the Home Secretary. He was previously Commissioner for Corrections and had effectively managed the £2.5 billion prison service budget.

The final adjournment debate of the Parliament was secured by Claire Curtis-Thomas, Labour MP for Crosby, on 6th April 2005. She referred to the earlier debate on 16th March 2005, which had raised concerns that were not adequately addressed because of time constraints. Issues being raised were similar to those of more than a year ago, though events that had surfaced during the intervening period added an extra frisson to some of the points made. On 7th May 2004, under cover of a letter from Martin Narey, the Home Office issued organisational and design proposals for NOMS. On 20th July 2004 the Minister withdrew the proposals. On 20th January 2005 I wrote to the Minister about the lack of progress and the paucity of information. Whether those or other concerns were the trigger to action is not known, but a brief flurry of information followed, issued by the Home Office and containing various descriptions of a NOMS end-state diagram. It is no different in essence from the proposed system that was withdrawn by the Home Office in July 2004. I should also like more information about the role and powers of local offender managers. I am concerned that the prison service seems to have opted out of NOMS and that offender managers will not be able to effect programmes in prison, as they will have no authority over prison governors. The unfolding debate on 6th April 2005 reinforced the importance of the local structure and of partnerships with the not-for-profit/voluntary sector. Discussion then moved on to the issue of contestability. The NOMS update magazine published in January 2005 had suggested that through separating offender management from interventions, existing providers would compete with private and voluntary sector providers to supply interventions in the community. It was suggested that if agencies had to compete for work then they would develop their own strategies; there would be secrecy and no sharing of best practice.

In the debate there were voices of implacable opposition to contestability and a restatement of the need to involve local people in work with offenders. There was also concern about how things might be done and it was suggested that there were different offender management targets in different prisons. It was suggested that public sector prisons had a target of keeping overcrowding below 24%, whilst in contracted prisons it is 34%. So there are clear disparities between contracted and publicly run prisons when it comes to targeting. The Minister was asked to respond. It was then suggested that the NOMS business plan had just been published on the Home Office website and appeared not to have been circulated to probation boards and Chief Officers. We seem to be descending into a quagmire. People do not know what is going on and communications are exceedingly poor. I understand that a cluster of prisons has already been put out to competition under the National

Offender Management Service, but the Bill has gone nowhere. The Minister wrote on 24th March that there was no intention of withdrawing the Bill but today, 6th April, the Bill has little likelihood of success. The NOMS business plan was then referred to as being extremely thin and attention was drawn to annex C of the plan, which was a summary risk register. It was pointed out that aspects of the plan had attached a colour relating to a traffic light code risk scale. It was also pointed out that some issues were thought to be so high risk that they were rated outside the traffic light system, at black. These were 'loss of key skills resulting in inadequate supervision of dangerous offenders'; 'failure to obtain GSI accreditation results in reduced cross-CJs collaboration leading to failure to deliver benefits of joined up for CJS' (this refers to failure of communication by email); 'inadequate supervision of cases leading to high profile media attention and unmanageable policy making'.

At the end of the 6th April 2005 debate the Minister, Paul Goggins, replied. He spoke of the difference between the business case and the business plan and said that the government would reconsider its refusal to publish the full business case. He then conceded that a copy of the five-page business plan may not have been sent to all Chairs and chief executives, but that they had been published on the website. He went on to say that one individual offender manager would be responsible for the whole sentence plan, whether in prison or the community. But there was an issue about where a prison governor's responsibility began and ended. The governor was responsible for good order and discipline in the prison and would continue to exercise that authority, but the system would not be composed of two distinct and unrelated parts. The offender manager would determine the plan, see it through and be accountable for its impact. At the end of this, the last debate of the Parliament on 6th April 2005, there were many questions that had not been answered and, whilst the Minister said that he would ensure that outstanding questions would be answered despite Parliament being prorogued, the debate itself had indicated the difficulty of holding a government to account.

Much can be learned through this briefest of reviews of the adjournment debates, not only about the democratic process itself but also the *modus operandi* of New Labour in its dealings with probation up to the general election of May 2005. The arrangements for NOMS had not been thought out clearly and, it could be said, were in fact shambolic. PBA and NAPO, together with other individuals, had usefully maintained the lobby and kept alive an important debate. It had exposed a crude plan for the privatisation of the probation service and near secrecy in the way in which government went about its business. There are so many questions that emerge from these parliamentary debates. As events continue to unfold, readers will judge for themselves how issues and concerns have been handled by government in what is a key development in our criminal justice system.

One issue seems to stand out at this juncture and that is related to the reply given by Paul Goggins at the end of the debate on 6th April 2005. In making the point about a prison governor's position with regard to maintaining good order and discipline in a prison establishment, he seemed to be suggesting that this issue was paramount. As such it would transcend any other issue that might be seen to get in the way of the principle. This is not a new position, but we need to remind ourselves that this tenet has so often in the past been used to frustrate initiatives and aspirations within the prison setting. Given the centrality of good order and discipline, if a prison wing was a member of staff down, for example, it could be used as an argument for not allowing prisoner movements and attendance at programmes or other activities. One absence would invalidate the programme should the same criteria be applied as those appertaining to programme delivery in the community. In such circumstances the offender manager could not see the supervision programme through; the need for attendance would quite simply have been subordinated to the discipline of the establishment. We would not seek to argue against this principle but would urge people to remain mindful of institutional dynamics; the needs of the institution can be used to frustrate initiatives. The minister's answer in effect revealed that prisons were not equal partners in NOMS. The problems of joined-up thinking between the two organisations, which had been seen to exist in the past (that is, since the aspiration to deliver throughcare in the 1960s), had manifested themselves again. The minister's moment of candour, in reinforcing the operational independence of prison governors, might lead to the conclusion that the NOMS initiative was, after all, an exercise simply to deconstruct the probation service, and to promote its privatisation. As if to reinforce this suspicion, a further and significant issue emerged, just prior to the general election and linked into our continuing theme of governance.

Governance and Correctional Services

A document was produced by the Home Office headed 'NOMS Design Workshop', which purported to explain the organisational arrangements of the correctional services. The paper (circulated within the service but not attributed to an identified author) sets out to clarify organisational arrangements for probation and prisons, which we will précis. It is suggested that the National Probation Service is not a statutory body because probation boards rather than the Secretary of State are responsible for delivering all probation services, either directly through their own staff or through contracts. However, paragraph 12 of Schedule 1 to the Criminal Justice and Court Services Act 2000 says that the functions and other powers of local probation boards must be performed in accordance with any directions given by the Secretary of State. Chief Officers in probation are statutory office holders not civil servants. As a consequence, there is no line management from the Secretary of State to the Chief Officer in probation as there is in the prison service. However, Chief Officers are accountable to the Secretary of State through the Director General, and NPD exercises functions on behalf of the Secretary of State (according to Carltona principles).

The difference between the two services is also illustrated by the audit arrangements. Prisons are subject to audit by the National Audit Office and probation by the Audit Commission. The paper then goes on to discuss the role of boards as employers and the implications for changing the employment status of probation employees. The final section is devoted to issues relating to the contracting out of functions, suggesting that under current arrangements only boards can let contracts for the delivery of probation services. This is a position that seems to be contradicted by: 'The Secretary of State can direct Boards to contract-out support services (see section 8 of the 2000 Act) but probably not any other. However it is arguable that the general power of direction which the Secretary of State has by virtue of paragraphs 12 and 14 of Schedule 1 of the 2000 Act, would allow him to direct Boards to contract-out other non-support services' (paragraph 14). This is a further development of the governance debate that has been a recurring feature in this book. The creation of NOMS has provided the need for clarification, but the exercise seems to be a further indicator of the route to probation privatisation and reinforces the concerns expressed in Parliament and elsewhere.

Summary and Conclusion

To some extent this chapter is self explanatory, particularly the first main section that recounts significant events occurring in a relatively short period of time. These events are sandwiched between the *Justice*

For All White Paper and a discussion on probation practice as a neglected feature of recent organisational and cultural change.

We have also developed an important theme that threads its way through the book, beginning in Chapter 2, namely changing governance structures, including: realigning the balance between local area autonomy and centrally determined prescription; the creation of a new organisational culture with the National Probation Directorate as its driving force; within the context of the National Offender Management Service. The emergence of NOMS, so soon after the creation of a National Probation Service, has caused disquiet amongst individual members of staff in addition to representative organisations. Even members of Parliament have been exercised, if not bemused, by the pace and nature of what has been happening since 2001.

So what now for probation services beyond the election of May 2005? What now for NOMS and the wider criminal justice system, including the supervision of individual offenders? We have much to think about in our final chapter as we begin to draw the salient threads of this book together, summarise the last seven chapters and look to the future.

NOTES – Chapter 7

[1] This is an interesting discussion in a helpful paper by Andrew Ashworth (2002) that can be found in the third edition of the *Oxford Handbook of Criminology*, edited by Maguire, Morgan and Reiner.

[2] We are specifically thinking about the Criminal Justice Act 1961 and Criminal Justice Act 1967. The Criminal Justice Act 1972 legislated for the community service order, suspended sentence supervision order, bail hostels and day training centres; we can also refer to the Criminal Justice Act 1991. For a genealogy of probation-relevant legislation beginning in 1861, see Whitehead and Thompson (2004) from pp69–77.

[3] We have referred to the Departmental Committees of 1909, 1922 and 1936 and Morison in 1962. Where the latter is concerned the committee was appointed on 27th May 1959 and reported in 1962, a much longer period of deliberation than reports referred to in Chapters 6 and 7 (for example, Halliday and Carter).

[4] In Teesside, for example, for 2004/05 the priority targets were:

Basic Skills: 501* starts and 125 awards
Enhanced Community Punishment completions 470*
Accredited Programmes completions 235*
DTTO starts 204*
DTTO 35% completion rate*
Offenders complying with their sentence: 70% compliance*
Timely breach action within ten days: 90% of relevant cases
Timely contact with victims of serious violent or sexual offences (8 weeks): 85% of cases*
Reducing staff sickness: 9 days per staff year
Accurate and timely race and ethnic monitoring of offenders: 95%*
Clear sentencing proposals for minority ethnic offenders. 95% of relevant PSRs*

   * = performance bonus scheme measures apply.

Reference to both national and local targets provides the reader with an understanding of the quantitative context within which the service has to operate.

Chapter 8

CONCLUSION: SUMMARY, EXPLANATIONS AND THE FUTURE

'In 1985 we had Labour out of power confronting a remorselessly increasing crime rate, bravely proposing to reduce imprisonment; today we have Labour in government, facing a decreasing crime rate, proposing exactly the opposite policy. The turnaround could not have been more complete.' *(Young 2003 p42)*

'The jury is therefore out. The new-style probation service, tightly managed and regulated, bears little resemblance to the probation service of even a few years ago ... Are we moving to a system of home confinement and surveillance, with probation officers acting as "soft cops"?' *(Goodman 2003 p219)*

Introduction: 1876 to 1962

We opened our account with a discussion of various themes and influences that seem pertinent when telling the story of probation, particularly during the early years: religion and humanitarianism standing against the Victorian prison; vestige of politics, power and control of working class people; the changing narratives around criminology, reform, rehabilitation and punishment. We have also touched upon the inward journey of psychology and, by contrast, the outward social dimension. Within the parameters established by these themes and influences, Chapter 2 selectively explored 1907 to 1979, those years sandwiched between reforming Liberals and radical Conservatives. The former introduced the Probation of Offenders Act 1907, enabling courts to make a probation order that was not a sentence or punishment but a reforming measure characterised by friendship, the personal influence of the probation officer and 'philanthropic assistance' (Oldfield 2002 p21). It was the relationship between officer and probationer that was intended to effect moral and spiritual influence conducive to conformity (Police Court Mission Diary). During the early years, and influenced by missionary endeavour, the inchoate system was more concerned with saving souls and mainly used for young and first offenders (McWilliams 1983).

Probation as a reforming and rehabilitative rather than punitive measure

247

was endorsed by the four Home Office Departmental Committees of 1909, 1922, 1936 and 1962. In a relatively benign political world after 1907 for criminal justice matters, notwithstanding the interruption of two world wars, probation was associated with assisting people and normalising behaviour (Garland 1985); promoting citizenship (Oldfield 2002 p31); welfare and treatment. As late as Morison (Home Office 1962) probation was pursuing rehabilitation through a casework relationship to correct individual dysfunction and probation officers were seen as the social workers of the court (Whitehead and Thompson 2004 p13f). By the 1960s we see the acme of the welfare-treatment model, particularly with juvenile offenders probation officers used to supervise, coming to its full flowering in the Children and Young Persons Act 1969. But ten years before, *Penal Practice in a Changing Society* (Home Office 1959) marked the apotheosis of a treatment approach for adult offenders. Even though by the mid-1960s probation was at the heart of the Labour government's penal policy, the wheel was beginning to turn. In fact we want to suggest that during the years 1963 to 1979 we can identify seven significant events that sowed the seeds of change and altered the mission of first saving souls and then curing the individual by casework. These events, or disturbances, have already been discussed but we place more emphasis upon them here because they are largely responsible for the service altering its shape. Notwithstanding ideological changes (McWilliams 1983, 1985, 1986), the probation service was the probation order premised upon the relationship between officer and probationer.

Seven Significant Events: 1963 to 1979

First, the report by the Advisory Council on the Treatment of Offenders on aftercare (Home Office 1963) was significant (Windlesham 1993 p104). Secondly, and related to the first point, by 1967 the re-badged Probation and After-Care Service was established with an expanded set of responsibilities for all forms of compulsory supervision and aftercare. By 1969 probation officers were filling posts in remand centres, detention centres and borstal allocation centres. Therefore, it is a time of expansion and diversification that took the system beyond predominantly supervising people on probation in the community. Having said that, we need to remind ourselves that by the early 1960s probation was involved in preparing court reports, matrimonial work, in addition to some responsibility for prison, approved school and borstal aftercare. Nevertheless, probation work was being propelled in a different orbit potentially aligned to more punitive influences. By contrast we can entertain the possibility of probation humanising custodial facilities at a time when it remained at the heart of rehabilitative penal policies in the 1960s. Be that as it may, we make the point that the diversification of probation duties in the direction of aftercare constituted a threat to the probation ideal.

Thirdly, we must draw attention to the Seebohm Report (Home Office 1968) which forced probation to choose between assimilation with the new local authority social services departments (which is what occurred in Scotland; Kilbrandon 1964) and preserving its independence and difference. To merge with other forms of social work constituted a threat because the probation system would have lost its identity as something other than mainstream social work (Murch 1969). But, in refusing to assimilate, we suggest a tension was created between social work ethos and values, and a different set of values created by closer allegiance with the wider criminal justice system. Therefore, in maintaining its independence, probation embarked upon a journey that weakened its place within the family of social work. It is interesting to observe that, in light of future battles over the competing ideologies of care and control, it was NAPO that stood against assimilation. Perhaps this was a more significant choice than we realised at the time because of future implications.

Fourthly, during the late 1960s Baroness Wootton (Home Office 1970), whose work contributed to the Criminal Justice Act 1972, proposed the Community Service Order (in addition to other new sentences as alternatives to custody). This was a hybrid sentence containing elements of rehabilitation, reparation, and punishment. Therefore, to what degree, if at all, did the Community Service Order further dilute the probation ideal as it had evolved between 1907 and the early 1960s?

Fifthly, a combination of IMPACT (1974, 1976), Martinson (1974) and Brody (1976) winded probation because empirical research and theoretical critiques questioned the efficacy of the rehabilitative and probation ideal. Sixthly, the Younger Report (in 1974), the Kent Control Unit (in 1980) and the *Cullen v Rogers* judgment (in 1982) illustrated the ideological disquiet that was present in probation by this time, resulting in the care–control battles following the collapse of the rehabilitative ideal. This was a time when probation was trying to define a new role for itself in what was becoming a post-rehabilitative age. The responses, as we have seen, were a number of models located at different points along the care–control continuum (Whitehead 1990).

The probation ideal was indubitably under pressure by the late 1970s because of the various factors just cited. Finally, the election of a new-right Conservative government in May 1979 detached itself from the previous criminal justice consensus by promoting a harsher law and order tone, despite the liberal influences of William Whitelaw and, later, the Indian summer of the Hurd, Patten and Faulkner years. This was a decisive moment that signalled the game was up. The service was fortunate to survive the Howard years of the mid-1990s and New Labour's euphemistically labelled modernisation programme hastened its demise even further. Of course, our reading of events is not as straightforward as it appears because New Labour embraced the What Works programme in 1997; committed itself to the Diploma in Probation Studies from 1998; considerably expanded the Trainee Probation Officer programme from 2001; and has better resourced the service in response to the additional demands expected by the Criminal Justice Act 2003 and NOMS. Yet all these developments are not tantamount to political support for the probation ideal but rather a very different type of organisation that has been evolving since the Thatcher and Major years.

Consequently, our first substantive point in this final chapter is to suggest that the period from 1963 to 1979 provides the framework within and background against which further critical changes occurred. These 16 years can be identified as the platform for the creation of the late or post-modern service that started to take shape after 1979. In fact, the early 1960s to late 1970s can be described as the 'surface of emergence' providing the 'conditions of existence' (Garland 1985, 2001) that enable us to explain why probation evolved in the way it has during the last 25 years from our vantage point in 2005. Therefore we suggest, in very broad terms, three distinct periods distilled from our analysis contained in Chapters 1 to 7: first, 1907 to 1962 saw probation progress from its religious, moral and spiritual influences to scientific casework, rehabilitation and treatment; secondly, 1963 to 1979 created the basis for radical change as a consequence of expanding aftercare duties, the Seebohm dilemma, the Community Service *mélange*, challenging empirical research, care–control debates, and a qualitatively different political climate after the election of the Conservatives in 1979. Part 2 of our book focuses on the third period, 1979 to 2001, and the clues to answering our *why* question posed in the Introduction are to be found here. Therefore, what are the major forces (themes and influences would bring us full circle with the construction in Chapter 1) since 1979 that help to explain the probation system in which we find ourselves in 2005? We draw attention to nine explanatory themes we think are significant.

Forces Undermining Probation: 1979 to 2005

New Politics

The political framework within which to think about and respond to offending behaviour and concomitantly probation work was different after 1979, although Brake and Hale (1992) trace important changes to the Labour government after 1976. To some degree political discourse decoupled more overtly offending behaviour from its wider social context, in marked contrast to the era of political and 'penological modernism' (Raynor and Vanstone 2002) that associated crime with social-economic factors. At one time the view that crime is a consequence of social deprivation requiring amelioration through improved social conditions, within a broader welfare state committed to rehabilitation, was the prevailing orthodoxy. This was a view accepted by the main political parties.

However, after 1979 Mrs Thatcher commented that 'the most direct way to act against crime is to make life as difficult as possible for the potential and actual criminal' (1995 p558), which changed the explanatory framework, tone of debates, and political culture for probation and sentencers. She also had a tougher approach to sentencing compared to some of her colleagues (1993 p307). We have seen that the penal politics of the 1890s to 1970s initially complemented social reforms under the Liberals after 1906 and then rehabilitation associated with the welfare state after 1945; accompanied by the language of treatment, help and social work (Garland 1985, 2001). By contrast, from the early 1980s we can identify a political realignment that placed greater emphasis on individual responsibility, discipline, authority, law, order and punishment, as the 19th century returned. This can be constructed as a shift from social democracy, embracing penal modernism and consensus politics between the main parties (on public spending, state provision of welfare services, full employment, rights, and a particular way of thinking about crime) to post-modernism that perceives a redefined and attenuated rehabilitation as one possible objective alongside others, including punishment (come to fruition in the Criminal Justice act 2003; see Appendix 2). As truth is no longer a moral or political absolute (Oborne 2005), neither is a commitment to rehabilitation. Therefore, it is reasonable to claim that new-right politics rebalanced the criminal justice system in a direction not conducive to the long-term health of probation values.

Of course, we need to maintain a sense of balance in our analysis at this critical historical juncture because after 1979 no one was seriously talking about abolishing probation. During the 1980s, as now, probation officers continued to write reports for magistrates and judges that drew attention to social factors at a time when unemployment rose to unprecedented levels. Even though the political climate was changing, we must recall that a commitment to social work values, putting crime into a social context, welfare and rehabilitation, persisted in the hearts and minds of individual probation officers (Whitehead 1990) despite the new political rhetoric. But as we progressed through the 1990s, initially with Mr Howard, then from 1997 with Mr Blair, the probation ideal was losing its brand appeal as offender deeds became more important than needs. In fact, from as early as 1992 when Mr Blair was shadow Home Secretary there were concerns expressed by his own leader that he was too punitive (Seldon 2004; Ryan 2003 p122f). Furthermore, in an interview with Lesley White in the *Sunday Times* on 1st May 2005, during the general election campaign, the Prime Minister is reported to have said, 'When I changed our position on crime, I didn't really analyse it – I just sort of felt it. You have to start with how you feel' (White 2005 p16). The political culture which has been in the ascendancy since the early 1980s has not been conducive to probation because it has diluted the explanatory power of the social; and punishment has overshadowed a welfare and rehabilitative response. The same political culture has redesigned probation by the language of toughness, enforcement, the benefit sanction, as more offenders have been committed to prison. This is not the vocabulary out of which intelligent and constructive probation work is fashioned and we think a proportion of staff have been too readily captured by the new politics to the detriment of clients and the probation ideal. It is easier to be blown along by the prevailing wind than stand against its force. We remain with a political theme in the next section, but from a different perspective.

Politics of Spin and Politicisation of Crime

Thirty years ago it was rarer than today for ministers to give an account of themselves by writing to newspapers as a more rigorous parliamentary process complemented democratic processes. In Chapter 7 we included extracts from parliamentary debates on issues affecting probation to demonstrate the growing powerlessness of Parliament. Members are recorded in Hansard expressing their disquiet at their own government's handling of certain issues, whilst at the same time expressing frustration at their own impotence. Additionally,

Peter Oborne (2005) chronicles incidents of political lying during the 1980s under Mrs Thatcher and 1990s under Mr Major that helped to create the groundswell for political change in 1997. He also conveys his own perception of events which shaped the emergence of New Labour and a style of government affected by spin and public manipulation.

The failure of Neil Kinnock and old Labour to beat the more unsavoury features of the Major years produced a substantial change of tactics. Mr Kinnock's defeat in 1992 was seen as a result of dissonance with the media, and a return to old-style Labour values no longer grabbed the interest of voters. Those who were better off under the Conservatives were not prepared to be less well off. Public sentiment was not to change about crime either and the idea that prison worked and was what offenders deserved was now the conventional wisdom. Therefore, the architects of New Labour set about creating a party that could be elected. The death of John Smith after Labour's election defeat in 1992 was a decisive moment in shaping events that culminated in the accession of Tony Blair and escalation of the black arts of media spin associated with Peter Mandelson and Alistair Campbell (Oborne 2005). It was recognised that for New Labour to be elected their relationship with the media had to be managed. The process of unattributed press briefings, instituted by Bernard Ingham and Mrs Thatcher to get government messages out to the public whilst avoiding political flak, was elevated to a different art form. It was ironic that Mr Blair should be elected in 1997 on the basis of honesty and a 'trust me' approach against a background of unsavoury attitudes associated with the previous government in the mind of the electorate (Oborne 2005). Perhaps a philosophical defence might be that not telling the truth is different to telling lies, and does this matter anyway in a world in which results are everything (in other words, the end justifies the means in politics).

The evidence provided by Oborne and others is of a New Labour government so ruthlessly determined first to seize and then maintain power that political and media manipulation was too great to resist, notwithstanding moral arguments to the contrary. Furthermore, no public institution was exempt from the change agenda and within the probation service we grew accustomed to the manipulation of figures and statistics. A particular example involved budgets and it should be acknowledged that the outcome of the spending round was always difficult to predict because the probation budget was subsumed within the Home Office budget set by the Treasury. New Labour was determined to exercise control over public expenditure in order to ensure it could avoid media criticism and virtually adopted the same approach as the previous Tory regime. This left probation services in difficulty because of Michael Howard's abolition of probation training and the consequent shortage of staff that had accrued from this decision, which was worsening all the time. Early in the life of the new government, the definitive probation budget figures were overdue and had been promised for a national meeting of Chief Probation Officers. It transpired that ACOP representatives were to visit the Home Office during the lunch break of this meeting to receive news of the budget from civil servants. The delegation duly returned to the meeting with illuminating figures. The headline message was that the service was to receive £3 million (this was not the true figure but we use £3 million to illustrate the point) in new money over the next three years. Many CPOs had a ready appreciation of the way in which the funding formula worked, and therefore the implications of extra funds for local services. As the meeting began to digest and extrapolate, it emerged that £3 million over three years was in fact an increase of $£^1/_2$ million for each of three years. The way civil servants represented this to Chiefs, following the script provided by ministers, amounted to double counting and sophistry. To make a very real $£1^1/_2$ million into £3 million of new spending required an imaginative approach to mathematics: Year 1 = $£^1/_2$ million; Year 2 ($£^1/_2$ m + $£^1/_2$ m) = £1 million; Year 3 ($£^1/_2$ m + £1 m) = $£1^1/_2$ million; grand total = £3 million.

For issues to be presented in this distorted way is nonsensical. Chiefs were not able to recruit double the staff as a result of misrepresented figures. The attempted legerdemain was transparent and self-defeating, but it did not prevent government continually presenting figures in this way. It was an approach that undermined confidence in communication with senior civil servants whose attitude towards ministers became obsequious. Their politicisation over the last 25 years has serious implications for democracy in Britain, particularly in light of the weakening of the parliamentary process that we have alluded to in this book. In fact, the position of civil servants was to become so serious it provoked comment from David Faulkner in an article published in the *Guardian* (Faulkner 2004). He confirmed that at the end of the Thatcher years there had been an expectation that civil servants would conform to political expectations, a trend he believed should be resisted. He suggests that the situation is now worse to the point that officials, in their desire to please, had moved on from the practice of helping to develop policy from a political perspective to helping to assist the personal situation of ministers. The implication of this is that ministers, senior civil servants, in addition to unelected 'advisers' beyond the gaze of parliamentary scrutiny, are part of an exclusive club fashioning government policy. Being a member of this exclusive club demands absolute loyalty. Moreover, the coterie forming part of what has become a more presidential as opposed to parliamentary style of government, contributed to the dynamics that afflicted the creation of a national probation service and later NOMS. By 2001 probation had become ensnared by these dynamics with power located at the centre without the balancing influence of probation chiefs and their local areas. Not only did a powerful centre have control of the budget; this power was also wielded to shape probation to fit the perceptions that drove its public utterances on crime.

The rivalry between government and media to influence public opinion, and the climate of dissimulation and manipulation infecting this culture, influenced the politicisation of crime. Just deserts, punishment in the community, what works, prison works, are catchphrases developed by government to appeal to the media. The consequences have been to create a sound bite world where informed debate on issues such as the moral climate, social ethics, public behaviour, imprisonment, how we should respond to crime and the kind of society we want, has less importance. It can be argued that the lack of courage to debate these issues openly and in a mature manner has been damaging. Also, there are contradictions at the heart of government policy that we can illustrate by referring to proposals to extend drinking hours, and the piloting of large-scale casinos, which could enhance the potential for those 'yobbish' social problems the government wants to stamp out. The contradiction is the creation of punitive measures like Anti-Social Behaviour Orders and extra prison places to mop up the consequences of such behaviour encouraged, it could be argued, by government policies. Consequently, the level of debate around important social issues has been reduced to superficial sound bites. Moreover, media discussion fails to get beyond headline issues and public fears are stoked up with reporting that lacks balance and often flies in the face of accepted data.

It is worth saying that probation does not stand alone because other public services have been snared by the superficial sound bite political and media crossfire: for example, the education system, which is seen as being solely responsible for both the educational achievements and behaviour of pupils. Consequently, the worrying number of excluded pupils reflects school decisions to rid themselves of those whose behaviour is disruptive and whose educational needs are beyond the scope of the national curriculum. League table results based on pupil performance lead to a concentration on a narrow range of targets and activities that ultimately invite tactics to manipulate outcomes. The centrally imposed government system seems to make little allowance for the characteristics of a challenging catchment area whose children have more limited academic potential. Consequently, these schools are portrayed in league tables as failing and they become preoccupied by the threat of special measures and means by which to extricate themselves from them. Instead they should be free to pursue educational innovation to meet the particular needs of each pupil on the school roll. What is clear is that there are complexities to the education process (as there are in probation) requiring mature and informed debate and, until government takes responsibility to promote this, those who work in education will continue to be unfairly criticised and the morale of the profession blighted by atrophy.

A final word on the presentation of crime statistics in the media is fraught with problems, as a piece in the *Guardian* illustrated (Hough 2005 p10). The differences between the British Crime Survey and the Police recording of crime make it difficult to define the true extent of crime. The Police have a vested interest in talking up crime, which they seem disposed to do. However, the fact that there has been a steady reduction in crime since 1995 is not readily appreciated, nor would a debate about its possible causes attract much sympathy because of the way in which crime is handled by the media. There seems to be a government-inspired agenda to ensure that crime remains high on the political agenda, and it was significant that one of government's first pronouncements after the 2005 general election was that offenders on community service might wear stigmatising uniforms. All this makes it impossible to have a mature debate about the nature and causes of crime or rehabilitation of offenders. In fact, as we have discussed throughout this book, criminal justice has become obsessed with punishment. The determination for the criminal justice system to deliver punishment means that probation has been marginalised because of its lack of fit with the way successive governments wanted to see themselves projected in a society whose own basic instincts have been influenced by a media diet lacking in balance or insight. Probation finds itself having to exist in a culture of negativism, punishment, manipulation, spin and the politicisation of crime.

Return of American Influences

The USA is credited with giving us the first probation officer because it was John Augustus in Boston who, from 1841, supervised offenders on bail at the courts' request. Moreover it was Miss E.P. Hughes, a former Principal of a Cambridge College for Women Teachers, who visited the USA in 1900 to 1901 to investigate the American probation system on behalf of the Howard Association (Bochel 1976). So right at the beginning of probation in England and Wales there was indebtedness to American influences.

It is instructive to take up this story of common interests with Mrs Thatcher, who in her 1995 autobiographical volume prevailed upon the work of Van Den Haag and J.Q. Wilson in support of her own views on crime. The work of these two American scholars endorsed an approach based upon the personal responsibility of offenders for their own behaviour; crime as a rationally chosen activity; less emphasis on the explanatory framework of social factors; more emphasis on deterrence and harsher punishment by sending people to prison. Consequently, probation does not sit happily within such a frame of reference (also see Young 2003 p39; Pitts 2003 p87).

Next, according to Tonry (2004 p3), Michael Howard in the 1990s was influenced by the zero tolerance policy pursued with alacrity in New York by Mayor Rudy Giuliani. Tonry proceeds to say that New Labour under Mr Blair has been influenced by the tough approach to criminal justice advocated by Bill Clinton's New Democrats (p51). In other words, political parties can no longer afford to be soft on crime; 'don't let your opponents get the better of you', is the political message being articulated on both sides of the Atlantic.

Furthermore, in an attempt to bring this American interlude up to date, Charles Murray provides us with a vision (more dystopian than utopian) of a criminal justice system in England and Wales based upon the American model. In an article for the *Sunday Times* (Murray 2005) the right-wing sociologist who popularised the notion of the underclass, states clearly that America has dealt with its crime problem not by addressing the causes of crime or pursuing rehabilitation; rather, it has simply removed the problem from the streets so that in 2005 there were more than 2 million Americans in custody. What Murray extrapolates from the American experience is that England and Wales can deal effectively with its crime problem and reduce crime by learning from America. To do so we would need to imprison approximately 250,000 offenders. Therefore the solution to crime is to write off the

NEETS (those not in education, employment or training). In fact, Murray's prognosis is that by 2020 the NEET problem, the underclass, will no longer be a problem in England and Wales because money will have been spent on building additional prisons. To some of us this is alarming because it is increasingly believable in a political culture and criminal justice system with a penchant for punishment. At the beginning of the probation system we were indebted to American influences; by 2020 we could still be indebted to America, but in a radically different way, if the prison population is allowed to increase from just less than 80,000 to 250,000. So what does this prospect mean for the probation ideal? Finally, the influence of New Public Management since the 1980s that injected managerial practices drawn from the private into the public sector, was inspired by American developments (Ryan 2003 p82).

New Relationship between Probation and Prison
During the period of the reforming Liberal government 100 years ago, Winston Churchill was interested in prison reform (Hattersley p143f.). On 20th July 1910, Churchill, as Home Secretary, made a speech in which he said: 'The mood and temper of the public, in regard to the treatment of crime and criminals, is one of the most unfailing tests of the civilisation of any country'. At this time the prison population was in the region of 22,000; dropped to just over 9,000 in 1918; but from the 1920s has been steadily rising.[1] From its inception probation was an alternative to the punitive legacy bequeathed by the Victorian prison. In fact this penal philosophy persisted, to some extent, up to the 1980s when Douglas Hurd, John Patten and David Faulkner tried to keep the lid on the prison population by pursuing a policy of alternatives to custody. Consequently, probation, notwithstanding a change of ideology from rehabilitation to punishment in the community during the 1980s, remained a serious alternative to prison because it inflicted less damage; it was cheaper; it was no less effective at preventing recidivism.

However, a more complex relationship between probation and prison has evolved, which began with Michael Howard in 1993 and has continued under New Labour since 1997. For many decades it is reasonable to argue that probation belonged to a fundamentally different species to custodial facilities. This was a difference in kind rather than degree so the decision was for *either* probation *or* prison. However, this clear distinction between custody (something damaging, negative and costly) and community (something potentially positive and constructive) has been diluted to such an extent that they are currently located on the same continuum of sentences. Both are now involved in the provision of degrees of punishment and various forms of programmes, facilitated by NOMS with its promotion of a closer association between probation and prison services (a seamless join so that one flows naturally into the other). In fact, the anticipated expansion of electronic monitoring and tagging over the next few years will further dilute the differences that once existed between the two organisations as we try to replicate prison conditions in the community. It is now 20 years since Stanley Cohen said that 'so fine, and at the same time so indistinct, are the gradations along the continuum, that it is by no means easy to know where the prison ends and the community begins ...'(1985 p57). The edges are now extremely blurred indeed. We are witnessing the hybridisation of probation that has tilted the probation ideal towards the punitive ideal within a criminal justice system that confuses and merges community and custody. End-to-end offender management under NOMS may well provide benefits to individual offenders but, at the same time, weaken important differences between probation and prison.

New Anti-Morality

The roots of probation, as we tried to explain in Chapter 1, were planted in the soil of evangelical religion and gave to the early system its underpinning ideology (McWilliams 1983). The Christian Church, rooted in New Testament theology, has a distinctive view of the nature of reality and attitude towards human beings (Kung 1976). In other words, the individual is unique and therefore important because created in God's image, a lofty ontological concept. God, through the Church, imbues the individual with inestimable value. People are thus perceived as ends in themselves, not means to an end, so they should not be used by others, including political elites, in games of power and control.

It may be argued that since 1979 the politics of the new-right has generated a moral discourse at odds with the morality underpinning the probation ideal at its best. It is somewhat tendentious to say an anti-morality has evolved, but let us stick with this emotive language for now to make a point. One example of what we are trying to capture here is to draw attention to the social and economic policies of Thatcherism during the early 1980s that saw unemployment rise to over 3 million. The message being promoted was that the macro needs of the economy take precedence over the micro needs of individuals and families, some of whom were being left behind through no fault of their own as the economy was restructured. This anti-morality was manifested in the way public expenditure was affected so there was less money for welfare. Homelessness and unemployment, the fallout from social and economic dislocation, were recast in terms of personal weakness and fecklessness. Welfare became the problem rather than the solution; there were political attacks on the miners and their families, who became the enemy within; a number of communities disintegrated. It felt as though society's values were being inverted; rewritten according to a different moral code on the back of a political ideology (Gilmore 1992).

These are examples not just of one set of social and economic policies preferred over others, regardless of how good the intentions were, but are indicative of acute moral issues touching on decency, humanity, social cohesion, and the value we invest in people, including those whom the political process labels as offenders. Probation clients as well as probation officers were deeply affected by the political, economic, social and moral dislocations of the 1980s, and some of us felt that certain categories of people were becoming less important than others. In fact, some appear to be expendable, a view with longevity under New Labour despite concerns over social exclusion and acknowledgement of connections between poverty, inequality and crime. In the probation system of the 21st century, help and opportunities continue to be provided to offenders, of that there is little doubt, but it is a more qualified type of help than formerly. If resources and opportunities are not fully grasped then the possibility of rejection looms large in the form of prison through committing new offences and/or non-compliance with a community sentence. Therefore, the new moral discourse is less tolerant and forgiving; there are more qualifications; there is a harsher tone to penal politics and the prevailing morality of help and opportunity can carry quite a punch if offenders do not (or, more importantly, cannot) conform because of acute personal problems. Those who have restructured and modernised probation seem ill-disposed to grasp that tolerance, discretion and understanding are needed when working with people with problems, many of whom have been burdened by experiences that have inflicted damage from childhood. Offenders are victims too. Consequently, it is an extremely difficult environment in which to defend and promote the probation ideal because the new politics and new morality have reshaped our view of the person. Is the benefit sanction, for example, moral or immoral?

One last point as we conclude this subsection. A case can be made for re-establishing a moral community as a counter to the forces of anti-morality along the lines suggested by Nils Christie (Rutherford 1996). Such a moral community should be drawn from the ranks of probation staff, academics, social responsibility committees within, but not exclusively, Christian Churches (one of which produced the Faith in the City initiative in the 1980s), education, social work, and also politicians and civil servants with liberal sensibilities. This would be an alliance committed to the principles of decency and humanity, not only expressed as concern for victims and communities affected by crime, but also impoverished and damaged offenders, many of whom are victims of circumstances not of their own choosing. Therefore, the shaping of social and penal policy during the next few years should not be the sole preserve of politicians in Whitehall. Rather this process should involve a wide constituency of people, including the views of offenders themselves, because the issue is too big and too serious to leave in the hands of our political representatives who are tempted to make decisions from mixed motives. A system of justice that aspires to live up to its name must be guided by a set of moral principles including decency, humanity, understanding and compassion for both victims and offenders. To work this out is a complex issue but we must pay attention to the moral dimension.

New Bureaucratic Managerialism
Managerialism, coupled with an expanding organisational bureaucracy is a relatively new phenomenon in probation, with roots reaching back to the 1963–79 period. In fact, McWilliams said that managerialism, in addition to radicalism and personalism, have become the three dominant ideologies over recent years (1987). We have clarified that by the early 1960s the probation service was characterised by a commitment to the rehabilitative ideal and the probation officer was involved in casework supervision. There was no managerial hierarchy but rather a vertical and hierarchical structure facilitating the professional casework of its officers, which had been developing since the 1930s.

However, with the expansion and diversification of the service in the 1960s, accompanied by complexity, politicisation and the rise of policy from the 1980s (McWilliams 1992), boosted by SNOP priorities in 1984, greater emphasis was placed on performance and accountability. Therefore, the hierarchical structure that once supported an enabling form of professional casework supervision was slowly transformed into a form of managerial accountability according to policy priorities (McWilliams 1987, 1992). This occurred in the post-rehabilitative era as probation sought a new rationale for its existence which, in the 1980s, became alternatives to custody for more serious offenders (from SNOP in 1984 to the CJA 1991). Additionally, this process influenced the meaning and value of probation being reduced to a set of activities amenable to quantitative measurement procedures; and in the 21st century there is an unhealthy obsession with statistical audits. The dominant political and managerial message seems to be that the only probation work of value is that which can be objectively measured, which is a gross distortion of practice. Sadly, this is an impoverished form of reductionism because it fails to grasp that people-based work, by its very nature, involves a qualitative and ineffable dimension that deserves recognition (Whitehead and Thompson 2004).

Raine and Willson state that the new-right government elected in 1979 viewed the criminal justice system as 'spendthrift, idiosyncratic and unaccountable' (1997 p82), resulting in a strategy with three main elements: cash limits; greater standardisation to reduce professional discretion and autonomy; more control and accountability by stronger political and managerial hierarchies, policies, objectives and targets, performance and monitoring. We can also add the 3Es (economy, efficiency and effectiveness) and VfM (Value for Money) to this list.

By the early 1990s the political, bureaucratic and managerial obsession with measurable objectives prevailed (Humphrey, Pease and Carter 1993). The initial concern with improving performance, being transparent, and demonstrating accountability, was allowed to drift into a politically inspired obsession to measure everything that moves in an organisation that has become more business oriented than people focused. This can be contrasted, it may be suggested, to the service from 1907 to the 1960s that was more people based; had a better understanding of the importance of (casework) relationships; perhaps had a better understanding of those qualitative dimensions and doctrine of the ineffable as key aspects of performance.

At this point we expand on recent developments by distinguishing between an uncomfortable and, some might say, irreconcilable tension, between political and practice-based agendas. In fact, this has become an acute tension for insightful practitioners because it illustrates a profound difference in outlook, view of probation work, discourse, a sense of what is important, including the way in which performance is being evaluated by politicians and managers. To explore this tension we want to establish a set of opposites that accentuates the gap, but with a view to creating a new synthesis by turning a negative into a positive. By trying to reconcile some of these opposites to forge a new synthesis, we are engaging in a dialectical process that should allow us to elicit support for the probation ideal:

Political Agenda	*Professional Practice-based Agenda*
Economy, efficiency, effectiveness	People-based practice
Value for money	Interviewing and communication
Policies and objectives	Listen, understand and explain
Cash-linked targets	Engage, relate, relationships
Performance indicators	Good thinking and curiosity
National standards	Imagination and creativity
Business plans and audits	Touch and feel
Bureaucracy and standardisation	Problem solving
Enforcement	Good judgment
Competence and codification	Artistry through reflection
Quantitative measurements	Passion, animation, commitment
Systems, processes, procedures	Social work values
Rule-based behaviour	Qualitative and ineffable features
	Autonomy and discretion
	People have needs

We suggest that, since the 1970s but particularly 1984 and the Statement of National Objectives and Priorities, some of us have experienced how probation has evolved into a Weberian inspired organisation (Gerth and Mills 1948; Garland 1990). This is manifested by a preponderance of rules, more business-like and impersonal features, officials and routines, policies, procedures, bulging files and information overload. It is a more prescriptive organisation with less professional discretion and autonomy. Applying a Weberian lens to probation developments over recent decades helps us to elucidate the nature of change that has been occurring. David Garland captures this point well when he articulates that social practices (we include probation) have become more 'instrumentally effective, but at the same time they become less emotionally compelling or meaningful for their human agents' (1990 p179). Such developments have the capacity to burden, oppress, demotivate and constrain employees in a people-based profession.

An example of the Byzantine bureaucracy within the probation domain is to refer to some of the language that has filtered down since 2001. Eithne Wallis, before her departure, and the National Probation Directorate bestowed upon the service the terms 'granuality', 'change streams' and 'transformational human relations'. There are those who have a vision of the NOMS 'end state' (but missed a trick by not using the word 'teleology') and the service has become riddled with jargon that contributes little to the work of practitioners. Furthermore, there are those within the organisation who pretend they understand this language, but others penetrate the veil of nonsense. Such language is more likely to obfuscate than elucidate and illustrates just how politically and managerially complex the job has become. The age of the bureaucratic technician in what is a person-focused enterprise has truly arrived (Millard 1977). Sometimes it feels the service has taken on the quality of a 21st century mystery religion that rivals the mysteries of Mithra from another age (Cumont 1956).

A final comment from another country rather than another age. Rutherford (1996) explores the Dutch penal system and comments that after 1945 criminal policy was characterised by a humanitarian approach and the prison population declined. But from the mid-1970s the prison population began to rise and the humanitarian approach drifted towards a system characterised by bureaucracy, efficiency, more business oriented, financial and quantitative concerns. So the developments described above are not unique to England and Wales.

Governance Old and New

The 1922 Departmental Committee (as we have seen) proposed the appointment of local justices to form a committee to oversee probation work. The committee became responsible for the administration of the local area service and eventually the Chief Probation Officer was the professional adviser. One of the main tasks of the committee was to appoint and pay probation officers and some of its powers could be delegated to the Chief. Moreover, during the 1920s and 1930s the probation case committee was responsible for supervising the work of its officers, a task handed on to the expanding hierarchy. It can be argued that as each area service evolved, a sense of balance existed between the major players within the organisation: probation committee; Chief Probation Officer; Home Office, which had a vested interest because of the money provided by central government that reached 80% in the 1970s; local authorities; NAPO; ACOP and CCPC. Importantly, there was a sense of balance between local development and national interest. As long ago as the 1930s the suggestion for a national service was made but the 1922 committee rejected this. For as Le Mesurier said: 'Probation is an instrument which depends for its success on an intimate connection between Courts of Summary Jurisdiction and their probation officers ... To take the probation officer away from the direct control of the Court would involve a disturbance of this valuable relationship, and might, contrary to constitutional practice, lead to undesirable interference by the executive in the functions of the judiciary' (1935 p32). Le Mesurier proceeded to make an impassioned plea for the local organisation of probation.

We have made it clear that this local–national balance was realigned from 1984 beginning with SNOP. This was followed by the development of a more rigorous Inspectorate following Grimsey in 1987 and then the imposition of centrally determined cash limits. The governance balance that once existed has been redefined in the interests of central power and control, a reflection of the new political culture (Statham 2000). By 2001 new governance arrangements were put in place with the creation of the National Probation Service illustrated by:

- Top down and centrally imposed power and control.

- Central controls over all 42 local areas.

- CPO became a civil servant and renamed Chief Officer.

- 100% funding by central government.

- Boards instead of Probation Committees.

- ACOP and CCPC abolished leaving Chief Officers muted.

What has happened to the organisation of probation reflects the changing nature of the new politics. Since 1997, and before, there is evidence to indicate a diminution of democratic principles manifested by a weakening of parliamentary democracy; attenuation of cabinet government; and the changing role of civil servants. On the last point, Oborne comments: 'Civil servants were supposed to be the disinterested servants of the state, owing their loyalty to the Crown, not to the government of the day' (2005 p152). This has been an important constitutional principle since Gladstone's reforms in the 19th century. But New Labour's attitude towards modernisation has disturbed checks and balances required in a democratic society by their headlong rush to control and direct from the centre. One serious problem with this is that it undermines, if not destroys, ancient wisdoms and trusted ways of doing things that have taken time to evolve, that rely upon mature discussion and the ability to compromise by all parties involved, not dictated to by a hard, uncompromising and know-all centre. In fact, Paxman says that, under Mrs Thatcher and then Mr Blair, power has been increasingly arrogated to the office of the Prime Minister and unelected staff rather than Parliament and Cabinet. This is the new political style and culture in Whitehall so much so that 'Ministers no longer run individual departments of government as they see fit. They do as they're told' (Paxman 2002 pp277–278) and so does probation. Governance changes in probation have centralised power and control in politicians and the National Probation Directorate in London. This has enormous implications for ownership, commitment, motivation and sense of belonging for individual members of staff in the remaining 42 areas. In the modernised probation service one could be forgiven for feeling that the only way to 'get on' is to acquiesce in all that the centre thinks and does; to do what we are told to do unthinkingly; simply to accept the new status quo without question. For individuals to think for themselves, question what is happening, say 'no' rather than 'yes', or challenge power and control emanating from the centre, is tantamount to disloyalty. This is not the way to run a mature country let alone an organisation staffed by people who want to make a positive contribution to work with offenders. The organisation of probation does not belong solely to politicians and elites with power, but all members of staff. We must listen to what they have to say.

Lack of Cohesion within Probation
When probation was evolving between 1907 and the early 1960s, when it was located at the heart of government's penal policy during the 1960s, there was also a consensus between the main political parties apropos the role of probation within the criminal justice. As far as we are aware it did not have to struggle to justify its existence. By contrast, as the service travelled into the 1970s and beyond, the probation ideal was put under pressure (as we have explained). At this critical juncture there was a discernible lack of organisational cohesion primarily because of leadership failures located in the representative organisations: Association of Chief Officers of Probation; Central Council of Probation Committees; National Association of Probation Officers. We argued in earlier chapters that for far too long service organisations were not united and spoke with a fragmented voice. Against the background of emerging problems with the service's product in the

form of rehabilitation, and ensuing ideological debates over care and control, the service lacked the political acumen to read the signs of the times. There was a lack of urgency and also vision to analyse what was happening, with a corresponding failure to plan effective strategies to defend and promote probation in the new political climate. We failed to grasp what was happening until it was too late and were out manoeuvred.

Of course, the years since 1979 have not been easy or kind. The uncompromising message emanating from the Leeds Castle seminar in 1987 was change or die. In these political circumstances we must question whether the existence of cohesiveness would have altered the course of probation history discussed in Parts 2 and 3 of this book. Nevertheless, the discernible lack of cohesive leadership put the service on the back foot and made it much more difficult to withstand the political battering that has occurred.

We also reflect upon the point that some senior managers have been too willing to embrace the new political *Zeitgeist*, particularly since 1997; too willing to be carried along by the winds of political change; too quick to acquiesce in a politically inspired bureaucratic culture that has diluted the people-based nature of the organisation with its social work values and welfare ideals. If leadership within the service had been more astute and cohesive, surer of itself and what the service stood for, then it is comforting to entertain the view that recent outcomes could have been more benign; a more robust local dimension respected; decent and humane values acknowledged; staff trusted to exercise discretion in pursuit of justice for offenders and victims. It is interesting to observe the extent to which a small coterie of elected representatives, a handful of powerful individuals based in London, have profoundly changed the culture of an organisation that has been in existence since Edwardian times. Not even the combined weight of ACOP, CCPC and NAPO, including service employees comprising thousands of individuals, have been able to resist those changes discussed in this book.

We are not making an argument here for no change. Rather, because we became unsure of our product, lacked leadership and political clout, and were not really sure of ourselves, we were not in a strong position to shape probation in new political circumstances according to those principles and values comprising the probation ideal. As a result, we find ourselves in a place not of our own choosing, but out of self-interest and other complex motives we have compromised our values in order to survive on the basis that what we now have is better than nothing at all. We want to expand on this point as follows.

Misunderstanding Management

Management was sometimes associated with authoritarianism in the minds of probation staff used to operating with a high degree of freedom. The culture reflected the history of a service with its roots in the mindset of the voluntary sector. What is surprising is that this culture had been sustained for so long, lasting as it did into the 1990s. Many CPOs, and other senior managers, who had grown up in an independent tradition found it difficult to see that management concepts had something valuable to contribute to probation's fidelity. The perception was, as in other parts of the public sector, that professionals simply needed the assistance of administrators in order to perform their duties. It was a naïve perception that could only be sustained by high public confidence. The belief that the service could escape accountability for its performance (as we have explored in previous chapters) was the ultimate naïvety, but probation had a culture that was deeply suspicious of management and only a minority practised it with any degree of commitment or understanding. We might go further and suggest that an opportunity was lost to create a comprehensive management structure that could inform the service nationally. For example, the regional training structure meant a differential approach to middle manager training and it was not until the 1980s that any thought was given to a national element, and even then it was a brief four-day programme which attempted to add a national perspective to the thinking of middle managers.

Attempts to develop a body of thinking about probation management received a muted response and even hostility in some quarters (Statham 1990, 1992; Statham and Whitehead 1992). The responses to what was being attempted reflected the narrowness and introspection of the probation service. Bill McWilliams, often quoted in these pages, became identified with anti-management rhetoric that had a mesmerising moral authority finding support in some of the academic exchanges of the time. However, these exchanges were to prove a distraction that defied the thinking driving both cultural and political change. As a result, the populist resistance to management weakened the service's bargaining position with government. By the 1990s, Chief Probation Officers were perceived as unable to deliver the change agenda desired by politicians, with the result that they could not shape the future criminal justice strategy according to probation values. This must be seen as a lost opportunity because probation could have developed its own management culture and led the way in promoting thinking about management in the public sector environment (Statham 1998, 1999). This was never achieved in any significant measure and, despite the efforts of some CPOs within ACOP and the advent of the Cranfield Conferences, collective leadership failed to ignite. There was instead almost a sense of phoney engagement with the idea as opposed to the reality of unified leadership, which occurred ultimately because of a lack of organisational maturity that was essential to achieving even the broadest consensus.

There has been little appreciation of these dynamics and, as recognition grew about the threat to probation, some speculation suggested that management had failed in the service. However, we would argue that such a hypothesis has to be extrapolated from a position that is itself resistant to an understanding of even the most basic attributes of management theory. Suggestions of management meltdown do not bear the weight of close analysis; in fact, there was no attempt on behalf of government to implement fully sound management theory and techniques with a view to testing out their success or failure. There were some examples of importing management techniques from the private sector and some small successes, but typically there was the same lack of discipline apparent in much of probation practice in relating theory to practice, and in many areas within the service management skills were often not practiced at all. Ultimately, this played into the hands of government administrators, now transmogrified into bureaucrats (as we have considered above), sitting in the wings. It is ironic that it was the failure to grasp the importance of politically astute leadership that would have manifested itself in good performance management, which left probation so vulnerable. The inability of Chief Probation Officers to convince ministers about their collective commitment led first to the National Probation Service and later to NOMS structures which are the epitome of bureaucracy, and which have so far failed to suggest any commitment to an appreciation of organisational dynamics. An increasingly centralised government machine, with its stranglehold on probation, has made the leap from the administrative aspirations of the post-war period to a process of bureaucratisation that, as it unfolds, resembles a Stalinist regime. These processes have not only begun to remove much of the personal discretion so prized by probation officers, but have also created a high degree of uncertainty. Even senior managers have been left attempting to second-guess the direction of the service, in a continuous waiting game for critical decisions. All of this is destined to have an accumulative impact on service culture and, in 2005, widespread disillusionment is palpable and growing.

Might a more open-minded approach to management have had an impact on this chain of events and reduced or even avoided probation's demise? We believe this is an issue worthy of exploration. Good management is about clarifying organisational purpose, structuring resources in a way that demonstrates a collective responsibility for the utilisation of those resources. It provides a structured approach to inclusive decision making and facilitates the effective contribution of all staff. It should not be about an autocratic approach that locates all decision making at its apex, denying others a voice – a caricature so beloved by management agnostics. Recourse to some basic management theory had the potential to be helpful in some basic aspects of organisational life. If we take as an example the issue of decision making in probation, an organisation famed for its individualism, achieving consensus was never going to be easy. However, all organisations or groups of people, which rely on collective action, need to develop ground rules for decision making. The academic world, which is devoted to management, has developed insights and techniques for such exercises and good consultation is at the heart of the success of businesses.

However, it is not just business organisations that have to make decisions if they are to prosper and achieve, and in widening our thinking we reflected on the dynamics within the Society of Friends. Neither of us has any affiliation with this organisation, but we felt it provided a credible example of an organisation with a set of clearly understood values grappling with the issue of corporate decision making. Morley (1993) suggests that a state of collective harmony can be achieved by reasonable people in search of a satisfactory decision, through a process of reconciling differences. Collective harmony falls short of consensus yet enables individuals to work together in the search for satisfactory solutions and strategies. For Quakers this is a sensitive and disciplined process of contribution and reflection that has transformation as its desired outcome. This is a commitment to sharing ideas and accommodating differences, enabling decisions to be made and owned. In the secular world, maturity could be used to describe the quality that would enable individuals to proffer views, listen to others and reconcile differences.

In the secular world of business organisations, the increasing pace of activity and change make decision making a less reflective process, but the need for acceptable mechanisms which facilitate consensus and change are critical. However, the ultimate challenge is the ownership of the decision making, the achievement of individual commitment. Even in the last decade of the 20th century probation team meetings were conducted in a culture where this level of mature cooperation could not always be relied upon. Perhaps even more tellingly it was not part of the culture of ACOP or CCPC. Meetings were not conducted with the expectation that there was a shared commitment to working together. In the year before the creation of the National Probation Service, within a problem-sharing exercise in a CPO learning set, it was clear that the senior management team in one local area was not operating with any degree of shared or corporate responsibility. Individuals left critical decision-making meetings not having the maturity to recognise they had lost the argument or owning the responsibility for joint decision making. The maturity of the Quakers would have been helpful.

Had Chief Probation Officers, as a group, been able to achieve this high level of unanimity it might have been possible to write a visionary new script for probation in the new political environment. Even simple strategic management exercises like SWOTs (defining an organisation's internal world through its strengths, weaknesses, opportunities and threats) and PESTs (defining the political, economical, sociological and technological dimensions of the external world), which provided frameworks for developing mutual understanding and consensus, were responded to in a lukewarm way. Even more tellingly, there could be no certainty that these ideas would be taken back to probation areas and used to build a consistent national approach. These were the basic tools of proactive strategic management and had the potential to become part of effective leadership in probation. They could have been used to build a robust service based on a probation consensus. In turn, such an organisation with clarity about its aspirations and performance could have promoted real debate as an antidote to the political rhetoric about crime. Surprisingly, the deteriorating political climate, particularly during the 1990s, did nothing to galvanise CPOs into a truly corporate group, which would have been an essential first step in joining with Central Council to create a strong lobby. The consultative framework that was developed by ACOP, although effective in some ways, was largely reactive and did not facilitate the mounting of serious political challenge.

What is clear is that, in 2005, chief officers in probation do not have a collective voice; they have been reduced to frustrated ciphers increasingly strangled by the tightening of the bureaucratic knot. What a pity that their predecessors, who had such freedom for so many years, were unable to harness their considerable talents in the exercise of cohesive leadership. There is also an enormous irony that probation should now succumb to the bureaucratic minds of the prison culture. The prison service is an organisation that never seems to be accountable for the failures of its regimes, exemplified by the growing numbers of prison suicides, or the catalogue of prison inspectorate criticisms; and has used privatisation to mask the serious industrial relations issues that have dogged the service for years. The successes in prison regimes are down to the initiatives of some governors rather than through an enterprise promoted from its bureaucratic centre. The ablest prison governors exercise their talents in an individualistic way in order to survive the system, to keep some of their reforming aspirations alive, and to achieve some rudiments of job satisfaction. It could be argued they have become practised in the art of apparent loyalty and probation chiefs may have something to learn from them.

Therefore, after reflecting upon a series of nine interlocking factors since 1979 which help us to understand and analyse the contemporary service, let us continue our reflections as we bring this book to its conclusion.

What Happened has not been Inevitable

This book could have recounted a different story. We are not historical determinists, so the story told from 1907 to the present day was not predestined to happen like this. It has not been fixed in the stars; we are not dealing with an inevitable outcome. So the fact we have told this story rather than another is a consequence of various themes, influences, forces, contingencies, and various individuals making important decisions at different times for various reasons. Such has been the impact of the decline of rehabilitation, the emergence of a new political culture, a different moral tone, burgeoning bureaucracy, and internal organisational weakness due to lack of cohesion, that one set of outcomes was more likely than another for probation. The combined weight of factors over a considerable period of time, beginning in the 1960s, explain how we have travelled from that point to where we are now. But it could have been different. If only the dramatis personae had been different and more kindly disposed; if only the political context had been more favourable. Therefore, *what if:*

- we had not become responsible for aftercare in the 1960s;

- we had become part of the reorganised social services departments following Seebohm in 1968 thus emulating what happened in Scotland;

- we had not become responsible for community service in the 1970s;

- we had not been distracted by the care–control debates of the 1970s and 1980s;

- Mrs Thatcher's government had not been elected in 1979 and we had avoided the influence of new-right politics;

- we had been more cohesive and astute and read the signs of the times, exercising robust leadership when it mattered and thus resisting the authoritarian, punitive and centralising pressures of New Labour?

In a sense, this line of questioning is futile because we cannot rewrite history. What has happened, been allowed to happen, can not be changed. But just as the course of our personal and professional lives within the context of 20th-century history could have been different, so probation history could have taken a different course if different decisions had been made at certain critical points. Yet the essence of history seems to be like this: this decision rather than that; accident and design; opportunity; mixed motives; the influence of the combined weight of certain people at different periods; the power of ideas to shape events and the way power is exercised by the few over the many.

We can not change the past but we can shape the future (as opposed to Hegelian and Marxist interpretations of history: Mazlish 1966).[2] The next 25 years do not have to replicate the last quarter century. For us this means learning from the past with a view to shaping the future according to a set of principles and values we have alluded to in this book but which have indubitably been diluted since 1979. Prior to concluding this book by explicating and underlining our commitment to the probation ideal, we want to reflect on an alternative vision for probation. The points we make in the next section are by no means unique, yet they draw attention to certain areas of practice we deem important.

Twenty-First Century Probation – an Alternative Vision

We want to consider an alternative vision, a differently weighted form of probation, to that currently taking shape within the NOMS structure, and indeed whatever else might evolve. We are not attempting to do this from an organisational perspective, as we have already explored some of these issues. However, it does seem important to reinforce the point that the changes now happening to the organisation we knew as probation do not reflect much understanding of the dynamics of organisations or the impact on individuals working within them. We are witnessing an iterative bureaucratic process, based on short-term tactical decision making that satisfies the omnipotent political machine's aspiration to be seen to be in control of crime. It recognises little of the values or human interactions which drive the engagement of individuals, ultimately reflected in commitment and loyalty. Indeed, for organisations to function effectively these factors require continuous attention and a culture of employee care is essential if people are to feel included. Organisational identity, clarity of purpose and task need to go hand in hand with good individual support, supervision and appraisal. Recent changes in moving probation from a National Probation Service to a National Offender Management Service structure seem to ignore these essentials.

The creation or re-creation of some semblance of cultural identity would be the first component of our probation service. This is a basic requirement if we are to ensure individual commitment and performance is not premised upon the automaton reflexes of bureaucratic demands. There would need to be an ongoing dialogue at all levels in the service to ensure ownership of the core tasks and purposes and realistic performance targets. This dialogue must reflect social, political and moral issues in a way that will not be possible until the climate of opinion shifts in this country and values can once again be discussed. Whilst we recognise there are few indicators to suggest the possibility at the present time, we would add our voices to those commentators who recognise the importance of debating these issues. An acute problem which has been escalating since the creation of the national service in 2001 is the ever-widening gap between the top of the organisation represented by the National Probation Directorate and senior managers; and an increasing number of staff at the bottom who have face-to-face contact with offenders. This has created cultural fragmentation rather than a sense of identity.

Despite the absence of debate about values we think probation, because of its work and collective experiences, could have some leverage in the discussions and developments within the criminal justice system. In our own thinking about alternative cultures and structures we recognise that a modern probation service would have to be capable of surviving the high-profile political rhetoric about crime. It would also need to develop a cohesive and robust alternative lobby, capable of widening the debate about crime into social and moral issues, and having the capacity for wide public understanding and appeal. Such debates would not be comfortable, as links would be made between social disadvantage, poor behaviour, disaffection and crime. We recognise the importance of not being captured by the sentiments of some nostalgic afterglow reflecting more liberal times, but the links between the social circumstances of offenders and behaviour is just as important as it ever was to understanding, explaining and addressing antisocial behaviour. We therefore invoke an important aspect of Underdown's work on effective practice in probation (HMIP 1998). We would argue that effectively challenging the behaviour of offenders requires insight into, and recognition of, attitudes and lifestyle that look beyond cognitive change programmes. Underdown highlighted the importance of cognitive behavioural programmes being underpinned by attention to social reintegration, accommodation, employment, financial circumstances and other factors, which require attention if lasting change is to be achieved. This is an aspect of effective practice that can be overlooked in the clamour for greater numbers on programmes to meet targets set by ministers and civil servants.

If an understanding of the relationship between offending behaviour and social factors is important for effective probation work, so is the management of risk. This aspect of the service's work is underdeveloped and unexploited in public debates on crime. Public perception of risk is often based upon the sensational headlines of a tabloid press seemingly incapable of providing dispassionate insight or discernment to its readers that in turn contributes to fear of crime. However, this fear can be real enough, illustrated when one of us attended a public meeting on Teesside in the late 1990s. It transpired that when there was a threat of a chemical leak from a nearby factory some people refused to be evacuated from their homes because they feared being burgled. This fear represented genuine anxiety derived from their everyday experience of living in a community in which burglary and petty theft were everyday experiences. However, much of the fear of crime is a result of displacement from headlines which have no link to any logical assessment of risk and often little likelihood of repetition. The preoccupation with such stories is both a reflection of irrational fear and a morbid interest in crime which is part of the human condition. Nevertheless, behind the headlines and distortions, individuals and communities have a legitimate aspiration to personal safety, free from the threat of victimisation.

Consequently, probation could occupy the middle ground between offenders and communities. There are good examples of restorative justice schemes and the long-term potential of an ongoing dialogue about crime and reparation should not be underestimated. Probation could be marketed as a community-based criminal justice agency that manages risk, thus promoting greater community safety and reassurance. Despite the aspirations of the past we may have to recognise it is impossible to achieve full social equality, yet the symbolism of inclusiveness, empathy and care remains essential for building a value base to counter social fragmentation. This is precisely the ground probation could occupy. This community-based concept is a considerable challenge to the situation in which probation finds itself in 2005, but is a legitimate one in a culture moving inexorably towards being desk and office bound. It must be forcibly stated that the probation officer role, due to the weight of bureaucracy being forced on the organisation, is being transformed into that of data entry technician. A disproportionate amount of time (perhaps as much as 70% of each working day for some members of staff) is now spent feeding data into computers, with the implication that the essence of good probation work – face-to-face contact with clients – is alarmingly being lost. Therefore, staff will begin to lose and have less time to acquire those people skills, such as listening and interviewing, necessary to facilitate insightful assessments and effective interventions. Probation staff want to work with people rather than respond to the insatiable demands being made by machines, but this is what is happening as we complete this book in the summer of 2005.

By returning to the theme of risk assessment, it should be acknowledged it has a long tradition in probation. The social enquiry report a few decades ago was to become the key document in the sentencing process in court, providing an exploration of risk that was reflected in the recommendation, or lack of it, and could then inform subsequent supervision. Risk assessment was more implicit than explicit in this process, because it was not part of the language or culture of those more therapeutic times. But social enquiry reports were becoming an art form in the probation service of the 1960s, and the very best exponents of this art could understand an individual in a way that produced valuable insights into attitudes and behaviour. These assessments also had the valuable extra dimension of an assessment of family dynamics and wider social influences because they were *social* enquiry reports. Therefore, home visits were an integral part of the intelligence-gathering process and individual behaviour and risk were located within wider social circumstances. Comprehensive social enquiry reports, later to become pre-sentence reports in 1991, provided sentencers with insights that were not available from the narrower office- or court-based assessment process. In other words, the social context added essential colour to the sentencing picture. The importance of the probation contribution to sentencing was fully explored in Chapter 5 when reviewing the implications of the Demonstration Project. Providing courts with community-based risk assessment information would be a further essential element of our probation service. We believe that, despite the pressure to expedite court processes and for sentencers to sentence in an increasingly formulaic way under the Criminal Justice Act 2003, justice to the individual is not only a basic human right, but at the heart of a just society that relies upon relevant information. Probation must continue to make this important contribution.

Whilst the probation service should provide risk assessments that strike a balance between risk and need at the point offenders are sentenced, there is a further contribution when those who have been sentenced to custody return to their community. Since the 1960s and the development of the parole system, probation has been the agency responsible for the supervision of those released from custody on licence. The provision of pre-release reports containing information on risk of re-offending and harm have been central to decisions made about release itself and licence conditions were part of the strategy to protect the community. This has been part of established practice for many years but not always appreciated by local communities. Little attention was given to explaining the significant powers of recall that probation possesses in circumstances where post-release risk was escalating. As the issue of risk began to emerge, sometimes within the emotionally charged atmosphere surrounding such issues, the probation service found it difficult to control the debate about the supervision of such cases, or the way in which surveillance was shared with other agencies. Equally, the probation service itself was involved in some accelerated learning and, as insights were developed into the way in which paedophiles, for example, groomed their victims, as domestic violence and child abuse became matters for public debate, public attitudes changed. In the subsequent media atmosphere it became difficult to promote a rational debate that might help the public to differentiate between levels of risk and dangerousness. It is to the credit of CPOs that they recognised the importance of having assessment tools that could provide greater objectivity to the risk assessment process. As a consequence the 1990s saw a range of experimentation in the use of risk assessment tools that ultimately led to OASys (Offender Assessment System) (see discussion in Whitehead and Thompson 2004 p80).

Almost in parallel there were other complementary developments, which led to greater cooperation between agencies in the management of risk in the community, and ultimately Multi Agency Protection Panel Arrangements (MAPPA), which is the joint statutory responsibility of the probation and police services. We would argue that probation has established a credible track record in the supervision of lifers and other high-risk offenders in the community, using risk assessment as an integral part of the process. What this experience has demonstrated is that some offenders capable of serious crimes can be released into the community to resume law-abiding lives. This too is an aspect of the probation service's work that deserves to be better understood.

The professional skills and techniques used in these cases are largely traditional to the work of the service but may not fit with prevailing political views. Research undertaken by Oxford University (2003), commissioned by the Home Office and curiously left unpublished by mid-2005, provided evidence of probation supervision with a group of 118 discretionary lifers distributed across England and Wales. These offenders had been convicted of some of the most serious crimes: 49% had been convicted of manslaughter and 22% had received life sentences for serious sexual offences. Only 16% of those released had any significant pre-release contact with their supervising officer. The major problems associated with resettlement were mental health, personal relationships, employment, alcohol and drugs, accommodation, family relationships, finance and other problems associated with physical health and institutionalisation. It is a list that has changed little over the years and the research provides insights into the traditional methods of effective one-to-one working at the heart of many of the planned supervision processes. Perhaps even more important was the finding that 46% of the sample had been recalled to prison at some stage. This is indicative of probation staff taking the risk management dimension of supervision seriously and using recall as a sanction when there were concerns about behaviour.

We would argue that the core purpose of probation should be rethought and rebalanced, and we have identified the components of practice that are essential to a credible vision of the service's contribution to criminal and social justice. It is our contention that an appropriate organisational structure would flow from clarity of purpose and tasks that must reflect the essential people-based nature of the work. This exercise would also facilitate a process that should be consistent with probation values and would allow staff that essential element of believing in and being animated by the organisation in which they are working. Importantly, such rethinking must be undertaken within the ethical framework derived from the probation ideal, to which we now turn.

The Probation Ideal

When we turn to clarify the tenets of the probation ideal we feel this is a complex task. The job has never been undertaken in an identical manner by all staff. There never was a golden age for this ideal, consequently it is more aspiration than reality, and it is in this sense we use the term here. We want to argue that it has the potential to be a force for good and can refine the way we currently think about probation and the wider criminal justice system. Before elucidating some of its main features we want to locate this ideal within a contemporary service that describes itself as a business.

The National Probation Service is perceived and promoted as a business which resonates with the notion of explaining the nature of the occupation in which it is involved. In this sense recourse to the term is legitimate. By contrast, it is not a business in the way shops and factories are, like Marks and Spencer or Marlow Foods, by being a commercial enterprise involved in buying and selling goods for profit. Rather, probation is a people rather than things-based enterprise. Probation works with people who cause problems for themselves and others. Accordingly it works with a complex set of human dynamics and contingencies that always exist where people are present, specifically probation clients who come from difficult backgrounds. Therefore this kind of enterprise requires careful thought and judgement by staff and sometimes differential responses in different situations to ensure the right outcome for different individuals. Yet political, managerial, and bureaucratic developments over recent years have attenuated discretion and judgement in favour of prescriptive systems, rules and procedures. Moreover, they have been imposed with a heavy hand and are not conducive to the artistry required in pursuit of just outcomes for offenders and victims. Hence the tension between bureaucratic technician and therapeutic imagination (Millard 1977); political and professional agendas; quantitative and qualitative dimensions; codification of knowledge and skills and the doctrine of the ineffable. Enforcement practice is a good example of the problem we are referring to here (Whitehead and Thompson 2004 p89f for discussion). With these thoughts in mind, what are some of those features that should comprise the probation ideal?

Some Aspirational Features of the Probation Ideal

- Probation officers are as concerned about the impact of offending behaviour upon victims and offenders themselves as politicians, sentencers and the public; it is not condoned nor colluded with.

- It is people focused and believes people can be helped to change, which is why it tries hard not to give up on those who repeatedly fail and struggle to learn from past experiences. Therefore the relationship between worker and client is at the heart of practice.

- It aims to keep people out of the criminal justice system for as long as possible; once inside the system, to keep them out of custody for as long as we can because it damages, negatively labels and prevents people from maturing. Only the most serious and dangerous offenders should be in custody, which is currently not the case.

- It supports a positive, constructive and educative approach *in the community* and works alongside other agencies to provide help and support. Therefore it is something 'other' than custody.

- It mitigates the punitive tendencies of the criminal justice system.

- The probation ideal has the imagination to understand and explain human behaviour and address those factors associated with offending. The pre-sentence report has a central role to play in achieving this objective by locating behaviour in its personal and social contexts. Sentencers need this information before making decisions about people.

- It promotes tolerance, decency, humanity, care and compassion, because it has a deep understanding of the human condition. In other words, there is a moral dimension to probation practice and it can be a force for good.

- It is aware of the distinction between the 'How' and 'What' of probation work (Whitehead and Thompson 2004 p207).

- It acknowledges that offenders can be victims too because, due to an accident of birth, they have not chosen their families, social circumstances or certain experiences which have shaped their lives.

- It makes an important contribution to a more fair and just society by its commitment to equal opportunities, diversity and anti-discriminatory practice (Home Office 2001c pp33f).

The principles and values running through the probation ideal should resonate with individuals and organisations beyond probation itself. This is why we reflected earlier on the viability of establishing a moral constituency of interested parties that would facilitate what we have in mind (Rutherford 1996). We think this is important because for far too long the political agenda and the exercise of political power have undermined the probation ideal. In its legitimate pursuit of improved performance, raising standards, targets and accountability, the new political culture has diluted aspects of the professional agenda comprised of ethical principles and humane values that emanate from being involved in a people-based occupation. Consequently, an argument for synthesis and reconciliation between conflicting priorities must be made. Both sides of the political–professional divide must acquire the maturity to listen to and learn from each other; it is unhealthy and immature for one side to dominate. The point we seek to establish is that if a mature conversation were possible then the probation ideal could be given a chance to inform thinking, which is primarily concerned with how best to achieve both criminal and social justice, consistent with principles of decency and humanity, for victims and offenders. However, this is premised upon a change of heart and mind within the Whitehall and National Probation Directorate political elites. This process could be given a helping hand by the restoration of a reconstituted ACOP body, thus giving Chief Officers a legitimate voice to promote the interests of the organisation and probation ideal. Without this the next few years will be extremely difficult and bleak.

For the foreseeable future probation, within the emerging NOMS structure, will continue to be convulsed by a change agenda that separates case management from interventions, with an emphasis on risk, performance and contestability. We will continue to feel the effects of centrally directed bureaucratic systems, computer demands, and quantitative measures of performance (internal organisational dynamics). Furthermore, the possibility of home confinement supported by electronic tagging, surveillance (Goodman 2003), enforcement, punishment, and the blurring of probation and prison within end-to-end offender management under NOMS, will characterise the criminal justice system. These are some of the features of New Labour's modernised world that can create a sense of dissonance for probation employees. Without doubt the modernised probation world is more technically efficient and accountable (Garland 1990), but not necessarily more human, meaningful or compelling. The main reason for this is that the people-based nature of the organisation is being transformed into a more rigid, authoritarian and centrally controlled bureaucracy. There is less local flexibility and lack of balance between local and national perspectives; less room for care and compassion, empathy and understanding, as the culture is transformed. The disorientating effects of the pace of relentless change undermine ideals and values.

Summary and Conclusion

Occasionally we have tuned in to the theme of the probation ideal, but with particular vigour in this final chapter. We acknowledge that others have attempted to define probation's core values, but our final sortie is an important reference point for this book. We have often wondered whether this ideal is capable of definition and, if it is, does it have an immutable quality or should it be subject to change? Questions of this nature are important but perhaps not capable of a satisfactory answer. Yet we have attempted our own philosophical exploration during the course of previous chapters.

We have explored the beginnings of probation and remind ourselves of pioneers like Mother Shepherd (Preece 1989) who combined Christian mission with the role of probation officer. Probation grew out of dissatisfaction with a punitive criminal justice system and the recognition that people could be assisted to change their lives, stop drinking and offending. From it flowed the aspiration and moral commitment of seeing value in everyone, regardless of what they have done. Within a religious context, arguments could be couched in terms of whether or not the individual was beyond redemption, and who was amenable to probation intervention. Subsequently, especially after the Second World War, the aspirations for the supervisory process shifted from moral and spiritual reformation to scientific treatment and rehabilitation through casework; from God's to man's intervention (McWilliams 1983, 1985).

Over time the emerging ideal was passed from one generation to the next as a cultural identity emerged, reinforced by systems established to recruit, induct and then train new entrants into the service. The Home Office occupied this role from the 1930s before handing it over to the academic world (Whitehead and Thompson 2004).

Moreover, selection processes were operated with a view to ensuring that those selected had the personal qualities to cope with what is often demanding work and to promote the ideal. These processes were effective at creating a culture comprising different individuals whose thinking was not always mainstream, who therefore had the capacity to be an irritant. Even though probation officers could be characterised by their individuality, they also had the capacity to argue for the rights and needs of individuals at the fringes of society. Whilst the probation ideal has been in decline over recent decades, the values traditionally associated with the service exist as a reminder of humanitarian influences in what is sometimes a rather bleak penal system that sends too many people to prison.

In the Introduction we made it clear that we wanted to produce a biography of an organisation, tell a story, to describe *what* has happened since the late 19th century, as we approach the centenary of the probation system in 2007. Moreover, and importantly, we wanted to explore *why* we have this service in 2005/06 rather than another. These constitute the analytical strands of the book, which we attempted to pull together in the final chapter by exploring a series of nine themes and influences since 1979.

We have examined the history of probation in relation to the dynamics of politics, power and cultural change, free of the prevailing confines which so clearly inhibit constructive debate. We hope that what we have done, in the way we have fused our individual perceptions, knowledge and experience of the probation world, has produced some challenging and innovative insights that will encourage a period of reflection as we approach 2007. Without doubt, this is a significant time for probation and the wider criminal justice system because of the emerging NOMS agenda. Our position is that we want those values associated with the probation ideal to create a more ethically based, anti-custodial and less punitive culture, as we move towards the next general election in 2009/10. The alternative, which we do not care for, is to see progress being made towards a vision based upon the work of Charles Murray which is one of more prison with its questionable morality and efficacy, in addition to the ever-increasing bureaucratisation of probation. So where do we go from here? What should we do now? How can we shape the future? Our responses to these questions will not only shape the future of criminal justice and probation's place within it, but also the kind of society in which we live. As we think about our future responses we are limited only by our imaginations.

NOTES – Chapter 8

[1] The prison population for selected years from 1908:

1908:	22,029
1918:	9,196
1928:	11,109
1938:	11,086
1948:	19,765
1958:	25,379
1968:	32,461
1978:	41,796
1980:	43,109
1987:	50,073
1996:	55,000
2001:	66,000
2003:	74,000
2005:	75,000 (by April)
2009:	80,000 (projected)

It is interesting to recall that in September 1987, when the Leeds Castle seminar was held (see Chapter 4), the projected prison population was 70,000 by 2000, which was both unimaginable and politically/morally/economically unacceptable. These concerns helped to shape the Criminal Justice Act 1991 by ensuring that only the most serious (sex and violent) offenders were committed to custody. When we were completing this book during the summer of 2005, the prison population had risen at one point to 75,000. One of the goals of NOMS is to stabilise the prison population at 80,000 by 2009 (NOMS update, Issue 4/2005, June 2005). We should remind ourselves that the Carter Report projected a prison population of 93,000 by 2009 (Carter 2003); David Blunkett revised this figure downwards to 80,000 (Home Office 2004c); Charles Murray (2005) talks about a prison population of 250,000 by 2015. However, during the week the manuscript was submitted to the publisher, *The Times* newspaper, on Wednesday 27th July 2005, stated that New Labour was hoping that judges will make a 15% cut in average prison sentences to keep prison numbers under control. This would mean reducing the average prison term of 17.1 months by more than 10 weeks. This is because the prison population has reached 76,506 'and officials say that it is growing faster than previously thought. It could top 90,000 by 2011, some 3,000 more than the worst-case scenario projection published in January. The Government has set a ceiling of 80,000 on the jail population' (p24).

[2] Georg Wilhelm Friedrich Hegel (1770–1831) was a German philosopher who considered the world was moving towards a predetermined end state through a complex dialectical process of thesis, antithesis and synthesis. This was understood and speculated of in terms of the unfolding of the Absolute; Spirit; Reason. For Marx the 'end' of the dialectical process was a communist society. In Christianity the 'end' to which the world is moving is the kingdom of God.

Therefore these are examples of understanding the historical process as a straight line with a beginning and end, rather than a cyclical process.

Appendices

Appendix 1

CHRONOLOGICAL SUMMARY OF PROBATION HISTORY

Before 1876

1841   Matthew Davenport Hill, Recorder of Birmingham, used bail to suspend sentence and then release offenders to suitable guardians. He used the term probationer.

1841   In the USA, John Augustus of Boston supervised offenders on bail at the court's request. Sometimes credited with being the first probation officer.

1870s   Edward Cox, Recorder of Portsmouth, released first and young offenders on recognisances entered into by parents or friends.

Chapter 1 – From 1876

1876   Appointment of first Police Court Missionary by the Church of England Temperance Society to supervise inebriates released by the courts.

1879   Summary Jurisdiction Act.

1887   Probation of First Offenders Act provided for the release on a recognisance of first offenders but did not include supervision by a probation officer. This had to wait until 1907.

Chapter 2 – 1907 to 1979

1906   Reforming Liberal government elected.

1907   Probation of Offenders Act and birth of probation order that was not a punishment and instead of sentencing.

1909   Departmental Committee.

1912   Creation of National Association of Probation Officers.

1914   Criminal Justice Administration Act.

1922   Departmental Committee proposed the appointment of local

Justices to form a committee to oversee probation work and 50% government grant towards the costs of the system. Every court should have a probation officer.

1925 and 1926   Criminal Justice Acts began to establish a more standardised administrative probation system.

1926   Probation Rules alluded to the possibility of Principal Probation Officers.

1930   First Home Office Training Scheme.

1933   Children and Young Persons Act and probation had an important role to play in supervising juveniles.

1936   Departmental Committee said the existing system needed trained staff and it must be a wholly public service administered by committees. Beginnings of the inspectorate and more senior and principal officers required. Beginnings of structural change from horizontal to hierarchical model.

1937   Summary Procedure (Domestic Proceedings) Act.

1938   *The Probation Service – Its Objects and its Organisation* published by the Home Office: provides an important glimpse into probation during the first 30 years. Governance structure was being established that comprised Home Office and local dimension manifested in the probation committee system that provided oversight of its officers.

1942   First Principal Probation Officer conference during the war.

1948   Criminal Justice Act amended the 1907 Act and became the primary legislation. 'Advise, Assist and Befriend' endorsed and the themes of welfare and rehabilitation promoted in the post-war welfare state.

1950s   Development of Divorce Court Welfare Service.

1959   Penal Practice in a Changing Society signalled the acme of the treatment model but there were concerns about the rising prison population.

1960   Creation of Central Council of Probation Committees.

1960   Ingleby Report.

1961   Criminal Justice Act.

1961   Streatfield Report on Business of the Criminal Courts.

1962   Departmental Committee (Morison Report).

1963   Children and Young Persons Act.

1963   ACTO report on aftercare.

1964   Longford Report.

1965   *The Child, The Family and the Young Offender* (White Paper).

1967   Criminal Justice Act.

1967   The Probation and After-Care Service established.

1968   *Children in Trouble* (White Paper).

1968   Seebohm Committee reported.

1969   Children and Young Persons Act: the apotheosis of the welfare approach to young offenders *if* it had been fully implemented.

1972   Butterworth Report looked at the relationship between probation officers and social workers apropos pay and duties.

1972   Central government grant increased from 50% to 80%.

1972   Criminal Justice Act introduced the Community Service Order etc.

1974   IMPACT research followed by Brody in 1976.

1974   Younger Report on Young Adult Offenders accentuated debates over care and control and future direction of the service.

1974   Local government reorganisation and areas reduced from 79 to 56.

1976   Home Office Working Paper: *A Review of Criminal Justice Policy* (a review of 1966 to 1976).

Some important themes during the 1970s: increasing managerialism and bureaucracy; rehabilitation and treatment questioned by empirical research; models of probation in response to the decline of the rehabilitative ideal; history of changing ideas in probation; and Home Office control mechanisms.

Chapter 3 – 1979 to 1984

1979   Election of Conservative government on 4th May that emphasised public sector efficiency, more law and order. Unemployment reached over 3 million during the early 1980s.

1980   Kent Control Unit; ongoing debates over care and control.

1981   Cash limits emphasised by the government.

1982   Association of Chief Officers of Probation created to replace the Chief Officers' Conference.

1982   Cullen and Rogers had implications for probation requirements.

1982   Criminal Justice Act and Schedule 11 requirements.

1982   Launch of Financial Management Initiative on 17th May.

1983   9th June: Conservatives re-elected.

1984   Statement of National Objectives and Priorities and the escalation of central control over the 56 areas.

Development of objectives; measurable outputs; performance; Value for Money; Efficiency, Economy and Effectiveness; better information for managers and the need for greater accountability. Local areas expected to get into line with SNOP priorities, including focusing on alternatives to custody.

Chapter 4 – 1985 to 1991

1985   Prosecution of Offences Act.

1985   ACOP commissioned study of local statements in response to SNOP. Differences over care and control, probation priorities and values. Ongoing cultural change due to emphasis on measurable objectives.

1986   Public Order Act.

1986   Deloitte, Haskins and Sells commissioned by Home Office to develop a Financial Management Information System to ensure the achievement of VfM and 3Es.

1987   11th June: third consecutive Conservative election victory.

1987   Joint Statement by ACOP, CCPC and NAPO: 'Probation – the next five years'.

1987 Grimsey Report on Inspectorate and Performance Indicators.

1987 28th September: the Leeds Castle seminar.

1988 *Punishment, Custody and the Community* (Green Paper).

1988 ACOP published *More Demanding than Prison,* which proposed a new sentence: Community Restitution Order.

1988 *Tackling Offending – An Action Plan* for 17–20-year-old youths and linked to the Green Paper of 1988.

1988/89 First appearance of National Standards.

1988 Criminal Justice Act.

1989 Coleman Report on Review of Probation Training.

1989 Audit Commission Report: *Promoting Value For Money in the Probation Service.*

1989 National Audit Commission Report on Home Office: *Control and Management of Probation Services in England and Wales.*

1989 Residential conference in Cambridge.

1989 Ditchley Park Conference.

1990 *Crime, Justice and Protecting the Public* (White Paper).

1990 9th November: Criminal Justice Bill.

1990 *Supervision and Punishment in the Community: A Framework for Action* (Green Paper) gave effect to the 1990 White Paper. It articulated how government expected probation to achieve its objectives and confirmed it was more criminal justice than social work service.

1991 *Organising Supervision and Punishment in the Community* (Blue Paper).

1991 Criminal Justice Act and probation becomes a sentence.

Chapter 5 – 1992 to 1997

1990 On 28th November John Major becomes Prime Minister replacing Margaret Thatcher.

1991 Introduction of cash limits following decision in November 1989 to cash limit the probation service.

1992   9th April: Conservative fourth consecutive election win.

1992   National Standards; RMIS replaced FMIS.

1992   First Three-Year plan that superseded SNOP in 1984.

1993   27th May 1993 to 1st May 1997: Michael Howard was Home Secretary.

1993   Jamie Bulger killed on 12th February.

1993   Stephen Lawrence killed on 22nd April.

1993   Michael Howard announced 27-point plan on law and order that signalled the end of the Hurd, Patten and Faulkner approach. The new doctrine of Prison Works.

1993   Criminal Justice Act reversed certain features of the CJA 1991.

1993   Performance Indicators evolved into Key Performance Indicators and ongoing development of measurable targets.

1994   Home Office review of training following Coleman Report.

1994   Criminal Justice and Public Order Act.

1995   National Standards revised again.

1995   *Strengthening Punishment in the Community* proposed a new sentence to give more flexibility that required new legislation. Not implemented because of two Demonstration Projects that gave existing legislation a chance to be effective.

1995   Decisions made on future of probation training that would detach probation from social work education. Home Office sponsorship of Diploma in Social Work ceased from 1995/96 so that the service did not have any new recruits for four years.

1997   Launch of Demonstration Projects in Teesside and Shropshire in response to the 1995 Green Paper (from April 1997 to March 1998).

1997   Protection from Harassment Act.

1997   Crime (Sentences) Act.

1997   Sex Offender Act.

Chapter 6 – 1997 to 2001

1997   1st May: Labour elected with 179-seat majority.

1997   Prisons–Probation Review announced in July.

1997   What Works/Accredited Programmes introduced.

1997 to 2001   Five Cranfield Conferences attempted to promote leadership from within probation and greater cohesiveness amongst Chief Probation Officers.

1998   *Joining Forces To Protect The Public: Prisons–Probation*, a Consultation Document revealed that government had decided not to merge the two organisations at this stage.

1998   Teesside Judgment by Mr Justice Collins on staffing.

1998   Diploma in Probation Studies began in nine consortia.

1998   Crime and Disorder Act.

1998   Human Rights Act.

1999 to 2000   Creation of Youth Offender Teams.

1999   Government launched review of courts by Lord Justice Auld.

2000   16th May: the Halliday review of sentencing began.

2000   Powers of Criminal Courts (Sentencing) Act.

2000   Criminal Justice and Court Services Act established the National Probation Service (began on 1st April 2001) and renamed certain court orders.

2000   Child Support, Pensions and Social Security Act legislated for the benefit sanction, piloted in 4 areas (ongoing in 2005).

2000 and 2002   National Standards (revised); stricter enforcement.

2001   Children and Family Court Advisory and Support Service resulted in probation losing its responsibility for civil work.

2001   National Probation Service began when 54 areas became 42 and 100% funded by central government.

Chapter 7 – 2001 to 2004

2001   New Labour's ten-year plan for criminal justice.

2001   Creation of the National Probation Service on 1st April.

2001   New Labour re-elected on 7th June.

2001   In July, Halliday Review on sentencing published: *Making Punishments Work* (that began on 16th May 2000).

2001   First NPS conference and D. Blunkett's response to Halliday.

2001   *A New Choreography* published in August.

2002   In March, Patrick Carter asked to review correctional services.

2002   *Justice For All* White Paper published in July.

2002   Criminal Justice Bill published in November.

2003   Criminal Justice Act 2003, partially implemented 4th April 2005.

2003   In December, Carter Report published: *Managing Offenders, Reducing Crime: A New Approach*.

2003   D. Blunkett's response to Carter: *Reducing Crime–Changing Lives*, giving support for a National Offender Management Service.

2003   *Heart of the Dance* diversity strategy published.

2004   *Setting the Pace*: review of the first 1,000 days of NPS.

2004   *Bold Steps*: new business plan replacing *New Choreography*.

2004   *National Offender Management Service–Next Steps*: summary of responses to two consultation exercises.

2005   Latest version of National Standards.

2005   In April, first NOMS conference held at Nottingham.

2005   New Labour re-elected on 5th May with reduced majority.

Appendix 2

CRIMINAL JUSTICE ACT 2003: SENTENCING FRAMEWORK

CUSTODIAL SENTENCES – Province of the Crown Court

Life – mandatory.

Life – discretionary for public protection in cases of 'serious offence' and 'serious harm' to the public.

Extended Sentence – for sex and violence specified offences. An extended period of licence to protect the public.

Custody – discretionary 12 months and over.

Normally offenders will be released at the halfway point of sentence and remain on licence until the end of sentence.

Dangerous Offenders – Specified Offence terminology

Section 224 defines the new terminology of 'specified offence', 'serious offence' and 'serious harm':

> *Specified Offences* are sexual or violent offences listed at Schedule 15 to the Act and all these offences carry a maximum penalty of two years' custody or more.

> *Serious Offence* is a *specified* sexual or violent offence which carries a maximum penalty of 10 years' imprisonment or more, including life.

> *Serious Harm* means death or serious personal injury, whether physical or psychological.

It should be clarified that the *Standard Determinate Sentence* of 12 months' custody and over can be used for specified offences if there are no serious risk of harm issues. Consequently, the probation service, by providing pre-sentence reports to the courts containing information on offence seriousness, risk of harm, and an assessment of needs, will contribute to the sentencing process.

OTHER CUSTODIAL SENTENCES OF LESS THAN 12 MONTHS

Custody 'Plus' at sections 181–182 has two parts. The custodial period must be for at least 2 weeks and not more than 13 weeks for one offence. The second is the licence period, which must be at least 26 weeks. Conditions can be attached to the licence as follows:

ECP	Prohibited Activity	Supervision
Activity Requirement	Curfew	ACO
Programme	Exclusion	

Intermittent or Part-Time Custody: ss 183–186.

Suspended Sentence/Custody 'Minus': ss 189–193. This is a prison sentence of at least 28 weeks but not more than 51. The offender must comply with certain requirements selected by the court. They have 12 to choose from (the same as the generic community sentence), which are listed immediately below.

GENERIC COMMUNITY SENTENCE

1. ECP (s 199): 40–300 hours.

2. Activity Requirement (s 201).

3. Programme Requirement (s 202): Think First etc.

4. Prohibited Activity Requirement (s 203).

5. Curfew and Electronic Monitoring (s 204).

6. Exclusion Requirement (s 205).

7. Residence Requirement (s 206) to reside at a specified place; hostel.

8. Mental Health Treatment Requirement (s 207).

9. Drug Rehabilitation Requirement (s 209).

10. Alcohol Treatment Requirement (s 212).

11. Supervision Requirement (s 213).

12. ACO Requirement (s 214) where offender is under 25.

Offenders must give **consent** to (8), (9) and (10).

The number of requirements will be determined by: the level of seriousness; risk of re-offending and harm; restriction of liberty required; and an assessment of individual need. NPD guidance specifies that:

Low   = 1 requirement

Medium = 1–2 requirements

High   = 1–3 requirements

Note on breach, revocation and amendment of community orders

Section 179 invokes Schedule 8 to the CJA 2003 (formerly Schedule 3 to the PCC(S) Act 2000). Normally, two failed appointments within 12 months (following final warning and intention to breach action) will lead to the supervising officer laying an Information to return an offender to court in breach/prosecution proceedings. A breach will now be dealt with as follows:

(a) amend the order by imposing more onerous requirements;

(b) revoke and re-sentence;

(c) if offender is aged 18 and over and persistently fails to comply, revoke and re-sentence to custody.

Paragraphs 13–15 deal with revocation in the interests of justice re: changed circumstances and good progress (where the offender *can not* comply rather than *will not*).

Paragraphs 16–20 deal with amendments to orders: deleting, adding, extending and substituting.

FINES AND DISCHARGES – OTHER ORDERS

Deferment of Sentence at Magistrates' and Crown Courts: s 278 and Schedule 23.

Individual Support Orders.

Parenting Orders and Referral Orders.

Additional Note: ss 199–223 deal with requirements that can be used with:

(a) generic community sentence (all 12 available);

(b) custody 'plus' restricted choice;

(c) licence arrangements – restricted;

(d) intermittent custody – restricted;

(e) suspended sentence/custody 'minus' (all 12 available).

If more than one requirement is imposed they must be compatible and also not conflict with religion, employment and education.

Finally, it should be acknowledged that from 4th April 2005 the new provisions introduced under the CJA 2003 were:

(a) public protection sentences for dangerous offenders;

(b) the new generic community sentence;

(c) custody 'minus';

(d) the new release and recall arrangements for all custodial sentences of 12 months and over.

REFERENCES

Allatt, P. and Yendle, S. (1992) *Youth Unemployment and the Family: Voices of Disordered Times*, London and New York: Routledge.

Ashworth, A. (2000 3rd edition) *Sentencing and Criminal Justice*, Butterworths: London, Dublin and Edinburgh.

Ashworth, A. (2002 3rd edition) 'Sentencing' in M. Maguire, R. Morgan and R. Reiner (eds) *The Oxford Handbook of Criminology*, Oxford University Press: Oxford, New York.

Association of Chief Officers of Probation (1988) *More Demanding than Prison, a draft discussion paper*, 24th May 1988.

Association of Chief Officers of Probation (1989) *Surviving Poverty*, ACOP: London.

Association of Chief Officers of Probation (1992) *A Sense of Justice: Offenders as Victims of Crime*, ACOP: London.

Association of Chief Officers of Probation (2001) *A Brief Chronicle and Review*, ACOP: London.

Association of Chief Officers of Probation, North-East Region Occasional Paper (1987) *Unemployment in the North East: A Probation Perspective*, ACOP: London.

Audit Commission (1989) *Promoting Value For Money in the Probation Service*, HMSO: London.

Auld, Lord Justice (2000) *Criminal Courts Review – Progress Report No. 1*, May 2000.

Beaumont, B. (1984) '1984 and Ahead: Prospects for the Penal System', *Probation Journal*, Volume 31, 1.

Beaumont, B. (1986) *Annual Report for 1985–86*, NAPO.

Benefit Sanction Report 198 (2003/04) www.dwp.gov.uk/asd/

Benyon, J. (1994) *Law and Order Review 1993. An Audit of Crime, Policing and Criminal Justice Issues*, Centre for the Study of Public Order, University of Leicester.

Biestek, F.P. (1961) *The Casework Relationship*, George Allen and Unwin Ltd: London.

Boateng, P. (1999) *Speech to Chief Probation Officers and Probation Committees*, HMSO: London.

Bochel, D. (1962) 'A Brief History of N.A.P.O.: Part 1 – The Edridge Era', *Probation Journal*, Volume 10, 3.

Bochel, D. (1976) *Probation and After-Care: Its Development in England and Wales*, Scottish Academic Press: Edinburgh and London.

Bottoms, A.E. (1974) 'On the decriminalisation of English Juvenile Courts' in R. Hood (ed.) *Crime, Criminology and Public Policy: Essays in Honour of Sir Leon Radzinowicz*, Heinemann: London.

Bottoms, A.E. (1980) 'An introduction to "The Coming Crisis"' in: A.E. Bottoms and R.H. Preston (eds) *The Coming Penal Crisis: A Criminological and Theological Exploration*, Scottish Academic Press: Edinburgh and London.

Bottoms, A.E. and McWilliams, W. (1979) 'A non-treatment paradigm for probation practice', BJSW, 9, 2.

Bottoms, A.E., Gelsthorpe, L. and Rex, S. (2001) 'Introduction: the contemporary scene for community penalties' in A.E. Bottoms, L. Gelsthorpe and S. Rex (eds) *Community Penalties: Changes and Challenges*, Willan Publishing: Cullompton, Devon.

Box, S. (1987) *Recession, Crime and Punishment*, Macmillan Education Ltd: Houndmills, Basingstoke.

Brake, M., and Hale, C. (1992) *Public Order and Private Lives: The politics of law and order*, Routledge: New York and London.

Brittan, L. (1984) 'Interview with the Editor', *Probation Journal*, Volume 31, 1.

Broad, B. (1991) *Punishment Under Pressure: The Probation Service in the Inner City*, Jessica Kingsley Publishers: London.

Brody, S.R. (1976) *The Effectiveness of Sentencing*, HMSO.

Brown, M. (1969) 'Management and the Senior Probation Officer', *Probation Journal*, Volume 15, 3.

Brown, M.J. (1973) 'The Probation Service: Structure, Management and Future', *Probation Journal*, Volume 19, 1.

Brownlee, I. (1998) *Community Punishment: A Critical Introduction*, Longman: London and New York.

Bryant, M., Coker, J., Estlea, B., Himmel, S. and Knapp, T. (1978) 'Sentenced To Social Work?' *Probation Journal*, Volume 25, 4.

Buchanan, J. and Millar, M. (1997) 'Probation: Reclaiming social work identity', *Probation Journal*, Volume 44, 1.

Burnham, D. (1981a) 'Probation: A New Orthodoxy?' *Probation Journal*, Volume 28, 1.

Burnham, D. (1981b) 'The New Orthodoxy: In The Place of Confusion', *Probation Journal*, Volume 28, 4.

Butler, T. (1983) 'The Financial Management Initiative' in *Future Directions of the Probation Service*, Bournemouth Residential Conference, 12th–13th May 1983.

Cadbury Report (1992) *The Financial Aspects of Corporate Governance – The Cadbury Committee*, HMSO: London.

Carter, P. (2003) *Managing Offenders, Reducing Crime. A new approach*, Strategy Unit.

Cavadino, M. (1997) 'Pre-Sentence Reports: The Effects of Legislation and National Standards', *BJ Criminology*, 37, 529.

Cavadino, M. and Dignan, J. (2002 3rd edition) *The Penal System: An Introduction*, Sage Publications: London, Thousand Oaks and New Delhi.

Cavadino, M., Crow, I. and Dignan, J. (1999) *Criminal Justice 2000: Strategies for a New Century*, Waterside Press: Winchester.

Central Council of Probation Committees (1987) *The Probation Committee: Role and Function*.

Chui, W.H. and Nellis, M. (2003) (eds) *Moving Probation Forward: Evidence, Arguments and Practice*, Pearson Longman: London and New York.

Clarke, A. (1971) 'The APPO and Middle Management', *Probation Journal*, Volume 17, 1.

Clarke, R.V.G and Cornish, D.B. (1983) (eds) *Crime Control in Britain: A Review of Policy Research*, State University of New York Press: Albany.

Cohen, S. (1985) *Visions of Social Control: Crime, Punishment and Classification*, Polity Press: Cambridge.

Coleman, D. (1989) *Review of Probation Training*, Home Office: London.

Colley, R.D., Lloyd-Owen, D.M., Ollerhead, D., Pearce, M., Ruth, J.W., Southwell, B.W.J. and Turner, K.T. (1970) 'Administration and Individual Responsibility', *Probation Journal*, Volume 16, 3.

Collins, Mr Justice (1998) *Approved Judgment in the High Court of Justice. R v Teesside Probation Committee ex parte National Association of Probation Officers*.

Crampton, R. (2005) 'The Main Man' in *The Times Magazine*, 30th April 2005.

Crow, I. (2001) *The Treatment and Rehabilitation of Offenders*, Sage Publications: London, Thousand Oaks and New Delhi.

Cumont, F. (1956) *The Mysteries of Mithra*, Dover Publications, Inc: New York.

Davies, M. (1969) *Probationers in their Social Environment: A study of male probationers aged 17–20*, Home Office Research Study, HMSO.

Davies, M. (1982) 'Community-based alternatives to custody: the right place for the probation service'. Unpublished address to a conference of Chief Probation Officers.

Department of Employment (1972) *Report of the Butterworth Inquiry into the Work and Pay of Probation Officers and Social Workers*, Cmnd. 5076.

Downes, D. (1988) *Contrasts in Tolerance: Post-War Penal Policy in The Netherlands and England and Wales*, Clarendon Press: Oxford.

Downes, D. (1997) 'What the Next Government Should Do About Crime', *The Howard Journal*, Volume 36, 1.

Downes, D. and Morgan, R. (1997 2nd Edition) 'Dumping the "Hostages to Fortune"? The Politics of Law and Order in Post-War Britain' in M. Maguire, R. Morgan and R. Reiner (eds) *The Oxford Handbook of Criminology*, Oxford University Press: Oxford, New York.

Downes, D. and Morgan, R. (2002 3rd edition) 'The skeletons in the cupboard: The politics of law and order at the turn of the millennium' in M. Maguire, R. Morgan and R. Reiner (eds) *The Oxford Handbook of Criminology*, Oxford University Press: Oxford, New York.

Drakeford, M. (1988) 'Privatisation, Punishment and the Future of Probation', *Probation Journal*, Volume 35, 2.

Drew, P. (1992) 'The Probation Service: A Few Valedictory Comments', *Probation Journal*, Volume 39, 2.

Driver, S. and Martell, L. (1998) *New Labour: Politics after Thatcherism*, Polity Press: Cambridge.

Elliot, N. (1997) 'The Qualification of Probation Officers: Thoughts for the Future', *Probation Journal*, Volume 44, 4.

Farrall, S. (2004) 'Supervision, motivation and social context: what matters most when probationers desist?' in G. Mair (ed.) *What Matters In Probation*, Willan Publishing: Cullompton, Devon.

Faulkner, D. (1984) 'The Future of the Probation Service' in *Probation; Direction, Innovation and Change in the 1980s*. York Conference, 11th–13th July, NAPO.

Faulkner, D. (1989) in R. Shaw and K. Haines (eds) *The Criminal Justice System: A Central Role For The Probation Service*, Institute of Criminology, University of Cambridge.

Faulkner, D. (2004) 'Why Officials Must Make Their Voices Heard', *Guardian* newspaper, 22nd December 2004.

Field, S. and Hough, M. (1993) *Cash-Limiting The Probation Service: A Case Study In Resource Allocation*, Research and Planning Unit Paper 77, Home Office: London.

Fletcher, H. (1987) 'Survive and Prosper?' in 'Back to the Future? Four Views on the Next Five Years', *Probation Journal*, Volume 34, 3.

Flynn, N. (2000) 'The Government's Approach to Performance Management', *Criminal Justice Matters*, no. 40, Summer 2000, CCJS: London.

Folkard, S., Fowles, A.J., McWilliams, B.C., McWilliams, W., Smith, D.D., Smith, D.E. and Walmsley, G.R. (1974) *IMPACT Vol.1, The design of the probation experiment and an interim evaluation*, HMSO.

Folkard, S., Smith, D.E. and Smith D.D. (1976) *IMPACT Vol.2, The Results of the Experiment*, HMSO.

Fraser, D. (1973) *The Evolution of the British Welfare State: A History of Social Policy since the Industrial Revolution*, Macmillan: London and Basingstoke.

Frayne, L. (1993) 'The History of Change', in D. Whitfield. and D. Scott (eds) *Paying Back – Twenty Years of Community Service*, Waterside Press: Winchester.

Fullwood, C. (1984) *FMI and the Probation Service*, Association of Chief Officers of Probation.

Garland, D. (1985) *Punishment and Welfare: A history of penal strategies*, Gower: Aldershot and USA.

Garland, D. (1989) 'Critical Reflections on the Green Paper' in H. Rees and E.H. Williams (eds) *Punishment, Custody and The Community: Reflections and Comments on the Green Paper*, LSE: London.

Garland, D. (1990) *Punishment and Modern Society: A Study in Social Theory*, Oxford University Press: Oxford, New York.

Garland, D. (2001) *The Culture of Control: Crime and Social Order in Contemporary Society*, Oxford University Press: Oxford, New York.

Garland, D. and Sparks, R. (2000) 'Criminology, Social Theory, and the Challenge of Our Times' in D. Garland and R. Sparks (eds) *Criminology and Social Theory*, Oxford University Press: Oxford, New York.

Garland, Mr. Justice P. (1997) Text of Speech at Launch of Demonstration Project, Teesside Probation Archive.

Gelsthorpe, L. (2003) 'Theories of Crime' in W.H. Chui and M. Nellis (eds) *Moving Probation Forward: Evidence, Arguments and Practice*, Pearson/Longman: Harlow, London and New York.

Gerth, H.H. and Mills, C.W. (1948) (eds) *From Max Weber*, Routledge: London.

Gibson, B. (2004) *Criminal Justice Act 2003: A Guide to the New Procedures and Sentencing*, Waterside Press: Winchester.

Gilmore, I. (1992) *Dancing With Dogma: Britain Under Thatcherism*, Pocket Books: London.

Glennerster, H. (2000 2nd edition) *British Social Policy since 1945*, Blackwell: Oxford.

Glover, E.R. (1956 revised 2nd edition) *Probation and Re-Education*, Routledge and Kegan Paul Ltd: London.

Goodman, A. (2003) 'Probation into the millennium: the punishing service?' in R. Matthews and J. Young (eds) *The New Politics of Crime and Punishment*, Willan Publishing: Cullompton, Devon.

Grieve Smith, J. (1997) *Full Employment: A Pledge Betrayed*, Macmillan: Basingstoke and London.

Griffiths, W. (1982a) 'A new Probation Service', *Probation Journal*, Volume 29, 3.

Griffiths, W. (1982b) 'Supervision in the Community', *Justice of the Peace*, 21st August 1982.

Grimsey, E.J. (1987) *Efficiency Scrutiny of HM Probation Inspectorate*, Home Office.

Hall, S., Critcher, C., Jefferson, T., Clarke, J. and Roberts, B. (1978) *Policing the Crisis: Mugging, the State and Law and Order*, London: Macmillan.

Handy, C. (1985) *Understanding Organisations*, London: Penguin.

Harris, R. (1977) 'The Probation Officer as Social Worker', BJSW, 7, 4.

Harris, R. (1980) 'A Changing Service: The Case for Separating "Care" and "Control" in Probation Practice', BJSW, 10, 2.

Harris, R. (1988) 'Taming the Whitehall Machine', *The Sunday Observer*, 21st February 1988.

Hattersley, R. (2004) *The Edwardians*, Little, Brown: London.

Haxby, D. (1978) *Probation: A Changing Service*, Constable: London.

Hedderman, C. and Hough, M. (2004) 'Getting tough or being effective: what matters?' in G. Mair (ed.) *What Matters In Probation*, Willan Publishing: Cullompton, Devon.

Hedderman, C., Ellis, T. and Sugg, D. (1999) *Increasing Confidence in Community Sentences: The Results of Two Demonstration Projects*, Home Office Research Study 194, HMSO: London.

HMIP (1988) *Performance Indicators For The Probation Service*, Home Office, HMSO.

HMIP (1998) *Strategies for Effective Offender Supervision: Report of the HMIP What Works Project*, Home Office, HMSO.

Hollin, C.R. (2002 3rd edition) 'Criminological Psychology' in M. Maguire, R. Morgan and R. Reiner (eds) *The Oxford Handbook of Criminology*, Oxford University Press: Oxford, New York.

Home Office (1909) *Report of the Departmental Committee on the Probation of Offenders Act 1907*, Cmnd. 5001, HMSO.

Home Office (1922) *Report of the Departmental Committee on the Training, Appointment and Payment of Probation Officers*, Cmnd. 1601, HMSO.

Home Office (1927) *Report of the Departmental Committee on the Treatment of Young Offenders*, Cmnd. 2831.

Home Office (1936) *Report of the Departmental Committee on the Social Services in Courts of Summary Jurisdiction,* Cmnd. 5122, HMSO.

Home Office (1938) *The Probation Service – Its Objects and its Organisation,* HMIP.

Home Office (1959) *Penal Practice in a Changing Society: Aspects of Future Development (England and Wales),* Cmnd. 645, HMSO.

Home Office (1960) *Report of the Committee on Children and Young Persons* (Ingleby Report), Cmnd. 1191, HMSO.

Home Office (1961) *Report of the Inter-Departmental Committee on the Business of the Criminal Courts* (Streatfield Report), Cmnd. 1289, HMSO.

Home Office (1962) *Report of the Departmental Committee on the Probation Service* (Morison Committee), Cmnd. 1650, HMSO.

Home Office (1963) *The Organisation of After-Care. Report of the Advisory Council on the Treatment of Offenders,* HMSO.

Home Office (1965) *The Child, The Family and The Young Offender,* Cmnd. 2742, HMSO.

Home Office (1966) *Report of the Inquiry into Prison Escapes and Security,* Cmnd. 3175, HMSO.

Home Office (1968) *Children in Trouble,* Cmnd. 3601, HMSO.

Home Office (1968) *Committee on Local Authority and Allied Personal Social Services* (Seebohm Report), Cmnd. 3703, HMSO.

Home Office (1970) *Report of the Advisory Council on the Penal System. Non-Custodial and Semi-Custodial Penalties* (Wootton Report), HMSO.

Home Office (1974) *Young Adult Offenders* (Younger Report), HMSO.

Home Office (1976) *A Review of Criminal Justice Policy,* Home Office Working Paper, London: HMSO.

Home Office (1981) *The Brixton Disorders 10–12 April 1981. Report of an Inquiry By the Rt. Hon. The Lord Scarman OBE,* Cmnd. 8427, HMSO.

Home Office (1983a) *Probation Service in England and Wales: Statement of National Purpose and Objectives,* Draft.

Home Office (1983b) *Future Direction of the Probation Service,* Draft, June.

Home Office (1984) *Probation Service in England and Wales. Statement of National Objectives and Priorities.*

Home Office (1988a) *Punishment, Custody and The Community,* Cmnd. 424, HMSO.

Home Office (1988b) *Tackling Offending: An Action Plan,* HMSO.

Home Office (1989a) *A Financial Management Information System (FMIS) For Area Probation Services. Report on Stage 3A of the FMIS Project,* London, C6 Division.

Home Office (1989b) *HM Inspectorate of Probation,* Inspection Programme 1989–1990.

Home Office (1990a) *Crime, Justice and Protecting The Public,* Cmnd. 965, HMSO.

Home Office (1990b) *Supervision and Punishment in the Community: A Framework for Action,* Cmnd. 966, HMSO.

Home Office (1991) *Organising Supervision and Punishment in the Community,* HMSO.

Home Office (1992) *The Probation Service: Three Year Plan for the Probation Service, 1993–1996.*

Home Office (1993) *The Probation Service: Three Year Plan for the Probation Service, 1994–1997.*

Home Office (1994) *The Probation Service: Three Year Plan for the Probation Service, 1995–1998.*

Home Office (1995a) *National Standards for the Supervision of Offenders In The Community,* Home Office: London.

Home Office (1995b) *New Arrangements For The Recruitment And Qualifying Training For Probation Officers.* Discussion Paper by the Home Office.

Home Office (1995c) *Strengthening Punishment In The Community: A Consultation Document,* Cmnd. 2780, HMSO.

Home Office (1997) *The Probation Service: Three Year Plan for the Probation Service, 1997–2000.*

Home Office (1999) *Diploma in Probation Studies,* Home Office.

Home Office (2000, revised 2002) *National Standards for the Probation Service,* Home Office: London.

Home Office (2001a) *Criminal Justice: The Way Ahead,* Cmnd. 5074, HMSO.

Home Office (2001b) *Making Punishments Work, The Report of a Review of the Sentencing Framework for England and Wales* (Halliday Review), Home Office Communication Directorate: London.

Home Office (2001c) *A New Choreography: An Integrated Strategy for the National Probation Service for England and Wales. Strategic Framework 2001–2004*. National Probation Service.

Home Office (2002) *Justice For All* (White Paper) Cmnd. 5563, Home Office: London.

Home Office (2003) *The Heart of the Dance. A Diversity Strategy for the National Probation Service for England and Wales 2002–2006.*

Home Office (2004a) *Bold Steps: National Probation Service for England and Wales. 2004–2005 Business Plan.*

Home Office (2004b) *National Offender Management Service: Next Steps. Summary of responses to the two Government consultation exercises.*

Home Office (2004c) *Reducing Crime – Changing Lives. The Government's plans for transforming the management of offenders.*

Home Office (2004d) *Setting the Pace – how the National Probation Service has delivered A New Choreography.*

Home Office Circular (225/66) *Structure of the Probation and After-Care Service.*

Hoover, K. and Plant, R. (1989) *Conservative Capitalism in Britain and the United States: A Critical Appraisal*, Routledge: London.

Hough, M. (2005) 'Surveys vary on direction of trend', *Guardian* newspaper, 22nd April 2005.

Hudson, B.A. (1987) *Justice Through Punishment: A Critique of the 'Justice' Model of Corrections*, Macmillan: London.

Hudson, B.A. (2003 2nd edition) *Understanding Justice: An introduction to ideas, perspectives and controversies in modern penal theory*, Open University Press: Buckingham and Philadelphia.

Hudson, R. and Williams, A.M. (1989) *Divided Britain*, Belhave Press: London.

Hugman, B. (1977) *Act Natural*, Bedford Square Press: London.

Humphrey, C. (1987) *The Implications of the FMI For the Probation Service*, Department of Accounting and Finance, University of Manchester.

Humphrey, C., Pease, K. and Carter, P. (1993) *Changing Notions of Accountability in the Probation Service*, University of Manchester.

Hurd, D. (2003) *Memoirs*, Little, Brown: London.

Ignatieff, M. (1978) *A Just Measure of Pain: The Penitentiary in the Industrial Revolution, 1750–1850*, Macmillan: London and Basingstoke.

James, A.L. (1995) 'Probation Values for the 1990s – and Beyond?' *The Howard Journal of Criminal Justice*, Volume 34, 4, Blackwell Publishers for the Howard League.

Jarvis, F.V. (1972) *Advise, Assist and Befriend: A History of the Probation and After-Care Service*, National Association of Probation Officers.

Joint Negotiating Committee for the Probation Service (1980) *Report of the Working Party on Management Structure in the Probation and After-Care Service*, JNC.

Jordan, W. (1983) 'Criminal Justice and Probation in the 1980s', *Probation Journal*, Volume 30, 3.

Kendall, K. (2004) *'Dangerous Thinking: a critical history of correctional cognitive behaviouralism'* in G. Mair (ed.) *What Matters In Probation*, Willan Publishing: Cullompton, Devon.

Kennedy, H. (2005) *Just Law: The Changing Face of Justice – and why it Matters to Us All*, Vintage: London.

Kilbrandon Report (1964) *Children and Young Persons: Scotland*, Cmnd. 2306, HMSO: Edinburgh.

King, J.F.S. (1964 2nd edition) *The Probation Service*, Butterworths: London.

Kung, H. (1976) *On Being a Christian*, William Collins, Sons and Co. Ltd.: London.

Le Mesurier, L. (1935) *A Handbook of Probation and Social Work of the Courts*, NAPO: London.

Leeson, C. (1914) *The Probation System*, P. and S. King and Son: London.

Lishman, J. (1994) *Communication in Social Work*, Macmillan: Basingstoke.

Lloyd, C. (1986) *Response to SNOP*, Institute of Criminology, University of Cambridge.

Lustig, R. (1987) 'The Crisis In Our Prisons', *The Observer*, 11th October 1987.

McWilliams, W. (1979) 'Paradigms of Practice'. Notes of Session at First National Seminar on Community Service at Keele University.

McWilliams, W. (1983) 'The Mission to the English Police Courts 1876–1936', *Howard Journal of Criminal Justice*, 22, 129–47.

McWilliams, W. (1985) 'The Mission Transformed: Professionalisation of Probation between the wars', *Howard Journal of Criminal Justice*, 24, 257–74.

McWilliams, W. (1986) 'The English probation system and the diagnostic ideal', *Howard Journal of Criminal Justice*, 25, 241–60.

McWilliams, W. (1987) 'Probation, pragmatism and policy', *Howard Journal of Criminal Justice*, 26, 97–121.

McWilliams, W. (1992) 'The rise and development of management thought in the English Probation system' in R. Statham and P. Whitehead (eds) *Managing the Probation Service: Issues for the 1990s*, Longman: Harlow.

Mair, G. (1989) *Some developments in probation in the 1980s*, Home Office Research and Planning Unit, Research Bulletin No. 27.

Mair, G. (1996a) 'Developments in probation in England and Wales 1984–1993' in G. McIvor (ed.) *Working With Offenders*, Research Highlights in Social Work 26, Jessica Kingsley: London and Bristol.

Mair, G. (1996b) '*Intensive Probation*' in G. McIvor (ed.) *Working with Offenders*, Research Highlights in Social Work 26, Jessica Kingsley: London and Bristol.

Mair, G. (2004) 'The origins of What Works in England and Wales: a house built on sand?' in: G. Mair (ed.) *What Matters In Probation*, Willan Publishing: Cullompton, Devon.

Mair, G. and May, C. (1997) *Offenders on Probation*, Home Office Research Study 167.

Major, J. (2000) *The Autobiography*, Harper Collins: London.

Major, J. (1993) in *The Mail on Sunday*, 21st February 1993.

Mark, R. (1978) *In The Office of Constable*, Collins: London.

Martin, R. (1989) 'The Political Economy of Britain's North–South Divide' in J. Lewis and A. Townsend (eds) *The North–South Divide: Regional Change in Britain in the 1980s*, Paul Chapman Publishing Ltd.: London.

Martinson, R. (1974) '*What Works? – Questions and Answers about Prison Reform*', *The Public Interest*, 34, 22–54.

Masters, G. (1997) 'Values for Probation, Society and Beyond', *The Howard Journal*, Volume 36, 3, Blackwell Publishers.

Matthews, B. (1979) 'Probation and Punishment', *Probation Journal*, Volume 26, 2.

Matthews, R. (1999) *Doing Time: An Introduction to the Sociology of Imprisonment*, Palgrave: Hampshire and London.

May, C. (1995) *Measuring the Satisfaction of Courts with the Probation Service*, Home Office Research Study 144, London.

May, C. (1997) *Magistrates' Views of the Probation Service*, Home Office Statistical Bulletin 48/97, London.

May, T. (1991) *Probation: Politics, Policy and Practice*, Open University Press: Milton Keynes and Philadelphia.

Mazlish, B. (1966) *The Riddle of History: The Great Speculators from Vico to Freud*, Minerva Press: USA.

Millar, M. and Buchanan, J. (1995) 'Probation: A Crisis of Identity and Purpose', *Probation Journal*, Volume 42, 4.

Millard, D.A. (1977) 'Literature and the Therapeutic Imagination', BJSW, 7, 2.

Monger, M. (1964) *Casework in Probation*, Butterworths: London.

Morgan, R. (2002 3rd edition) 'Imprisonment: a brief history, the contemporary scene, and likely prospects', in M. Maguire, R. Morgan and R. Reiner (eds) *The Oxford Handbook of Criminology*, Oxford University Press: Oxford, New York.

Morley B. (1993) *Beyond Consensus: Salvaging Sense of Meeting*, Pendle Head: Pennsylvania.

Morrison, B. (1997) *As If*, Granta Books, London.

Morrison, W. (1995) *Theoretical Criminology: from modernity to post-modernism*, Cavendish Publishing Limited: London.

Muncie, J. (1984) *The Trouble with Kids Today*, Hutchinson: London.

Murch, M. (1969) 'Seebohm: A Painful Dilemma for Probation', *Probation Journal*, Volume 15, 1.

Murray, C. (2005) 'The advantages of social apartheid', in News Review, p 6, *Sunday Times*, 3rd April 2005.

National Association of Probation Officers (1970) *The Future Development of the Probation and After-Care Service.* A Statement by the National Association of Probation Officers.

National Association of Probation Officers (1988) Punishment in the Community, *NAPO News*, No. 1, July 1988.

National Association of Probation Officers (1988) *Punishment, Custody and the Community. The response of the National Association of Probation Officers*, December 1988.

NAPO, ACOP and CCPC (1987) *Probation – the next five years. A joint statement by the: Association of Chief Probation Officers, Central Council of Probation Committees and National Association of Probation Officers*, July 1987.

National Audit Office (1989) *Home Office: Control and Management of Probation Services in England and Wales*, H.C. 377, 1988/89 Session, HMSO: London.

National Probation Directorate (April 2005) *National Standards 2005, National Offender Management Service*.

Nellis, M. (1995) 'Probation Values for the 1990s', *The Howard Journal of Criminal Justice*, Volume 34, 1, Blackwell Publishers for the Howard League.

Nellis, M. (2001) 'Community penalties in historical perspective' in A.E. Bottoms, L. Gelsthorpe and S. Rex (eds) *Community Penalties: Changes and Challenges*, Willan Publishing: Cullompton, Devon.

Nellis, M. (2004) '"Into the Field of Corrections": the end of English probation in the early 21st century', *Cambrian Law Review*, Volume 35, pp 115–134.

Nolan (1997) *Report on the Committee on Standards in Public Life*, HMSO: London.

Oborne, P. (2005) *The Rise of Political Lying*, Free Press: London.

Oldfield, M. (2002) *From Welfare to Risk: Discourse, Power and Politics in the Probation Service*. Issues in Community and Criminal Justice, Monograph 1, NAPO.

Oxford University Centre for Criminological Research and Probation Studies Unit (2003) 'The Resettlement of Discretionary Life-Sentenced Offenders', unpublished research.

Parliamentary All-Party Penal Affairs Group (1980) *Too Many Prisoners*, Barry Rose Publishers Ltd: Chichester and London.

Patten, J. (1988) 'A "New World of Punishment": The View from John Patten's Window of Opportunity', interview with Nigel Stone, *Probation Journal*, Volume 35, 3.

Paxman, J. (2002) *The Political Animal: An Anatomy*, Penguin: London and New York.

Pease, K. and Statham, R.S. (1979) 'Community Service Background Issues'. A paper for the First National Community Service Conference at Keele University.

Pitts, J. (2003) 'Youth Justice in England and Wales', in R. Matthews and J. Young (eds) *The New Politics of Crime and Punishment*, Willan Publishing: Cullompton, Devon.

Pointing, J. (1986) (ed.) *Alternatives to Custody*, Basil Blackwell: Oxford.

Police Court Mission Report Book for the Borough of Sunderland. Diary for the period April 1918 to April 1923.

Preece, C. (1989) *Woman of the Valleys – the Story of Mother Shepherd*, New Life Publications: West Glamorgan.

Probation Boards Association (2002), Newsletter No. 2, February.

Pugh, D.S. (1984) (ed.) *Organisation Theory: Selected Readings*, Penguin: London.

Radzinowicz, L. and Hood, R. (1990) *The Emergence of Penal Policy In Victorian and Edwardian England*, Clarendon Press: Oxford.

Raine, J.W. and Willson, M.J. (1997) 'Beyond Managerialism in Criminal Justice', *The Howard Journal*, Volume 36, 1, Blackwell Publishers.

Ramsbotham, D. (2003) *Prison Gate: The Shocking State of Britain's Prisons and the Need for Visionary Change*, Free Press: London.

Raynor, P. (1984) 'National Purpose and Objectives: A Comment', *Probation Journal*, Volume 31, 2.

Raynor, P. (1985) *Social Work, Justice and Control*, Basil Blackwell: Oxford.

Raynor, P. (2002 3rd edition) 'Community Penalties: Probation, Punishment, and "What Works"' in M. Maguire, R. Morgan and R. Reiner (eds) *The Oxford Handbook of Criminology*, Oxford University Press: Oxford, New York.

Raynor, P. and Vanstone, M. (2002) *Understanding Community Penalties: Probation, policy and social change*, Open University Press: Buckingham, Philadelphia.

Rees, H. and Williams, E.H. (1989) (eds) 'Punishment, Custody and the Community: Reflections and Comments on the Green Paper'. Papers presented at the second International Criminal Justice Seminar, April 1989, at the London School of Economics.

Rex, S. (1997) 'Offenders and their Supervisors' Views of Probation: Help within a Restrictive Framework'. Paper presented to the British Criminology Conference.

Rock, P. (1990) *Helping Victims of Crime: The Home Office and the Rise of Victim Support in England and Wales*, Clarendon Press: Oxford.

Rutherford, A. (1994) *Criminal Justice and the Pursuit of Decency*, Waterside Press: Winchester.

Rutherford, A. (1996) *Transforming Criminal Policy: Spheres of Influence in The United States, The Netherlands and England and Wales during the 1980s*, Waterside Press: Winchester.

Ryan, M. (1983) *The Politics of Penal Reform*, Longman: London and New York.

Ryan, M. (2003) *Penal Policy and Political Culture in England and Wales. Four Essays on Policy and Process*, Waterside Press: Winchester.

Saint Augustine (1961) *Confessions*. Translated with an Introduction by R.S. Pine-Coffin, Penguin Books: Middlesex.

Sargeant, J. (2005) *Maggie: Her Fatal Legacy*, Macmillan: London.

Sartre, J.P. (1973) *Existentialism and Humanism*. Translation and Introduction by Philip Mairet, Eyre Methuen Ltd: London.

Savage, S.P. and Robbins, L. (1990) (eds) *Public Policy Under Thatcher*, Macmillan: London.

Seldon, A. (2004) *Blair*, Free Press: London.

Seldon, A. and Collings, D. (2000) *Britain Under Thatcher*, Longman: Harlow, London and New York.

Senior, P. (1984) 'The Probation Order: Vehicle of Social Work or Social Control?', *Probation Journal*, Volume 31, 2.

Sennet, R. (2005) 'What Our Grannies Taught Us', *Guardian* newspaper, 19th May 2005.

Shaw, R., and Haines, K. (1989) *The Criminal Justice System: A Central Role for the Probation Service*, Institute of Criminology, University of Cambridge.

Sked, A. and Cook, C. (1979) *Post-War Britain: A Political History*, Penguin Books: London and New York.

Smith, D. (1996) 'Social Work and Penal Policy' in G. McIvor (ed.) *Working with Offenders*. Research Highlights in Social Work 26, Jessica Kingsley: London and Bristol.

Smith, D. (2004) 'The uses and abuses of positivism' in G. Mair (ed.) *What Matters in Probation*, Willan Publishing: Cullompton, Devon.

Spencer, J. (1995) 'A Response to Mike Nellis: Probation Values for the 1990s', *The Howard Journal of Criminal Justice*, Volume 34, 4, Blackwell Publishers for the Howard League.

Statham, R.S. (1980a) 'The Rise and Fall of Community Service: A Sketch in four scenes', Staffordshire Probation Service.

Statham, R.S. (1980b) 'Project Provision in Community Service'. Paper produced for Second National Seminar on Community Service at Keele University, Stoke on Trent: Staffordshire Probation Service.

Statham, R.S. (1990) 'The Probation Service in a Market Driven World', Cleveland Probation Service.

Statham, R.S. (1992) 'The Growth of the Management Culture in Probation and the Practice Ideal'. Paper presented to the Fullbright Colloquium at Stirling University, 1st–4th September.

Statham, R.S. (1998) 'The Shape of Things to come in Probation – Quality at the Core', *The Probation Manager*, 1.

Statham, R.S. (1999) 'Probation – A Life Beyond The Reviews', *Probation Journal*, Volume 46, 1.

Statham, R.S. (2000) 'New Governance Structures for Probation Boards: The Implications for Chief Probation Officers', 3rd International Conference on Corporate Governance and Direction. Henley Management College, 16th–18th October.

Statham, R.S. and Whitehead, P. (1992) (eds) *Managing the Probation Service: Issues for the 1990s*, Longman: Harlow.

Stevenson, L. (1974) *Seven Theories of Human Nature*, Oxford University Press: New York and Oxford.

Stevenson, O. (1981) *Specialisation in Social Service Teams*, George Allen and Unwin: London.

Stewart, G. and Stewart, J. (1993) *Social Circumstances of Younger Offenders Under Supervision. A research report for the Association of Chief Officers of Probation*, ACOP.

Stone, N. (1984) 'The Home Secretary: An Interview', *Probation Journal*, Volume 31, 1.

Stone, N. (1988) 'A "New World of Punishment": The View from John Patten's Window of Opportunity', *Probation Journal*, Volume 35, 3.

Stone, N. (1994) '1991 And All That', *Probation Journal*, Volume 41, 4.

Stoner, J.A.F. and Wankel, C. (1986) *Management*, Prentice Hall: New Jersey.

Stott, D.H. (1952) *Saving Children from Delinquency*, University of London Press Ltd: London.

Tarnas, R. (1991) *The Passion of The Western Mind: Understanding the Ideas that have shaped our world view*, Pimlico: London.

Tayler, C. and Nuttall, B. (1989) 'Measuring up to the Future – a Businesslike Service', NAPO News, May/June 1989, No. 10.

Taylor, I., Walton, P. and Young, J. (1973) *The New Criminology: for a social theory of deviance*, Routledge/Kegan Paul: London, Boston and Henley.

Taylor, R., Wasik, M. and Leng, R. (2004) *Blackstone's Guide To The Criminal Justice Act 2003*, Oxford University Press: Oxford, New York.

Thatcher, M. (1993) *The Downing Street Years*, HarperCollins: London.

Thatcher, M. (1995) *The Path to Power*, HarperCollins: London.

The Management of Structure Review (1980) *Probation Journal*, Volume 27, 4.

Thornborough, M.M. (1970) 'The Satisfaction of Being A Senior Probation Officer', *Probation Journal*, Volume 16, 1.

Thorpe, D.H., Smith, D., Green, C.J. and Paley, J.H. (1980) *Out of Care: The Community Support of Juvenile Offenders*, George Allen and Unwin: London.

Tonry, M. (2004) *Punishment and Politics: Evidence and emulation in the making of English crime control policy*, Willan Publishing: Cullompton, Devon.

Traux, C.B. and Carkhuff, R.R. (1967) *Towards Effective Counselling and Psychotherapy*, Aldine: Chicago.

Vanstone, M. (2004) 'Mission Control: The origins of a humanitarian service', *Probation Journal*, Volume 51, 1.

Walker, M. and Beaumont, B. (1981) *Probation Work: Critical Theory and Socialist Practice*, Blackwell: Oxford.

Walklate, S. (2003 2nd edition) *Understanding Criminology: Current Theoretical Debates*, Open University Press: Buckingham and Philadelphia.

Ward, D. and Spencer, J. (1994) 'The Future of Probation Qualifying Training', *Probation Journal*, Volume 41, 2.

Wargent, M. (2002) 'The New Governance of Probation', *Howard Journal*, Volume 41, 2.

Weston, W.R. (1973) 'Style of Management in the Probation Service', *Probation Journal*, Volume 20, 3.

White, L. (2005) 'The great persuader marches on' in News Review section of the *Sunday Times*, 1st May 2005.

Whitehead, P. (1988) 'Models of Probation', Doctor of Philosophy, University of Durham, unpublished.

Whitehead, P. (1990) *Community Supervision for Offenders: A New Model of Probation*, Avebury: Aldershot, Brookfield USA.

Whitehead, P. (1992) 'The Probation Service and the Church: A Theoretical Rationale for Partnership', *Crucible*, April to June 1992.

Whitehead, P. and Macmillan, J. (1985) 'Checks or Blank Cheque: Justifying Custody of Juveniles', *Probation Journal*, Volume 32, 3.

Whitehead, P. and Thompson, J. (2004) *Knowledge and the Probation Service: Raising Standards for Trainees, Assessors and Practitioners*, John Wiley and Sons Ltd.: Chichester.

Whitehead, P., Turver, N. and Wheatley, J. (1991) *Probation, Temporary Release Schemes and Reconviction: Theory and Practice*, Avebury: Aldershot, Brookfield USA.

Whittington, C. (1988) 'Literature Review: The Efficiency and Performance Assessment Debate', BJSW, 18, 2.

Wilkins, L.T. (1958) 'A small comparative study of the Results of Probation', *British Journal of Delinquency*, 8, pp 201–209.

Windlesham, Lord (1993) *Responses to Crime, Volume 2: Penal Policy in the Making*, Clarendon Press: Oxford.

Windlesham, Lord (2001) *Responses to Crime, Volume 4: Dispensing Justice*, Clarendon Press: Oxford.

Worrall, A. (1997) *Punishment in the Community: The Future of Criminal Justice*, Longman: London and New York.

Young, J. (1999) *The Exclusive Society: Social Exclusion, Crime and Difference in Late Modernity*, Sage Publications: London, Thousand Oaks, New Delhi.

Young, J. (2002 3rd edition) 'Crime and social exclusion' in M. Maguire, R. Morgan and R. Reiner (eds) *The Oxford Handbook of Criminology*, Oxford University Press: Oxford, New York.

Young, J. (2003) 'Winning the fight against crime? New Labour, populism and lost opportunities' in R. Matthews and J. Young (eds) *The New Politics of Crime and Punishment*, Willan Publishing: Cullompton, Devon.

Young, P. (1976) 'A sociological analysis of the early history of probation', *British Journal of Law and Society*, 3, 44–58.

INDEX